Frommer's™

Florida

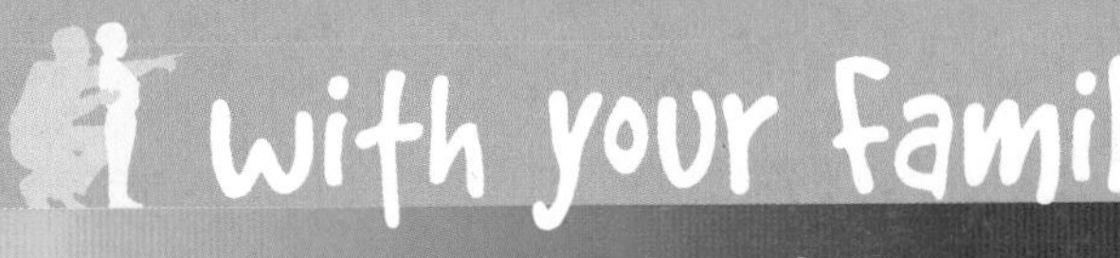

From theme park fun to sunny beach getaways

by Lesley Anne Rose

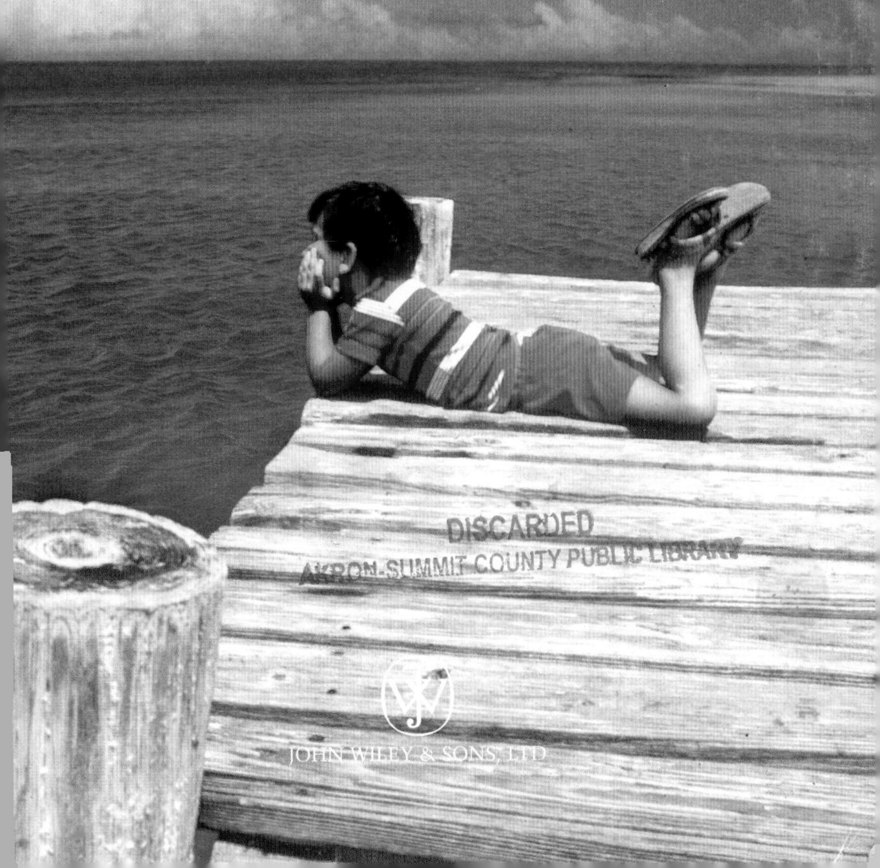

JOHN WILEY & SONS, LTD

ISBN: 978-0-470-51864-9

UK Publisher: Sally Smith
Executive Project Editor: Daniel Mersey (Frommer's UK)
Commissioning Editor: Mark Henshall (Frommer's UK)
Development Editor: Sasha Hasaltine
Content Editor: Hannah Clement (Frommer's UK)
Cartographer: Tim Lohnes
Photo Research: Jill Emeny (Frommer's UK)
Typeset by Wiley Indianapolis Composition Services
Printed and bound in China by SNP Leefung Printers.

A catalogue record for this book is available from the British Library

This book is printed on acid-free paper responsibly manufactured from sustainable forestry in which at least two trees are planted for each one used for paper production.

Wiley also publishes its books in a variety of electronic formats. Some content that appears in print may not be available in electronic books.

5 4 3 2 1

Contents

6 The North & Central East Coast 137

7 Miami & the South East Coast 165

8 The Florida Keys & Everglades 197

9 The Panhandle & Big Bend 229

About the Author

Lesley Anne Rose is a freelance writer specialising in travel and scriptwriting. She has developed a substantial portfolio of travel writing over the past decade, including writing a travel column, guidebooks, articles and promotional materials, and her specialist areas include the Southern Caribbean, North America and the UK. Lesley Anne has made short documentary films and, as a commissioned playwright, has seen her work produced in regional theatre. She also teaches travel writing and film studies.

Dedication

To Martin Chester – 'the navigator'.

Acknowledgements

Thank you to all the PR agencies, tourist information organisations and various businesses that helped in the research and organisation of my trip including: Lisa Cooper and Kate Burgess-Craddy at KBC-PR; Stefanie Douch at gosh pr; Lee Rose at the Lee County Visitor & Convention Bureau; Kate Allen at Virgin Atlantic; Aby Farsoun at Trimedia Harrison Cowley; Chloe Handy at Fleishman-Hillard; Kevin Gibson at Hills Balfour Synergy; Oliver Kugler; Helen Mitchem at Orlando/Orange County Convention & Visitors Bureau; Lynda Daboh at First Public Relations; Megan Falls at Disney Destinations International; Alana France & Kathy Farris at Daytona International Speedway; Kevin Brett at Attractions Collection; Katy Martin at Central Florida Visitors and Convention Bureau; Carol Shaughnessy at Stuart Newman Associates; Jeanne L Bigos; Jessica Taylor at Greater Fort Lauderdale Convention & Visitors Bureau; and Tangela Boyd at Daytona Beach Area Convention & Visitors Bureau.

For cat and house sitting beyond the call of friendship thanks to Hilli McManus, Leon Gurevitch, Jane Twyman and Corrie and Martha. And thanks to my husband Martin Chester for taking time off to travel with me, helping with research, formatting, map reading, editing and unending support.

An Additional Note

Please be advised that travel information is subject to change at any time and this is especially true of prices. We therefore suggest that you write or call ahead for confirmation when making your travel plans. The authors, editors and publisher cannot be held responsible for experiences of readers while travelling. Your safety is important to us however, so we encourage you to stay alert and be aware of your surroundings.

Star Ratings, Icons & Abbreviations

Hotels, restaurants and attraction listings in this guide have been ranked for quality, value, service, amenities and special features using a star-rating system. Hotels, restaurants, attractions, shopping and nightlife are rated on a scale of zero stars (recommended) to three (exceptional). In addition to the star rating system, we also use five feature icons that point you to the great deals, in-the-know advice and unique experiences. Throughout the book, look for:

FIND	Special finds – those places only insiders know about
MOMENT	Special moments – those experiences that memories are made of
VALUE	Great values – where to get the best deals
OVERRATED	Places or experiences not worth your time or money
GREEN	Attractions employing responsible tourism policies

The following **abbreviations** are used for credit cards:

AE American Express
MC Mastercard
V Visa

A Note on Prices

In the Family-friendly Accommodation section of this book we have used a price category system.

An Invitation to the Reader

In researching this book, we discovered many wonderful places – hotels, restaurants, shops and more. We're sure you'll find others. Please tell us about them, so we can share the information with your fellow travellers in upcoming editions. If you were disappointed with a recommendation, we'd love to know that too. Please write to:

Frommer's Florida with your family, 1st edition
John Wiley & Sons, Ltd
The Atrium
Southern Gate
Chichester
West Sussex, PO19 8SQ

Photo Credits

Cover Credits

Main Image: © Gabe Palmer / Alamy
Small Images (L-R):
© Anthony Cox / PCL
© Disney
© sodapix – f1 online / Alamy
© Colin Paterson / PCL
Back Cover: © David Noble / PCL

Front Matter Credits

Pi: © Gabe Palmer / Alamy; piii: © Anthony Cox / PCL; © Disney; © sodapix – f1 online / Alamy; © Colin Paterson / PCL; piv: © Anthony Cox / PCL; © Disney; © sodapix – f1 online / Alamy; © Colin Paterson / PCL.

Inside Credits

© **Busch Entertainment Corporation:** p73.

Courtesy of Alamy: p83 (© Amy Mikler); p137 (© Paul Wayne Wilson – PhotoStockFile); p141 (© Andre Jenny); p158 (© Lynne Siler Photography); p162 (© David Osborn); p219 (© Jeff Greenbery); p224 (© Khaled Kassem); p229 (© M Timothy O'Keefe).

Courtesy of Daytona Beach Area Convention and Visitors Bureau: p7, p24, p152.

Courtesy of Florida Keys & Key West / *www.fla-keys.co.uk***:** p206, p214 (© Bob Krist); p208 (© Andy Newman).

Courtesy of Greater Miami Convention & Visitors Bureau: *www.gmcvb.com*: p5a, p176, p178, p182, p192.

Courtesy of Lee County Visitor & Convention Bureau: p4, p107, p119, p123.

Courtesy of Little Harbor Resort: p9, p128.

Courtesy of Orlando / Orange County Convention & Visitors Bureau, Inc.®: p91b, p94, p99.

Courtesy of PCL: p1, p11, p197, p216, p227 (© Gregory Wrona).

Courtesy of Theatre of the Sea: p213.

Courtesy of The Travel Library (TTL): p124 (© Tom Mackie); p143, p145 (© Stuart Black); p165 (© Clare Roberts); p172 (© John Lawrence).

© **David Woods:** p10.

© **Daytona International Speedway:** p6.

© **Discovery Cove:** p71.

© **Disney:** p45, p49, p58, p59, p60, p77.

© **Kennedy Space Center:** p75.

© **Lesley Anne Rose:** p5b, p35, p39, p89, p91a, p96, p103, p110, p114, p117, p126, p129, p136, p149, p151, p154, p169, p179, p184, p185, p186, p188, p195, p204, p209, p210, p211, p234, p238, p240, p244, p247, p253.

© **2007 Universal Orlando Resort.** All rights reserved: p3, p63, p66, p67, p78.

1 Family Highlights of Florida

When I first travelled to Florida nearly 20 years ago, I, like many first-time visitors, had my heart set on nothing else but doing Disney. While each subsequent visit to the Sunshine State has involved whatever new theme park or new rides there were to enjoy, each has also taken me further and further away from Florida's tourist-dominated central region and to its farthest flung nooks and crannies, where I discovered just how much this diverse state has to offer all ages.

For the millions of families who travel to Florida each year, its larger than life theme parks are the biggest draw, and an ever-increasing number of direct flights make it easier than ever to travel to Orlando from inside the US and internationally. With accommodation options from luxury self-catering villas to budget motels, all set up for visiting families and of a high standard built on strong competition, it's equally easy once you get there.

However, an expanding number of tours and fly-drive deals are opening up many possibilities further afield. I now regularly hear a whole host of international accents on the beaches of the Deep South–influenced Panhandle, where a slower way of life prevails, or on the vibrant streets of Key West, where a Caribbean-infused culture and lifestyle hold sway. And it's only when you consider just how different these two places are that the myriad of possibilities and experiences this vast state offers becomes clear.

After its glittering theme parks, Florida's award-winning, sun-drenched beaches are its biggest draw. And, apart from the curve of the Big Bend, each coastal region has more than its fair share of both tourist-filled beaches, such as Tampa Bay's Clearwater, and practically deserted sands epitomised by the likes of Fernandina Beach in the north east. Away from the sands, Florida's glorious outdoors offers first class snorkelling, endless kayaking and canoeing and miles of great cycling. Plus many chances to learn all about the state's intricate ecosystems, abundant wildlife and endangered species.

Families should never underestimate the appeal of Florida's cities, each shaped by an influx of different cultures. Big name destinations such as the stylish Miami, thoroughly modern Jacksonville and Cuban-influenced Tampa contain a range of excellent interactive museums and family-friendly attractions. While others, including St Augustine, North America's oldest surviving European settlement, and state capital Tallahassee, are places to live and breathe Florida's diverse history.

Once you start breaking down geographical constraints by taking internal flights or incorporating road trips into a visit, you can cover a lot of ground in a single trip. Yet, as the growing number of families from outside of Florida buying property here suggests, this is a place with enduring appeal at the heart of which is the endless excitement generated by the ever-changing tourist areas, contrasted with the timeless allure of areas like the eternal Everglades and laid-back Keys.

TOP 10 UNMISSABLE FLORIDA FAMILY HIGHLIGHTS

1. **Getting** up close to the amazing animals at Disney's majestic Animal Kingdom; p. 58.

2. **Taking** to the skies in a vintage biplane at Fantasy of Flight; p. 90.

3. **Searching** for seashells on the shores of Sanibel Island; p. 118.

4. **Experiencing** the thrill of the race track at Daytona International Speedway; p. 150.

5. **Discovering** Miami's amazing Art Deco district; p. 175.

6. **Picnicking** on Honeymoon Island; p. 116.

7. **Exploring** St Augustine's historic streets; p. 143.

8. **Snorkelling** at John Pennekamp Coral Reef State Park; p. 215.

9. **Swimming** in sparkling spring waters at Wakulla Springs; p. 246.

10. **Learning** about the care of injured sea turtles at the Gumbo Limbo Nature Center; p. 186.

BEST FAMILY EXPERIENCES

Best Theme Park For families with young children, nothing beats getting up close to the amazing wildlife in Disney's newest park, **Animal Kingdom**. See p. 58. While families with

Universal's Islands of Adventure.

teens who like nothing better than hurling themselves through the air on an array of white-knuckle rides, should aim for **Universal's Islands of Adventure,** where they won't know which thrill to head for first. See p. 65.

Best Family Event Each night **Disney's MGM Studios** draws the day to an end with its dazzling **Fantasmic!** show, for which the 10,000 seats and standing room places fill up most nights. This water and fireworks spectacular, loosely based around the classic animation *Fantasia* and featuring characters from *The Lion King*, *Jungle Book*, *Beauty and the Beast* and many other Disney favourites, is a classic tale of good versus evil, played out in an epic style that will entertain all the family. See p. 57.

Florida's Best Family-Friendly Beaches

Florida's fantastic coastline is holiday heaven for the beach-loving family, and regional highlights for those travelling with children are:

Along the Panhandle – **Seaside**, with its vibrant child-friendly community and powdery sands. See p. 242.

In the south west – **Fort Myers Beach**, a vast swathe of wide, white sands with the lively Times Square at the north end and opportunities for solitude further south. See p. 118.

In the Florida Keys – **Bahia Honda State Park** offers visitors the combination of fine sands, great swimming and snorkelling, and compelling views of an old wooden road bridge, worn away by hurricanes and time. See p. 215.

In the north east – **Fernandina Beach** is a charming mix of windswept shores and an historic downtown. See p. 148.

In the south east – **Fort Lauderdale's beach** is well used by local families, and visitors can choose between the bustling Beach Place, great if you're travelling with older children, or chilling out in quieter areas with youngsters. See p. 183.

In Central Florida – **Cocoa Beach** is a must for surf-loving teens (see p. 146) and the artificial beach at **Disney's Typhoon Lagoon** is a convincing alternative for those who can't get to the coast. See p. 93.

Best City Cities aren't always the first destination of choice when planning a family holiday to Florida, but those looking for some city life to spice up their time in the Sunshine State won't be disappointed with **Miami**. You'll find all the ingredients for a great family holiday including fine beaches, world class

Playing on a Fort Myers beach

South Beach, Miami

attractions, shopping to suit all ages and tastes plus the world famous Art Deco district. See p. 175.

Best Natural Attraction **The Everglades** are a vast, subtropical wilderness that sprawl across Florida's southern tip and are best visited via the tours and trails owned and operated by **The Everglades National Park.** There's simply nowhere else like this in the world and once you start delving into the land and water scapes that make up this unique, but shy, region, the glades will reward you with a glimpse of just how fabulous they really are. An added bonus for children is the **Junior Ranger programme**, an activity booklet full of ways to educate and entertain young visitors, with the chance of being enrolled as a Junior Ranger at the end. See p. 216.

Best Aquarium **The Florida Aquarium** is both one of the world's top aquariums and one of the state's best family attractions. The aquarium contains thousands of different types of marine plants and animals and a visit includes plenty of children's games for all ages and the opportunity to take an eco tour out onto the waters of Tampa Bay. See p. 122.

Best Outdoors Activity Unbeknown to many UK visitors, Florida is one of the best places in the US to kayak, and even young children who've never lifted a paddle in their lives will find plenty of opportunities to take to the water and give it a go.

Seaside

Daytona International Speedway

Adventures Unlimited, located in **Blackwater River State Park**, organise excellent kayaking, canoeing and tubing along the slow, wide river that runs through the heart of the forest (see p. 248). And **Captiva Kayaks and Wildside Adventures** on **Captiva Island** will take all ages out into the wonderful world of Florida's coastal waterways. See p. 126.

Best Snorkelling Florida's underwater realms are just as stunning as its endless beaches, and the best way for families to peer into this wonderful marine world is via an organised snorkelling tour at **John Pennekamp Coral Reef State Park** at Key Largo in the Florida Keys. The Keys' reefs are the only living coral reef barrier in North America and home to masses of colourful tropical fish and weird and wonderful marine plants. Look out for the famous underwater 'Christ of the Deep' statue and bring an underwater camera. See p. 215.

Best Tour Climb aboard a specially created swamp buggy and take a tour on the wild side with **Babcock Wilderness Adventures Eco Tours**. These fabulous child-friendly tours take visitors through Telegraph Cypress Swamp and an authentic south Florida ranch, which still farms in a traditional, eco-friendly style. Expect to encounter cracker cattle, big cats, alligators, wild pigs (and piglets if you're lucky) and maybe the odd cowboy.

Best Nature Centre Located inside Boca Raton's Red Reef Park, **Gumbo Limbo Nature Center** is a fantastic facility where children can get up close to sick and injured animals being nursed back to health and engage with Florida's plants, animals and natural environments via displays, activities and trails. See p. 186.

Best Family Adventure At **Fantasy of Flight** a family of four can board a vintage biplane and take to the skies above central Florida for a trip of a lifetime. And if the Biggles bug bites your child along the way, there are plenty of wonderful old planes inside the attraction itself, plus opportunities to learn just how and why they fly. See p. 90.

Best Sporting Attraction **Daytona International Speedway** is the home of NASCAR (National Association for Stock Car Racing), which was founded on the famous sands of Daytona's Beach. With roots that reach into the Deep South, stock car racing is one of the most popular sports in the US, and this electrifying race-track brings you right up close to its history, drivers and high-speed thrills. See p. 150.

Best Journey Break The rest stops at either end of the **Sunshine Skyway Bridge** are brilliant places to get out of the car and stretch your legs. Each stop provides glorious views of this graceful architectural master-piece and the magnificent Tampa Bay it arches over.

Best Road Trip Stretching the length of Florida's east coast from Fernandina Beach in the north to Miami's South Beach, **SR-A1A** takes in the likes of the Kennedy Space Center, Daytona Beach, the secluded coastal man-sions of the rich and famous, some cool surfing spots and Miami's Art Deco, making for a gentle yet diverse road trip with something to interest all groups along the way.

Best Place to Explore History **St Augustine** offers an unusual experience of history in North America, embodying the Spanish intervention in this region in the 16th century and is basically one big, living museum. This old city is fascinating to walk around and contains a number of attrac-tions where children can learn about this very special slice of Florida history. See p. 143.

Best All American Experience Infused with the same magic ingredient that makes cricket so quintessentially English, **base-ball** is uniquely American in ways that not even America can put its finger on. Matches are very popular with local families and you can catch a Minor League game at venues such as

The Daytona Cubs

Daytona Beach's Jackie Robinson Ballpark (see p. 148), one of the Major League training matches that take place throughout the state in spring (see p. 21) or a regular Major League match in Tampa or Miami.

BEST ACCOMMODATION

Best Theme Park Accommodation Themed in the style of an African Game Reserve, Disney's sumptuous **Animal Kingdom Lodge** is such a great resort for children that you might struggle to tear them away from its swimming pools, playgrounds and special activities and actually get them into the theme parks. See p. 76. However, for older children and teens, **Universal's Hard Rock Hotel** is too cool to be true. See p. 77.

Best Family-focused Beach Resort **Cheeca Lodge and Spa** in the Florida Keys offers laid-back luxury in a paradise setting and organises one of the best children's programmes of any resort in Florida. Its many facilities cater for both young guests and adults who want time alone to relax. See p. 222. At the other end of the family spectrum, **Ron Jon's Cape Caribe** near Cocoa Beach is a large, colourful and lively resort bursting at the seams with child-focused activities and entertainment, and is close to some of Florida's biggest attractions. See p. 161.

Best Family-friendly Bed and Breakfast Right in the heart of Key West's historic old town, **Island City House Hotel** is a wonderfully rambling complex of three old houses, tropically landscaped gardens and shady swimming pool. One of the few historic bed and breakfasts in Key West to accept children, this beautiful old hotel is close to the hustle and bustle of Duval Street and yet in a tranquil world all of its own. See p. 221.

Best Seaside Hotel Standing at the quieter north end of Fort Lauderdale's beach, the **Pelican Grand Resort** has its own private stretch of sand where children can play while adults relax in rocking chairs on the hotel's wooden beachfront balcony. Some serious thinking about a family's needs went into the design of the rooms, while the staff are wonderfully friendly. See p. 193.

Best Self-catering Situated on the east side of Tampa Bay, close to both Tampa and Sarasota, **Little Harbor** is an ideal place to stay for families who want to explore Florida's west coast attractions but feel far away from the tourist-saturated areas. The apartments and town homes are well set up for families who prefer to self cater and there's the added bonus of a good range of on-site restaurants if you don't want to cook after all. See p. 128.

Best Cowboy/Cowgirl Friendly Accommodation **Westgate River Ranch** in central Florida is a place where

Little Harbor Apartments

American families hire cabins or park their RVs and enjoy the outdoors and time together. The ranch is relatively isolated but there are plenty of activities such as airboat rides, hayrides and bike hire to occupy children during the day and family-orientated entertainment, such as a Saturday night rodeo, to fill the evenings. See p. 103.

The Best of the Rest You'll find a real mix of European and American families at the **Outrigger Beach Resort**, which backs onto a wonderfully wide stretch of Fort Myers beach. This is simply a very friendly, relaxed resort where children make new friends on the sand and whole families gather around the Tiki bar in the evening to play and watch the sunset. See p. 132.

BEST EATING OPTIONS

Best Child-friendly Restaurant **Morada Bay**, with its fantastic food, glorious sunset views and surrounding child-friendly sands, could be the best restaurant in so many categories, and is a highly recommended family-friendly dining experience for anyone spending time in the Florida Keys. See p. 226.

Best Seafood Perched on the edge of Apalachicola Bay, **Boss Oyster** serves up seafood fresh from its surrounding waters, and while oysters are its speciality, there are plenty of other more child-friendly dishes to please all ages. See p. 255.

Best Family-friendly Restaurant with an Airstrip **Chalet Suzanne**, in central Florida's Lake Wales, is probably the state's only restaurant with an airstrip, but is so good it's worth

Lily Pond at Chalet Suzanne, Lake Wales

a mention in its own right. This glorious Swiss-style restaurant has sent its homemade soups into space to nourish NASA's astronauts, and Florida families come here to celebrate special events or just treat themselves to this establishment's divinely good food. See p. 105.

Best Breakfasts Spanning the corner of Collins Avenue and Espanola Way in Miami's South Beach, **Jerry's Famous Deli** is an iconic Art Deco diner, the décor and ambience of which is purely authentic and not specially created for the tourists. The breakfasts are delicious, but the menu is so long it might be lunchtime before every family member has made up their minds what to eat. See p. 194.

Best Theme Park Dining Experience Eating out with your children doesn't come wackier than MGM Studios' wonderfully bizarre **Sci Fi Dine-In**, where diners sit in recreated vintage convertible cars in a weird world of 1950s drive-ins and low-budget 'B' movies. See p. 80.

Best British Pub Grub Any Brit pining for a plate of fish and chips or bangers and mash should head for the **Rose & Crown** pub in Epcot's British Pavilion for a taste of what your local could look like if Disney took it over. Outside of the theme parks, the **Mucky Duck** on Captiva Island is popular with both locals and tourists and serves up good food and beer on the edge of a glorious and child-friendly beach.

Best Quick Bite **Mama Maria's** restaurant and takeaway on the edge of the Alt-19 highway as it travels through Tarpon Springs serves up mouth-watering Greek food, which you can either eat in or take on a picnic to one of the region's glorious beaches. See p. 115.

Best Picnic Spot Just about all of Florida's State Parks are perfect places to picnic and well set up with shady tables and often barbeque grills. However, **Honeymoon Island** on the central west coast, just north of Dunedin, is a wild and wonderful beach where seabirds nest, children play and the sunsets are spectacular. See p. 116.

2 Planning a Trip to Florida

FLORIDA

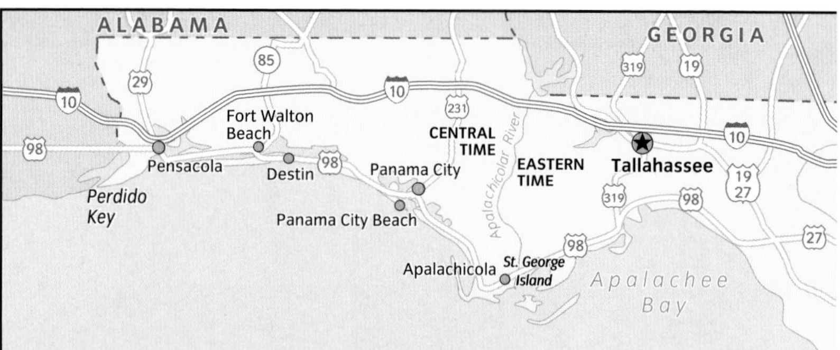
ALABAMA
GEORGIA
85
29
10
319
19
231
98
Fort Walton Beach
CENTRAL TIME
EASTERN TIME
Apalachicola River
Tallahassee
Pensacola
Destin
Panama City
Perdido Key
Panama City Beach
19 27
27
Apalachicola
St. George Island
Apalachee Bay
Gulf of Mexico

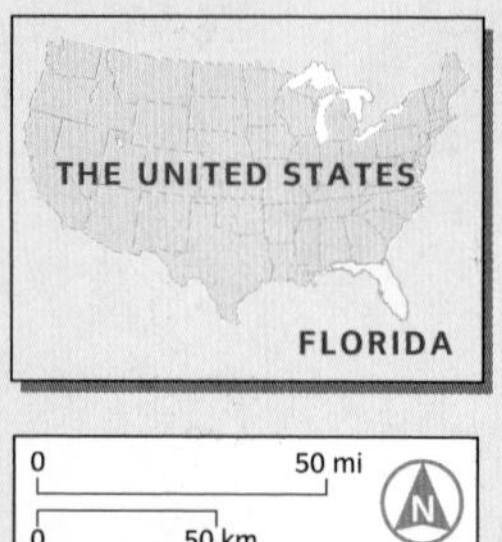
THE UNITED STATES
FLORIDA
0
50 mi
0
50 km
N

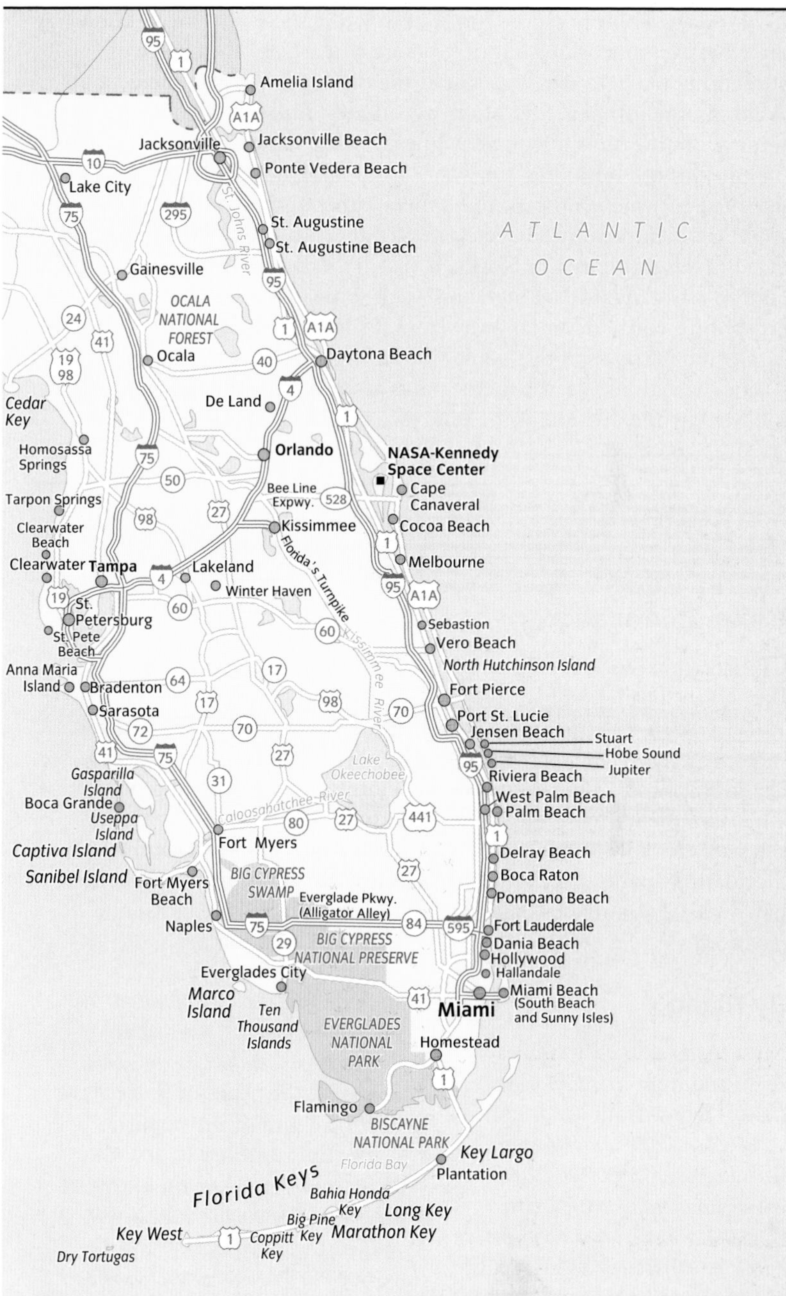
Amelia Island
Jacksonville
Jacksonville Beach
Ponte Vedera Beach
Lake City
St. Johns River
St. Augustine
St. Augustine Beach
ATLANTIC OCEAN
Gainesville
OCALA NATIONAL FOREST
Ocala
Daytona Beach
Cedar Key
De Land
Homosassa Springs
Orlando
NASA-Kennedy Space Center
Bee Line Expwy.
Cape Canaveral
Tarpon Springs
Clearwater Beach
Kissimmee
Cocoa Beach
Florida's Turnpike
Clearwater
Tampa
Lakeland
Melbourne
Winter Haven
St. Petersburg
St. Pete Beach
Sebastion
Vero Beach
Anna Maria Island
Bradenton
Kissimmee River
North Hutchinson Island
Fort Pierce
Sarasota
Port St. Lucie
Jensen Beach
Stuart
Hobe Sound
Jupiter
Lake Okeechobee
Gasparilla Island
Riviera Beach
Boca Grande
West Palm Beach
Palm Beach
Useppa Island
Caloosahatchee River
Fort Myers
Captiva Island
Delray Beach
Sanibel Island
Fort Myers Beach
BIG CYPRESS SWAMP
Boca Raton
Everglade Pkwy. (Alligator Alley)
Pompano Beach
Naples
Fort Lauderdale
BIG CYPRESS NATIONAL PRESERVE
Dania Beach
Hollywood
Hallandale
Everglades City
Marco Island
Miami Beach (South Beach and Sunny Isles)
Miami
Ten Thousand Islands
EVERGLADES NATIONAL PARK
Homestead
Flamingo
BISCAYNE NATIONAL PARK
Florida Bay
Key Largo
Plantation
Florida Keys
Bahia Honda Key
Long Key
Big Pine Key
Marathon Key
Key West
Coppitt Key
Dry Tortugas
95
1
A1A
10
75
295
24
41
19
98
40
4
50
528
27
60
64
17
70
72
31
80
441
84
595
29

Planning is the essential part of any trip and, far from being boring, if children are involved from the word go, preparing a trip to Florida as a family can be fun. The key to a successful trip is knowing what everyone wants out of it before you arrive. The choice of attractions and activities is as vast as the distances between them, so to avoid disappointment, and often save money, find out what everyone wants from the Sunshine State, while allowing some flexibility to fit in the unexpected. Also find out what's happening in the places you want to visit when you plan to be there, otherwise carefully laid plans could get disrupted by a large event or public holiday. The big advantage of taking children to Florida is that it's a popular destination for families, so standards are high and, with some off the beaten track exceptions, you're never far away from 24-hour facilities.

For the purposes of this book Florida has been divided into the Major Attractions (i.e. the theme parks around Orlando and Tampa), followed by the division of the state into six large geographical regions.

INTERNAL US TRAVEL

Visitor Information

Contact **Visit Florida**, P.O. Box 1100, Tallahassee, FL 32302-1100 (✆ *888/7-FLA-USA; www.visitflorida.com*), the state's official tourism marketing agent, for a free comprehensive guide to the state. For information on Florida state parks, check out the new website *www.floridastateparks.org*.

By Plane

Most major domestic airlines fly to and from many Florida cities. Choose from **American** (✆ *800/433-7300; www.aa.com*), **Continental** (✆ *800/525-0280; www.continental.com*), **Delta** (✆ *800/221-1212; www.delta-air.com*), **Northwest/KLM** (✆ *800/225-2525; www.nwa.com*), **United** (✆ *800/241-6522; www.united.com*), and **US Airways** (✆ *800/428-4322; www.usairways.com*). Of these, Delta and US Airways have the most extensive network of commuter connections within Florida.

Several so-called no-frills airlines – with low fares but few, if any, amenities – also fly to Florida. The biggest and best is **Southwest Airlines** (✆ *800/435-9792; www.southwest.com*) which has flights from many U.S. cities to Fort Lauderdale, Jackson, Orlando, and Tampa.

Others flying to Florida include **AirTran** (✆ *800/AIR-TRAN; www.airtran.com*); **American Trans Air** (✆ *800/435-9282; www.ata.com*); **Carnival Air** (✆ *800/824-7386*), an arm of the popular cruise line; **JetBlue** (✆ *800/538-2538; www.jetblue.com*); **Midwest Express** (✆ *800/452-2022; www.midwestexpress.com*); **PanAm** (✆ *800/FLY-PANAM; www.flypanam.com*); and **Spirit** (✆ *800/722-7117; www.spiritair.com*).

Frommers.com: The Complete Travel Resource

It should go without saying, but we highly recommend Frommers.com, voted Best Travel Site by *PC Magazine.* We think you'll find our expert advice and tips; independent reviews of hotels, restaurants, attractions, and preferred shopping and nightlife venues; vacation give-aways; and an online booking tool indispensable before, during, and after your travels. We publish the complete contents of over 128 travel guides in our **Destinations** section covering nearly 3,800 places worldwide to help you plan your trip. Each weekday, we publish original articles reporting on **Deals and News** via our free **Frommers.com Newsletter** to help you save time and money and travel smarter. We're betting you'll find our new **Events** listings (http://events.frommers.com) an invaluable resource; it's an up-to-the-minute roster of what's happening in cities everywhere—including concerts, festivals, lectures, and more. We've also added weekly **podcasts, interactive maps,** and hundreds of new images across the site. Check out our **Travel Talk** area featuring **Message Boards** where you can join in conversations with thousands of fellow Frommer's travelers and post your trip report once you return.

Internet resources such as **Travelocity** (***www.travelocity.com***) and **Microsoft Expedia** (***www.expedia.com***) make it easy to compare prices and purchase tickets.

Family Friendly

Florida is a great family destination, with Walt Disney World leading the list of theme parks geared to young and old alike. Consequently, most Florida hotels and restaurants are willing, if not eager, to cater to families travelling with children. Many hotels and motels let children age 17 and younger stay free in a parent's room (be sure to ask when you reserve).

At the beaches, it's the exception rather than the rule for a resort not to have a children's activities program (some will even mind the youngsters while the parents enjoy a night off!). Even if they don't have a children's program of their own, most will arrange babysitting services.

Recommended family travel websites include **Family Travel Forum** (***www.familytravelforum.com***), a comprehensive site that offers customized trip planning; **Family Travel Network** (***www.familytravelnetwork.com***), an online magazine providing travel tips; and **TravelWithYourKids.com** (***www.travelwithyourkids.com***), a comprehensive site written by parents for parents offering sound advice for long-distance and international travel with children.

Surfing for Hotels

In addition to the online travel booking sites **Travelocity**, **Expedia**, **Orbitz**, **Priceline**, and **Hotwire**, you can book hotels through **Hotels.com**, **Quikbook** (***www.quikbook.com***), and ***Travelaxe*** (***www.travelaxe.net***).

HotelChatter.com is a daily webzine offering smart coverage and critiques of hotels worldwide. Go to **TripAdvisor.com** or **HotelShark.com** for helpful independent consumer reviews of hotels and resort properties.

It's a good idea to get a confirmation number and make a printout of any online booking transaction.

America's love affair with the Internet has revolutionised planning for a trip to the States. Florida's official tourism website ***www.visitflorida.com*** is a huge information portal, with updated articles, accommodation information, links to tourist information for cities and communities around the state and a section specifically for UK visitors ***http://international.visitflorida.com/uk***, which includes special deals in UK prices and up-to-date currency exchange information. Create your own e-magazine as you browse by collecting articles to be emailed to you. The Florida section of the Visit USA site (***www.visitusa.org.uk***) is also worth consulting and is tailored to a UK audience.

Other websites to explore are: ***www.floridabeaches.com*** and ***www.florida-secrets.com***.

Details of regional visitor information websites have been included in each chapter.

Child-specific Websites

Visit Florida's site has a section specifically for families and children, which includes special deals at large hotel chains, special family-focused articles, itineraries and a list of resorts offering children's programmes. Family Travel Times ***www.familytraveltimes.com*** is a US-based newsletter dedicated to improving family holidays; some articles are free and some are for subscribers only. For tips on surviving theme parks with children visit ***www.familyfun.go.com/family-travel/***. Other, more general, sites geared towards travelling families are ***www.travellingwithchildren.co.uk***, ***www.takethefamily.com*** and ***www.babygoes2.com***.

UK & INTERNATIONAL TRAVELLERS

ENTRY REQUIREMENTS & CUSTOMS

Passports & Visas

Most British visitors to the US travel under the US Visa Waiver Programme, which allows you to stay in the United States for up to 90 days if you're travelling on holiday.

You will only qualify for this programme if you are described as a 'British Citizen' on the photo page of your passport. If you are described as a 'British Subject', 'British National (Overseas)', 'British Overseas Territories Citizen', 'British Dependent Territories Citizen', 'British Protected Person' or 'British Overseas Citizen', you need a visa.

All family members, including children and babies, travelling to the US must have individual passports with at least six months left from the final day of your visit before it expires (if you update your passport early, the British authorities will add the months left on to your next passport). In addition, if your passport is not a new biometric version, it must have a machine-readable zone (marked by three chevrons on the photo page).

Restrictions are in place for anyone who has a criminal record or has overstayed on a previous visit. If you've any concerns about your passport or whether or not you qualify for the US Visa Waiver Programme, check the tourism section of the US Embassy's website ***www.usembassy.org.uk***, where you can download an information booklet called *Welcome to the United States*, or call their Visa Information Line *0904 245 0100*. Be warned, calls are charged at £1.20 per minute and the embassy may keep you hanging on for quite a while.

During your flight you will be issued with an immigration form, on which you have to state the length of your stay in the US and an address (including postcode) for at least the first night of your visit. Part of this form will be stapled to your passport when you pass through immigration and it must remain there until it is removed by an airline official when you leave. Also, on entry into the US, all visitors aged between 14 and 79 will have their fingerprints scanned and be digitally photographed.

Airport Security & Flying Restrictions

At the time of writing, airport security and flying restrictions have been relaxed, but remain in place. For up-to-date information check ***www.dft.gov.uk/transportforyou/airtravel/airportsecurity***

The main to points to remember when flying to the US are:

- Passengers are restricted to one item of cabin baggage with a maximum size of 56 cm x 45 cm x 25 cm. Other bags (e.g. handbags) may be carried inside this single item of cabin baggage.
- All items containing liquids or creams must go into your hold baggage, as there are strict restrictions on the quantity of liquids that can be taken on board. Passengers can only carry separate containers, with a capacity not greater than 100 ml, of liquids and creams onto a plane. These containers must be placed inside a transparent, re-sealable plastic bag, which itself must not exceed one litre in capacity (approximately 20 cm x 20 cm). Each passenger is limited to one bag and must present it separately for examination at the airport.

- Liquid baby food or sterilised water, sufficient for the journey, can be taken on board, however the accompanying adult may be asked to taste it to prove that it's baby food. The same applies to essential liquid dietary foodstuffs.
- If you need to take on board any essential medicines that you'll need in quantities higher than 100 ml, you must obtain permission from your airline and the airport you are departing from. Bring supporting documentation from a relevant qualified medical professional when you travel.

INSIDER TIP

Never make a flippant remark about bombs or terrorism when in a US airport.

Customs

Entering the US

Visitors aged 21 and over may bring one litre of alcohol, 200 cigarettes, 100 cigars or three pounds (1.4 kilograms) of tobacco and gifts worth up to £50 (US$100) into the US without paying duty. Any product of Cuban origin, including cigars, may not be brought into the US and a number of food items, including cheese, fresh fruit and meat products, are prohibited.

Coming Home

Visitors to Florida can bring home 200 cigarettes or 100 cigarillos or 50 cigars or 250 g of tobacco, 60 ml of perfume, 250 ml of eau de toilette, 2 litres of still table wine, 1 litre of spirits or strong liqueurs over 22 per cent volume or 2 litres of fortified wine, sparkling wine or other liqueurs and £145 worth of all other goods including gifts and souvenirs.

INSIDER TIP

Take photocopies of all your essential travel documents and carry them in a separate bag to the originals. If you can access your email account online, email yourself passport and ticket numbers, travel insurance details and the emergency telephone numbers you'll need to cancel any credit cards. If you can't access your normal email account away from home, open a free Hotmail ***www.hotmail.com*** or Yahoo ***www.yahoo.com*** account.

MONEY

The US Dollar

Florida, along with the rest of the US, uses the dollar as its currency. There are 100 cents to a dollar, with notes for US$1 – US$100 and coins for 1 – 25 cents. Older notes (still in circulation) are green and all look very similar. The dollar amounts and pictures of different presidents differentiate each one. Newer bills are also distinguished by colour. In 2007 a new US$1 coin was also introduced into circulation. These coins also feature presidents in the order that they served, with four different ones being introduced each year. At the time of writing, the US dollar–sterling exchange rate is US$2.032 to £1; making approximate calculations is therefore easy, just halve everything to get the sterling price. For up-to-date exchange rates and a currency converter, see ***www.xe.com***.

There's no limit on the amount of money you may bring with you into Florida. However, if you're travelling with more than £5,000 (US$10,000) in currency or travellers' cheques, you must declare it to a Customs Inspector.

INSIDER TIP

25 cent coins, known as quarters, are useful to collect, as they're used in a variety of situations from laundry machines in motels to parking meters.

Credit & Debit Cards

It's essential to carry a credit card when travelling in Florida, as you'll need one to secure accommodation, organise car hire and sometimes to show at immigration to prove that you've enough funds to finance your stay. Most accommodation and dining options, shops and petrol stations accept credit cards. The best ones

What Things Cost in Florida

A gallon of petrol	US$3.25 (£1.62)(and rising)
Hire of a medium-sized car for a week	US$400 (£200)
Round trip airfare between Orlando and Key West	US$459 (£230)
Admission to a zoo, adult	US$11 (£5.50)
Admission to a zoo child aged 3–12	US$8 (£4)
British newspaper	US$2.25 (£1.12)
Fixed price child's menu at a mid-priced restaurant	US$4.99 (£2.50)
Road toll	US$1 (50p)
Parking at a theme park	US$10 (£5)
Tub of popcorn in Walt Disney World	US$2.75 (£1.38)
Tub of popcorn in Walt Disney World in a souvenir bucket	US$3.75 (£1.88)
Slice pizza from a takeaway counter	US$3 (£1.50)
A litre of milk in a supermarket	US$1.30 (65p)
A litre of orange juice in a supermarket	US$1.80 (90p)
A litre and a half of still water in a supermarket	89¢ (45p)
1 lb of bananas in a supermarket	50¢ (25p)
A pack of 40 disposable nappies	U$13 (£6.50)
750 grams of baby formula	US$17 (£8.50)
Jar of baby food	US$3 (£1.50)

to travel with are Visa and Mastercard, as many small establishments don't accept American Express and Diners' Club is fading from popularity.

I've used credit cards all over Florida and have never been asked for a PIN, but make sure you know yours just in case. Inform your card company that you're going away so they don't block your card when they see it being used frequently in an unusual place.

You will not be able to use debit cards in shops or restaurants, but can use them at ATMs to withdraw cash.

INSIDER TIP

The Post Office credit card does not add commission on purchases overseas, making it the cheapest way to buy things on credit abroad as long as you pay it off as soon as you get home. Visit ***www.postoffice.co.uk*** for more information.

For lost or stolen cards see p. 43.

Travellers' Cheques

Although now relatively obsolete in a world crammed with 24-hour ATMs, travellers' cheques are the safest way to travel if you want to take large amounts of money with you and they are accepted at most locations. Keep a record of the serial numbers so you can make a claim in the event of loss or theft, and carry them separately from your money and any form of identification.

Cash Points

You'll find 24-hour cash points or ATMs in banks (look out for drive thru ATMs), grocery stores, shopping malls, petrol stations, supermarkets and theme parks. Those located in smaller establishments, such as convenience stores, may charge a fee to use and limit the amount you can withdraw to US$100 (£50).

Saving on Ticket Prices

It can work out cheaper to buy tickets to Florida's major attractions in advance of your visit.

Cheap tickets are available in the UK from Attraction Tickets Direct ☎ *0845 130 3876* ***www.attraction-tickets-direct.co.uk***. While in Florida you can find discount booklets containing vouchers to attractions, accommodation and restaurants all over the place, including visitor information centres, supermarkets and petrol stations.

If you're planning to visit a lot of historic sites, joining the Florida Trust might save you money. A household membership, which includes two adults and all under 18s, costs US$50 (£25) and allows free or reduced entrance to around 80 historic sites in the state; check ***www.floridatrust.org*** for details.

Average temperatures in the different regions of Florida (°F/°C)

	Jan	Feb	Mar	Apr	May	June	July	Aug	Sept	Oct	Nov	Dec
North	53/12	56/13	63/17	68/20	72/22	78/26	81/27	81/27	77/25	74/23	66/19	59/15
Central	60/16	63/17	66/19	71/22	78/26	82/28	82/28	82/28	81/27	75/24	67/19	61/16
South	68/20	70/21	71/22	74/23	78/26	81/27	82/28	84/29	81/27	78/26	73/23	70/21
Keys	69/21	72/22	74/23	77/25	80/27	82/28	85/29	85/29	84/29	80/27	74/23	72/22

WHEN TO GO

Different areas of Florida have different high and low seasons determined by the weather. South Florida, with its subtropical climate, has a high season from mid-December to mid-April when everyone escapes cold temperatures elsewhere. In the north, high season lasts from May until September when the temperatures are high but not as unbearably hot as the south. Spring and autumn can be pleasant times in all areas of the state and all tourist areas are busy and expensive at Christmas, Easter and other public holidays (see p. 42 for a list of Florida's public holidays).

Be wary of American college students' Spring Break holidays, up to a six-week span beginning in late February. Some beach destinations are very popular with spring breakers and these have been indicated in the main body of this book. In addition, each spring major league baseball teams from all over North America travel to Florida to train and pre-season games pull in huge crowds, making it difficult to find accommodation in the towns and cities where they are playing. Details of when and where matches are played can be found on the Major League Baseball's website ***www.mlb.com*** and the Florida Sports Foundation's website ***www.flasports.com*** from late January onwards.

WHAT TO PACK

The important factors to consider when packing for children travelling to Florida are how to keep them entertained while travelling long distances and how to protect them from the heat and mosquitoes. For details on how to keep children entertained on car journeys, see p. 32 and for advice on staying safe in the sunshine, see p. 23.

There's always a tendency to over-pack when travelling with children and flying is far easier the lighter you travel. Toiletries, nappies, clothes and feeding equipment are all available and inexpensive in Florida, so there's no need to travel with too many bulky items. When packing clothes, remember that the dress code is casual wherever you stay. Child safety seats for cars can be rented from car-hire companies and buggies can be rented at the main attractions. Almost all accommodation options have cots, coin-operated washing

Hurricane Season

A hurricane is a tropical storm that forms over the Atlantic with wind speeds of over 75 mph. These storms are categorised via the Saffir–Simpson Scale, starting at a category-one storm containing gusts of less than 77 mph, which cause minor damage, and rising to a potentially catastrophic category-five hurricane with wind speeds of over 175 mph.

Hurricane season officially lasts from June to November, with August to October being the most active months. There's no reason not to travel to Florida then; it's unlikely that one will affect your holiday and if it does, most resorts have evacuation procedures in place and most package tour operators will work with airlines and hotels to ensure that minimum disruption occurs. However, if you plan to travel to Florida during hurricane season, check both your tour operator's small print and travel insurance. For up-to-date hurricane information, check the National Hurricane Center's website ***www.nhc.noaa.gov***.

machines and dryers on site, many resorts rent baby monitors (check ahead) and most restaurants have highchairs.

The following are essential items to travel with or buy as soon as you arrive:

- Sunglasses – check ***www.frubishades.com*** for funky and effective child sunglasses
- Sun hats and high-factor sun screen
- Basic first-aid kit including rehydration salts
- Wet wipes
- A nightlight if your child is afraid of the dark
- A fold-up cooler bag if you intend to picnic
- Rain ponchos for the inevitable downpour
- Lightweight, long-sleeved shirts to avoid your child getting sunburnt
- Lightweight jackets
- Comfortable shoes
- Mosquito repellent

www.travellingwithchildren.co.uk stocks an excellent range of clothes, shoes and accessories for young travellers including inexpensive child identity wrist bands, a must for small children in any theme park.

HEALTH, INSURANCE & SAFETY

Travel Insurance

Never travel to Florida without adequate insurance for all family members, as paying for medical attention while you're there costs a small fortune. If your package tour operator does not offer insurance, shop around, as prices vary enormously from one provider to the next. The Post Office ***www.postoffice.co.uk*** and Columbus Direct ***www.columbusdirect.com*** both offer reasonably priced travel insurance, also check ***www.travelinsuranceweb.com*** for a comparative quote.

Staying Healthy

The primary health concerns when travelling to Florida are the heat and sun. Always protect yourself and your children with a high factor sunscreen or sun block (SPF 45 for children) at least half an hour before exposure and remember to reapply several times during the day, especially after swimming. Make sure your children wear sunglasses and attach them on a cord around their necks so they don't lose them, and protect children's heads with a sun hat. If you're hiring a car, buy a car shade (they are relatively inexpensive), as temperatures soar when cars are parked in the sun. The hottest times are 11am–3pm, when it's a good idea to be inside or in the shade.

Dehydration can occur with prolonged exposure to the heat and sun, even in Florida's winter months, and if your children are suddenly cranky for no good reason, the chances are they're dehydrated. If you plan to be out all day, carry bottled water – Florida's tap water is fine to drink – and salted crisps. Salt replacement drinks are plentiful in supermarkets and convenience stores, with Gatorade being the most popular brand; these should be drunk on a regular basis. Carry rehydration salts with you – while it's easy to buy them with no added sugar in the UK, it's impossible to find sugar-free options in the US.

INSIDER TIP

Dehydration can also occur on a car journey if the windows are closed and air conditioning turned on, as this creates a very dry atmosphere.

Florida's Beach Warning Flags

Florida's public beaches operate a flag system, alerting visitors to unsafe surf conditions. These are what the different coloured flags mean:

- Red with a line crossing out a swimmer – Water is closed to the public.
- Red – High hazard, high surf and/or storm currents.
- Yellow – Medium hazard, moderate surf and/or currents.
- Green – Low hazard, calm conditions but still exercise caution.
- Purple – Dangerous marine life is present, e.g. jellyfish.

The absence of a flag doesn't necessarily mean the water is safe. Check with a lifeguard to be sure.

Mosquitoes are often a problem in Florida, so have a repellent handy, especially in southern Florida, in parks and on trails. Ask 10 people for advice on keeping mosquitoes away and you'll get 11 answers, I swear by Avon Skin So Soft, soft and fresh dry oil body spray ***www.avon.uk.com.*** Although it's not meant to be a repellent, mosquitoes hate the stuff and I've never been bitten while wearing it. However, whatever product you choose, remember that many people are allergic to DEET. If you're travelling to the Keys or Everglades with a baby, buy a mosquito net for the cot. Although Florida's mosquitoes have been known to carry West Nile Virus, it's very rare.
No vaccinations are required for travelling to Florida. Check ***www.fitfortravel.scot.nhs.uk*** for full details on health risks in the US.

If You Fall Ill

If you or your youngsters fall ill in Florida, your tour representative or hotel or resort receptionist will provide information on the nearest doctors' surgery. If there's no one you can ask for help, look under 'clinics' or 'physicians and surgeons' in the Yellow Pages and try to find someone who will charge your insurance company rather than asking you to pay up front. If you do have to pay for treatment or medication, keep the receipts so that you can claim any expense incurred from your travel insurance company when you get home.

Travelling Safely with Children in Florida

With the exception of big cities, the crime rate is relatively low in Florida and you're unlikely to experience problems. However, always take basic precautions while travelling including:

- Keeping all valuables, airline tickets, passports and other travel documents locked in a hotel safe.
- Never leave purses, wallets, luggage or other valuables in sight in an empty car; if you

Having fun on Daytona Beach

Are Sting Rays Safe?

Following the death of naturalist Steve Irwin from a sting ray barb, some attractions in Florida offering visitors the chance to swim or snorkel with sting rays received a lot of attention from press and visitors who wanted to know if it's safe to get into the water with these marine animals. Some attractions, such as Discovery Cove in Orlando (see p. 70), file or trim sting rays' barbs. Others, including Theatre of the Sea in the Florida Keys, house sting rays that are many generations born into captivity and have no fear of humans. However, if you're concerned about letting your children get up close to sting rays, seek assurances from the keepers at the park you are visiting.

must leave them in your vehicle, lock them in the boot.

- If you're driving somewhere for a night out, park under a streetlight or in a well-lit area.
- If you're unsure about going somewhere at night, seek advice from your hotel reception.
- Drive with your car doors locked and try to stay on main roads.
- Carry credit cards or travellers' cheques instead of large amounts of cash.
- Avoid wearing expensive jewellery and carrying valuable items.
- If hit from behind while driving, indicate to the other driver to follow you to a public place and call ☎ *911* for police help.
- If you're hiring a car, have a mobile phone with you in case you break down in the middle of nowhere (for details of mobile phones, see p. 27).
- Have a plan in place in case you get separated in a large attraction.
- Always lock the sliding doors on to your hotel balcony.

INSIDER TIP

The UK's Foreign Office website contains up-to-date information and advice on travel safety ***www.fco.gov.uk/travel***.

Beach Safety

Rip currents or riptides are strong currents that can carry even the most experienced swimmer out to sea. More than a hundred people are killed by rip currents every year in the US. If you get caught in one, don't panic, they pull you out to sea but not underwater. Swim parallel to the shoreline (north to south direction) until you're out of the rip current's influence. If you are unable to swim, tread water until you are out of the current. Then swim diagonally back to shore. Check ***www.usla.org/ripcurrents*** for more information.

Topless sunbathing and thong bikinis are prohibited on Florida's beaches and it's illegal to take glass containers on to the sand. Always use wooden boardwalks to enter a beach where provided, as they are in place to protect sand dunes from erosion.

INSIDER TIP

If you're concerned about how clean a beach you're visiting is, check the website of the Blue Flag Programme, America's environmental certification programme for beaches ***www.cleanbeaches.org***. This site contains a list of all the clean beaches in the US.

Staying Safe on Off-road Trails

If you're taking your children on hiking trails, always avoid direct contact with, and never attempt to feed, any wild animals you may encounter. Be cautious near lakes and ponds, as they are prime habitats for alligators, and only ever swim in clear water. Although there are poisonous snakes in Florida, it's very rare to encounter one, but if you're taking your family into wilderness areas, buy a snakebite kit from a camping store as a precaution.

INSIDER TIP

An obvious sign that you're on holiday is the pile of post that builds up at the front door. To avoid this happening, Royal Mail operate a Keepsafe service through which all your post is held while you're away and delivered the first working day after you return. The cost of this service starts at £5.70 for up to 17 days. Call into a Post Office or visit ***www.royalmail.com*** for more information.

SPECIALISED RESOURCES

For Single Parents

The US-based website ***www.singleparenttravel.net*** is full of good advice about travelling in the States with children as a lone parent. I advise single parents to use resorts, as the lively pools, children's clubs and organised events give parents an opportunity to interact with other adults.

For Grandparents

Florida's population has a high percentage of retired people and their numbers are boosted considerably each year by thousands of older people from Canada and the northern US who travel to Florida to escape cold winters elsewhere (these annual visitors are known as snowbirds). As such, older people are well catered for and often enjoy discounts at attractions; some US airlines also offer reduced travel to 'seniors'.

If you're travelling alone with your grandchildren, carry a letter of consent from the parents giving permission for any emergency medical care that the child may need. If you have a medical condition yourself, either tell the child so they're aware of it or carry written details with you in case of an emergency – your grandchild may be unable to articulate what the problem is.

AARP's (American Association of Retired Persons) website ***www.aarp.org*** contains some useful travel tips and a message board through which you can search for and seek advice.

Families with Special Needs

Travelling with Essential Medical Equipment

Passengers are allowed to carry on board medical equipment essential for use during the flight. Where possible, the equipment should be contained within the one item of cabin baggage (see p. 17) and accompanied by supporting documentation from a relevant qualified medical professional.

Accessibility

All hotels and motels are required by law to have accessible rooms equipped for wheelchairs. Most parks and all public buildings, including museums, are wheelchair accessible (with some offering wheelchair hire) and have adapted toilets. All public transport is wheelchair accessible and there's plenty of accessible parking throughout the state, including at all the major attractions.

Most car-hire companies provide hand-controlled vehicles (book in advance) and to obtain a temporary, 90-day handicapped parking permit, bring your Blue Badge permit and at least one form of identification to a local tax collector's office upon entering the state. You cannot obtain one in advance online. For a list of tax collector locations and more information, visit ***www.hsmv.state.fl.us***.

The Orlando Visitor Center's website features an excellent section on travelling to central Florida with special needs ***www.orlandoinfo.com/specialneeds.*** Other useful resources include the Society for Accessible Travel & Hospitality ***www.sath.org***, and Holiday Care ☎ *0845 124 9971*; ***www.holidaycare.org.uk***.

If you're booking a package tour or flight, make the company aware of any special needs your family may have.

THE 21ST-CENTURY TRAVELLER

Mobile Phones

Before taking your mobile phone to the US, check that it will work there and what the charges will be, and remember to purchase an adapter so you can recharge it. Even if your company does have a network in Florida, it may be weak in rural areas, check the coverage section of your provider's website before you leave home. If you're hiring a car, it's essential to carry a mobile in case you break down. One solution is to hire a cellular phone

Finding a Bargain Online

There's a multitude of travel-related websites, through which the discerning traveller can find a bargain. Here's a few to get you started:

For holidays check: ***www.expedia.com***, ***www.ebookers.com***, ***www.travelzoo.co.uk***, ***www.shermanstravel.com*** and ***www.travelsupermarket.com***.

For flights check: ***www.cheapflights.co.uk***, ***www.dohop.com***, ***www.ufly4less.com*** and ***www.skyscanner.net***.

For hotel rooms and villas check: ***www.laterooms.com***, ***www.holiday-rentals.co.uk***, ***www.midashotels.com*** and ***www.hotelkingdom.com***.

with the car; most major rental companies offer this service. Alternatively, rent through companies such as Cellular Group Inc ***www.cellulargroupinc.com***, who aren't cheap, but offer family deals on renting two phones for short periods of time.

Other Phones

For information on telephones and making calls in the US, see p. 43.

The Internet

Visitors to Florida will have no problem accessing the Internet. If you're travelling with a laptop, most accommodation options have a wireless service that's free to log on to. Many hotels and resorts also have guest computer facilities, especially those that cater for business travellers, but some may charge a fee. Internet cafés are plentiful in tourist areas or head for the nearest public library, as they offer free computer and Internet access.

ESSENTIALS

Getting There

By Package Tour Most families travelling to Florida do so on a package tour, and the choice of locations that operators offer is growing all the time. Many operators offer the flexibility to incorporate more than one location into a holiday package. Your local travel agent will have full details of package tour operators to Florida or you can check out last-minute deals online. Booking online is often cheaper than through an agent or with tour operators on the telephone.

Tour operators to Florida include:

Airtours ☎ *0870 241 8942*; ***www.airtours.co.uk***

First Choice ☎ *0871 220 7799*; ***www.firstchoice.co.uk***

Funway ☎ *0870 44 40 770*; ***www.funwayholidays.co.uk***

My Travel ☎ *0871 664 7970*; ***www.mytravel.co.uk***

Thomas Cook 0870 750 5711; ***www.thomascook.com***

Travel City Direct 0871 911 2576; ***www.travelcitydirect.com***

Virgin 0870 990 4215; ***www.virginholidays.co.uk***

For additional tour operators or information on choosing a reputable company, consult ABTA ***www.abta.com*** or the Association of Independent Tour Operators ***www.aito.co.uk***.

If you're planning to visit Walt Disney World only, their UK website ***www.disneyworld.co.uk*** has full information on how to plan and book a holiday directly with them and ***www.wdisneyw.co.uk*** is a useful, unofficial, site for would-be Disney visitors. To book directly with Universal Orlando, check ***www.universalorlando.co.uk***.

INSIDER TIP

Save paper and view travel brochures online at ***www.onlinetravelbrochures.com***

By Plane If you're looking for a flight to Florida, the easiest option is to fly direct to Orlando, as a number of large airlines operate direct services between Orlando's airports (see p. 86) and British airports, both in London and around the country. Every year, 1,580 flights depart from Gatwick alone to Orlando, with hundreds more leaving from Manchester, Birmingham, Doncaster–Sheffield, East Midlands, Newcastle, Glasgow, Cardiff, Belfast and Dublin. The main companies to run these services are Virgin Atlantic ***www.virgin-atlantic.com***, British Airways ***www.britishairways.com***, Excel ***www.xl.com***, Thomas Cook Airlines ***www.thomascookairlines.co.uk*** and Thomson ***www.thomson.co.uk***. Virgin Atlantic also operates a regular, direct service between London Heathrow and Miami, while British Airways have a programme of regular flights between London Gatwick

Car Hire Pitfalls

It's not illegal to drive without car insurance in the US, and big companies often quote visitors a price for car hire that doesn't include insurance, without telling you that this is the case. Insurance costs about the same amount again as car hire, so when getting a quote make sure it includes adequate insurance to cover all occupants of your vehicle and third-party claims, including personal injury. When obtaining a quote, ask the company to send you the quote in writing or via email, and print and take it with you when picking up the car. There have been many incidents of visitors being assured that their quote covers everything, only to find on picking up the car they have to pay a whole lot more than expected or drive uninsured. If your deal isn't what you expected, complain loudly and ask for information on how to make a formal complaint.

and Tampa, as well as London Heathrow and Miami.

INSIDER TIP

If you're looking for inspiration on how to make your trip to Florida different for your children, check out ***www.dosomethingdifferent.com***. This company organises once in a lifetime experiences from astronaut training to hot air balloon rides over central Florida.

Getting Around

By Car Hiring a car is the only real option for most families travelling around Florida with children in tow. If car hire is not part of your package tour, the major companies who have outlets all over the state and at the main airports are:

Avis ***www.avis.com***

Budget ***www.budget.com***

Dollar ***www.dollar.com***

Hertz ***www.hertz.com***

Children under four or weighing less than 40 lbs (15 kg), must travel in an approved child car seat; these are available from car-hire companies. Additional extras that can be hired along with your car include cellular phones, satellite navigation systems and DVDs for children to watch in the car. Some companies, such as Hertz, offer green cars that emit less CO_2.

I've only ever been asked for the photo card part of my licence, but it's recommended that anyone wanting to drive in Florida carry an International Drivers Licence and the green paper part of their licence as well.

INSIDER TIP

Avoid petrol stations near car-hire centres when filling up before returning your vehicle, as they are often more expensive.

For details on getting around central Florida without a car, see p. 88, and for details of a ferry service between Fort Myers, Miami and Key West, see p. 168.

Driving – The Rules of Florida's Roads

Anyone planning to drive in Florida should take time to learn the rules of their roads, as there are some marked differences between driving in the US and the UK. These are the main points to consider before getting behind the wheel of your hire car:

- You have to be 21 or over to hire a car and have held a full driving licence for at least a year whatever your age.
- Most hire cars are automatic.
- Drive on the right side of the road.
- It's the law to wear seat belts.
- Carry a valid driving licence and proof of insurance at all times.
- Florida's official speed limit is 55 mph, which rises to 70 mph on some interstates and drops to as low as 20 mph in a school zone when children are present.

Sample Mileages in between Florida's Cities

Cities	Distance	Driving Time (hours)
Orlando to Apalachicola	296 miles	6
Orlando to Miami	296 miles	5
Orlando to Tallahassee	244 miles	5.5
Orlando to Fort Myers	152 miles	3
Orlando to Daytona	54 miles	1
Orlando to Tampa	85 miles	2
Tallahassee to Pensacola	191 miles	4
Tallahassee to Jacksonville	163 miles	3.5
Daytona to Jacksonville	89 miles	2
Miami to Fort Myers	144 miles	3
Miami to Fort Lauderdale	25 miles	0.5
Miami to Key West	153 miles	3.5
Pensacola to Key West	790 miles	19

- Interstate and major roads will also often have a minimum speed limit of 40 mph. Legal limits, which are posted on the right-hand side of the road, are strictly enforced and fines are doubled when road workers are present. Even if you're in the middle of nowhere on a Sunday afternoon and think you can get away with putting your foot down, you can't. There's always heavy police presence on Florida's roads.

- At a traffic light controlled junction you can turn right on a red light after coming to a complete stop, unless there's a sign stating 'no right on red'.

- You must turn your headlights on if it's foggy, raining or if there's smoke in the air, e.g. if you drive in an area near a forest fire, but turn your windscreen wipers off when stopping at a tollbooth.

- If you pass a police car parked on the hard shoulder helping a motorist or pulling someone over for speeding, you must move to the far lane, away from the police.

- It's the law to yield to buses and let them back into traffic.

- If a school bus stops to let children on or off, all other traffic stops. Even if you're driving on the opposite side of the road, you must stop when a school bus does.

- Driving under the influence of alcohol is illegal and considered to be a serious crime. The legal limit for blood alcohol level is lower than in the UK and a zero tolerance attitude prevails if you're caught driving over the limit. Fines and suspensions are heavy, especially if you're driving with children, and it's best not to drink at all if you plan to drive.

Keeping Children Entertained On the Road

Driving distances between towns and cities in Florida are vast and roads are generally boring for children – even driving from one side of Orlando to the other can take time and offer little in the way of interesting views. Larger car-hire companies offer the added extra of in-car DVD players and DVDs to keep back-seat passengers entertained. If you don't want your children to watch films in the car, keep them occupied with 'spot the number plates'. All US cars have number plates representing the state they're from and it's fun to look out for where cars have come from (double points if you get Hawaii). Before leaving home, check the 'Know How' section of the RAC's website ***www.rac.co.uk*** for ideas on how to keep children entertained on a long journey. In the States, Universal Map ***www.universalmap.com*** sell a range of Little Passenger travel activity maps and games to keep young travellers occupied.

- Road junctions are not marked in numerical order but after the mile along the road where they are situated, e.g. junction 55 is 55 miles from the start of the road.
- A flashing yellow light is a caution sign and they're usually found at crossroads or when emergency vehicles are present, e.g. outside a fire station. You have right of way but should be aware that other traffic may pull out onto the road.
- A flashing red light is a warning that there's a stop sign at a junction ahead where you must stop.
- When stopping at a red traffic light, remember there's no amber light and it will just change straight to green. There is an amber light between green and red giving drivers plenty of time to slow down and stop.
- At a four-way stop, which is basically a crossroads that's not controlled by traffic lights, all cars must stop and then proceed in the order they arrived, give way to the car on your right if in doubt.
- If a pedestrian is standing on the corner of the road waiting to cross, they have right of way and you must stop and let them cross (not that many drivers seem to, even though it's the law). Drivers must also always stop at zebra crossings, and if you need to drive across a pavement at any time, e.g. when driving out of a car park, you must stop before the pavement, check there are no pedestrians, and then drive to the edge of the road to check for traffic before turning.
- It's illegal to park against the flow of traffic and don't park within ten feet of a water hydrant; you'll get clamped or towed away.

● It's illegal to make a 'U' turn when an unbroken white line runs down the middle of the road – these are usually found on interstates.

● It's illegal to change lanes across double yellow solid lines, double white solid lines and a single yellow solid line on your side of a broken yellow line unless you're turning left into a private driveway. You can change lanes through a single white or yellow lines but it is discouraged – these are usually found at large junctions when traffic has committed to a lane and changing to another one could be difficult or dangerous.

● It's a good idea when approaching a junction to know whether you want to head north, south, east or west, as all roads are signposted in the direction they lead. On smaller roads there's often little in the way of prior warning before a junction, so you have to make instant decisions.

● If you break down, pull over onto the hard shoulder and put on your hazard lights so that local police and other drivers know you need help. Breakdown cover should be included with your car hire (check at the time of hiring) and they will issue you with a number to call for breakdown service. If you don't have breakdown cover or need police help, call ☎ *347* to reach Florida's Highway Patrol or call ☎ *911* in an emergency. There are emergency call boxes roughly every half a mile on major interstates.

● If you're pulled over by the police, remember that Florida's police aren't famous for their sense of humour, so don't try and crack jokes. Also, never reach into the glove compartment, as the police officer may assume that you're reaching for a gun. Stay in your car, sit with your hands off the steering wheel and put on the inside car light if it's dark. If you've been pulled over for an offence such as speeding or driving through a red light, you'll be fined and given a ticket. Don't try and pay the fine on the spot, this could come across as bribery, instead let the police officer tell you how, when or where to pay.

● If possible, don't drive as soon as you arrive. Stepping straight off a long-haul flight into a hire car is not the best time to get used to a new road system and its rules. Wait until you're feeling more refreshed before picking up a car.

● And finally, don't let any of the above put you off driving in Florida. These might seem like draconian rules and regulations compared with the UK, but once you're used to it, driving in the US is much easier than driving at home, and, outside of the traffic-clogged cities, it can be a lot of fun.

INSIDER TIP

Florida 511 is a free state-wide travel information service. ☎ *511* or visit ***www.fl511.com*** for real-time traffic information.

Different Types of Roads in Florida

Florida's road system consists of a number of different types of roads. The fastest and quickest to drive are interstates, which are the equivalent of motorways in the UK and identified by the letter 'I' in this book, e.g. interstate 4 is depicted as I-4.

One down from interstates, and similar to 'A' roads in the UK, are US highways, major roads that often travel directly through towns and cities, rather than bypassing them like interstates. They also have slower speed limits than interstates and in this book have been identified by Hwy- followed by the road's number, e.g. Hwy-41. Some 'scenic' versions of US highways exist, such as the A1A that runs down the east coast. These roads have lower speed limits but fantastic views.

More minor roads, and the equivalent of 'B' roads in the UK, are known as state or county roads (often called routes) and are identified by SR- in this book, e.g. SR-60.

Florida also has a system of fast toll roads, of which the Florida Turnpike is the longest.

By Plane Although flying isn't the cheapest way to travel around Florida, it is the quickest and all areas are served by internal flights operated by major American airlines. If you do decide to travel internally by plane, book as far in advance as possible, as this is far cheaper than leaving it until the last minute. To give you a general idea of flying times, flights from Orlando to Miami and Tallahassee last an hour and flights to Key West and Pensacola an hour and a half. For information, schedules and prices for internal flights check:

American Airlines *www.aa.com*

Continental Airlines *www.continentalairlines.com*

Delta *www.delta.com*

Gulfstream *www.gulfstreamair.com*

US Airways *www.usairways.com*

Responsible Tourism

Whales and Dolphins in Captivity

An enormous controversy rages around the ethics of keeping dolphins, whales and other marine animals in captivity for the purposes of entertaining humans, and the arguments of whether or not to 'Free Willy' are complex and not clear cut. If you would like your children to come into close contact with a dolphin or any other marine animal at one of Florida's attractions, but are concerned about animal cruelty, ask the organisation you're thinking of visiting where their dolphins have come from. A dolphin might have been born in captivity and therefore be unable to survive in the wild or it might be a rescue animal and equally dependent upon human care. However, many dolphins are captured in the wild, causing them great

Gator swimming in the Everglades

distress, and bought by some attractions to be trained to entertain. You might also want to ask how animals are trained, some organisations, such as Theatre by the Sea in the Florida Keys, do not withhold food from animals as a means of training, while others do. For more information visit the Whale and Dolphin Conservation Society's website ***www.wdcs.org***.

It's also worth remembering that while nothing beats seeing a dolphin, or any animal, in its natural environment, human intervention in that environment is often as cruel as keeping an animal in captivity. For more information check the Marine Conservation's website ***www.mcuk.org*** or Seafood Watch ***www.seafoodwatch.org***, which contains some good advice on the different types of seafood available in Florida's restaurants and supermarkets, such as which ones have been caught or farmed in environmentally friendly ways.

Florida's Wildlife in its Natural Habitat

When experiencing animals in their natural habitat, impress upon your children the difference between animals in the wild and those in captivity and be aware of the laws in place to protect Florida's abundant and magnificent wildlife. Just because a dolphin will roll over and be tickled in a theme park doesn't mean that it won't attack in the wild, and there have been many incidents of this happening when people get too close.

Also be aware that it's both a bad idea and illegal to feed animals such as alligators, dolphins and manatees in the wild, as this turns them into scavengers. There have been occasions when female dolphins will compete with their calves for food rather than teaching them how to hunt.

And, although it's overwhelmingly tempting to reach out and touch the docile manatee, this is also illegal, as any human interaction with this animal could potentially cause problems by taming them and diminishing their natural suspicion of humans.

Forest Fires

Forest fires are a constant problem in Florida and, although some are intentional and controlled, many are the result of lightning strikes or campfires that haven't been put out properly. In times of drought, such as summer 2007, when the risk of forest fires escalates, lighting ground fires or throwing away cigarette butts is prohibited. If you're considering lighting a campfire in one of Florida's state or national parks, look for the 'Smokey the Bear' sign – a cartoon brown bear in a ranger's hat – as he will indicate if the risk of forest fires in that area is low, moderate or high and whether or not you can light a fire.

Carbon Offsetting

An increasing number of travellers are choosing to carbon offset their flights. Although the only real 'green' solution is not to fly at all, carbon offsetting does reduce the negative impact on the environment that flying has. Two companies offer this service. Climate Care ***www.climatecare.org.uk*** will calculate your emissions and charge a set fee that's put towards sustainable energy and forest restoration projects. At the time of writing, this company charges around £14–15 per passenger to offset a return flight to Orlando, depending on which UK airport you depart from.

The Carbon Neutral Company ***www.carbonneutral.com*** offers the same service and provides the option to choose where you want your money to be spent. At the time of writing, this company charges £12–17 per passenger for a return flight to Orlando, depending where you fly from and where you choose to allocate your money .

If you're hiring a car, some companies, such as Hertz ***www.hertz.com***, hire vehicles that emit less CO2.

General Information about Responsible Travel

Numerous organisations exist to promote sustainable tourism practices. Below are a number that will help you plan a family trip that will be as environmentally friendly as possible:

www.responsibletravel.com helps travellers choose environmentally responsible tour operators and businesses.

www.tourismconcern.org.uk works with communities to help reduce tourism's negative impact.

www.thetravelfoundation.org is set up to help visitors care for the places they go on holiday and includes an excellent children's section so youngsters get involved too.

www.ecotourism.org, a US-based organisation, promotes travel to and preservation of natural areas and provides some useful definitions and facts around ecotourism.

ACCOMMODATION & EATING OUT

Accommodation

As a rule, accommodation is far cheaper and of a higher standard in Florida than in the UK. Accommodation options for families are either self-catering villas, large resorts, chain or privately owned hotels and chain motels. On the whole, exclusive boutique hotels and bed and breakfasts are where adults stay to be away from families and do not accept children. For the purposes of the reviews in this book, accommodation prices have been classified as:

Budget US$60–US$100 (£30–50)

Moderate US$100–US$200 (£50–100)

Expensive US$200–US$500 (£100–250)

Very Expensive US$500 plus (£250 plus)

Self-catering villas are abundant in tourist areas and often the most cost-effective form of accommodation for families. Details of villa rental companies can be found in the accommodation sections of relevant chapters.

Most families travelling on package tours will stay in one of the many large resorts which dominate Florida's popular tourists areas and are well set up to cater for children of all ages. All have swimming pools and most contain children's pools, games rooms, family dining packages and children's clubs at the very least. If you book through a tour operator, all taxes should be included, but if you book independently or arrive as walk-ins, expect to pay a resort tax of between US$5 and US$30 (£2.50 to £15)in order to use the facilities on top of the usual room rate, as well as Florida tax (see p. 43).

Big hotels are plentiful in the main tourist centres and along the coast, and are often the only option in city centres. Most have a swimming pool and on-site restaurants and all rooms are en suite with air conditioning, telephones and cable TV, but they're unlikely to be as family focused as resorts.

The most economical accommodation option for families travelling on fly-drives or independently is chain motels, which can be found everywhere from the popular tourist stops to junctions off major roads. Motel rooms can be excellent value for money, as all have private bathrooms and most contain two double beds, cable TV, iron, safe, telephone, fridge, microwave, coffeemaker and hairdryer. It's usual for each motel to have its own swimming pool, coin-operated laundry facilities, cots and extra rollaway beds (for a fee). Adjoining rooms are often available. The main motel chains, their toll-free telephone numbers and websites are:

Best Western *1-800 780 723*; ***www.bestwestern.com***

Days Inn 1-800 329 7466; *www.dyasinn.com*

Extended Stay America 1-800 426 7866; *www.extendedstayamerica.com*

Hampton Inn 1-800 426 7866; *www.hamptoninn.com*

Holiday Inn 1-800 465 4329; *www.holidayinn.com*

Howard Johnson 1-800 446 4656; *www.hojo.com*

La Quinta 1-800 642 4271; *www.lq.com*

Quality Inn, Comfort Inn and Econo Lodge 1-877 424 6423; *www.choicehotels.com*

If you're planning to use motel accommodation, pick up discount brochures from petrol stations, supermarkets and visitor centres, as you can save money by using the coupons they contain. However, it's unlikely you'll be able to use the coupons on Friday and Saturday nights when rates are higher than the rest of the week.

Unless you've booked through a tour operator, all accommodation options will require a credit card number to secure a reservation.

Eating Out

With a few notable exceptions, family dining in Florida is inexpensive compared with the UK, but limited. For the purposes of the reviews in this book, dining prices for a main course have been classified as:

Budget US$6–US$10 (£3–5)

Moderate US$10–US$20 (£5–10)

Expensive US$20–US$30 (£10–15)

Very Expensive US$30 plus (£15 plus)

Budget options are mainly the big-name chains, branches of which are everywhere in the main tourist areas. Of these chains, Olive Garden *www.olivegarden.com* and Denny's *www.dennys.com* are the healthiest options and Pizza Huts are generally not as nice as branches in the UK.

American families are early eaters compared with Europeans and even popular restaurants can stop serving dinner as early as 9pm, so call ahead if you plan to eat somewhere other than a chain restaurant after this time.

Outside the major chains, the vast majority of Florida's restaurants are seafood oriented, with most serving some meat options. Dining out with a vegetarian member of the family can be a serious challenge, a vegan or any other special dietary requirement, even more so. Any restaurant serving Mexican food usually has vegetarian options and most will rustle up something without meat, but they prefer to have advance notice. Theme parks are a particular challenge for vegetarians, especially as many do not allow visitors to take in their own food. See the Family-friendly Dining section of the Major Attractions

Ice-cream seller, Seaside

chapter for further information, p. 80.

Most restaurants provide a children's menu, but these often consist of little more than burgers, fries and hot dogs. If you want something a bit healthier for your children, there's always the option of ordering starters or an adult main course and splitting it between your children.

THE ACTIVE FAMILY

Even in the theme park soaked central region, active families will not be disappointed with a visit to Florida. As with everywhere in the US, the option of walking between places is limited, but what Florida lacks in pavements, it makes up for with its state parks. There are over 150 in Florida and each one is open from 8am until sunset daily. And, whether inland or on the coast, all parks are wildlife havens offering an abundance of outdoor activities, including swimming, snorkelling, cycling, hiking, kayaking and canoeing. For full details on the facilities that each park offers, and to find ones in the areas you plan to visit, check the Florida State Parks' website ***www.floridastateparks.org***.

Outside of its state parks, Florida's inland and coastal waterways are perfect for all ages to kayak and canoe. There are companies throughout the state which run kayak and canoe trips plus equipment hire. Florida's Professional Paddlesports

Association's website ***www.paddleflausa.com*** contains information on kayak and canoe tour companies and some helpful hints for those with limited paddling experience.

Cycling is increasingly popular in Florida and a network of trails both large and small is laced all over the state, along with numerous cycle-hire outlets. Visit Florida have created a booklet detailing Florida's main paved and off-road cycling trails and some bike rental locations. Details can be found on their website ***www.visitflorida.com***.

Also see the Active Families sections of each chapter for further information.

INSIDER TIP

If you rent bikes remember that, by law, any child aged under 16 must wear a helmet.

GETTING CHILDREN INTERESTED IN FLORIDA

Whether your children are preschool or hitting their teens, you should have no trouble sparking their interest in a trip to Florida. Most will be excited about visiting the theme parks, so get them involved at an early stage in finding out about the rides, attractions and animals at each, so they know what they want to do when they arrive.

The Internet has many brilliant resources to get children interested in the places you plan to visit. Google Earth is a free downloadable program with which you can obtain aerial views of just about anywhere in the world (yes, you can check how far the beach is from your hotel), watch video diaries made by residents and see photos taken in the area. Webcams are good to get up close to locations in Florida and are a smart way for children to get involved in planning the trip.

In addition, America's national parks, which in Florida include the Everglades, operate a Junior Ranger's Programme through which children are given a number of activities to undertake in their parks before being enrolled as a Junior Ranger. Copies of the activity booklets can be downloaded from the National Parks' website ***www.nps.org*** in advance of a visit.

For a child-friendly history of Florida that includes information on the Seminole Indians, check the 'kids' section of the My Florida website ***http://dhr.dos.state.fl.us/kids/*** which has been created by the state's Cultural and Historical Programs. Very young children may be interested in the 'kids' section of the US Geological Survey's South Florida Information Access (Sofia) ***http://sofia.usgs.gov/virtual_tour/kids/***, which features information on the animals and ecosystems of southern Florida.

Films are another good way to get children interested in Florida. A visit to the Kennedy Space Center is far more interesting after watching *Apollo 13,* for example, and with a history rich with the likes of Blackbeard and Gasparilla, any pirate film should raise children's interest in the state. Or you can prepare teens for the sights of Miami with the new film and old cop show, *Miami Vice.*

The older book-loving child can delve into the works of Ernest Hemmingway prior to a visit to Key West, while young children can relish the Disney classics before hitting their theme parks.

FAST FACTS: FLORIDA

Alcohol The minimum age for buying and drinking alcohol in Florida is 21 and proof of age is often requested, so carry photo ID stating your date of birth. No one is allowed to consume alcohol in public places such as beaches, parks, on the street or at a motel pool unless there's an adjoining bar. It's illegal to drive with alcohol within reach of the driver, so travel with it in the boot of your car – even there it must be sealed.

Business Hours Shopping malls are generally open 10am–9pm Mon–Sat and many large shopping complexes and department stores also open on Sundays from noon to 6pm. Smaller, privately owned stores typically open between 9am and 10am and close between 5pm and 6pm Mon–Sat, while large supermarkets are often open 24 hours.

Most banks are open 9am–4pm Mon–Fri and some open on Saturday mornings.

Car Hire see p. 130.

Chemists Most large communities and shopping malls contain a branch of the chain chemists Walgreens; some open 24 hours and many are drive thru. Large supermarkets such as Publix often have a chemist section.

Climate see p. 21.

Crime & Safety see p. 24.

Currency Currency can be exchanged at most major airports, banks, at private exchange offices such as American Express or Thomas Cook and at some hotels. Foreign currency exchange offices at international airports are usually open until the last international flight comes in, Mon–Sat.

Dentists All towns and cities will have dentists. Ask at your hotel reception for advice or look in the Yellow Pages. You're unlikely to find a dentist who'll charge your travel insurance company, so expect to pay upfront and make a claim when you return home – keep all receipts and proof of all expenses incurred.

Doctors See p. 24.

Driving Rules See earlier on in chapter p. 130.

Electricity The US uses 110–120 volts and 60 cycles is standard. If your small appliances use 220–240 volts, you'll need to bring a voltage converter and a plug adapter with two flat parallel pins.

Embassies & Consulates The main website for the British Embassy in the US is ***www.britainusa.com***. Main Florida consulates are:

British Consulate, Orlando ☎ *407 254 3300* Main Switchboard ☎ *407 254 3300* Consular ***www.britainusa.com/orlando/***

British Consulate, Miami ☎ *305 374 1522* Main Switchboard ☎ *305 374 3500* Consular ***www.britainusa.com/miami/***

Emergencies To reach the police, ambulance or fire brigade in an emergency ☎ *911* from any phone. For less urgent requests, call the local non-emergency number for the local police, which your hotel, visitor information or telephone book will be able to provide.

Holidays Banks, government offices and post offices are all closed on the national public holidays listed below. In addition, some attractions and many stores, restaurants and museums may be closed or have limited hours (call ahead to check).

New Year's Day – 1st January

Martin Luther King Jr. Day – 3rd Monday in January

Presidents' Day – 3rd Monday in February

Memorial Day – last Monday in May

Independence Day – 4th July

Labor Day – 1st Monday in September

Columbus Day – 2nd Monday in October

Veterans' Day – 11th November

Thanksgiving Day – 4th Thursday in November

Christmas Day – 25th December

Hospitals Most towns and cities have their own hospitals with emergency departments. Ask your hotel reception for advice or look in the telephone book.

Internet Access see p. 28.

Laundry Nearly all motels and some hotels and resorts will have coin-operated washing machines and dryers for guest use. Otherwise you'll have to pay for their laundry service.

Legal Aid Contact the British Embassy or consulate.

Lost Property Most attractions and public buildings will have a lost property department; find guest services or visitor information and they'll be able to help you. Outside of the attractions, call the local police to see if your property has been handed in.

Mail US post offices are normally open 9am–5pm Mon–Fri and 9am–noon Sat and blue mail boxes are easily identified on street corners. Many hotel receptions will also sell stamps and sort out postage for you.

Maps An up-to-date road map is essential for anyone hiring a car in Florida. Maps can be bought in advance from Stanfords ***www.stanfords.co.uk***. Most major bookshops with a travel department have a map section. Maps are available at petrol stations, supermarkets and visitor information centres in Florida and online maps can be printed from ***www.multimap.com*** and ***www.maps.google.com***.

Money & Credit Cards For lost or stolen credit cards call:

American Express *800-528-4800*

Diners' Club *800-234-6377*

Discover *800-347-2683*

MasterCard *800-826-2181* or *800 307 7309*

Visa *800-336-8472*

For lost or stolen travellers' cheques call:

American Express *800- 221-7282*

MasterCard *800-223-9920*

Thomas Cook *800-223-7373*

Visa *800-227-6811*

Newspapers & Magazines The main national US newspaper is *USA Today*, a copy of which is complimentary in most hotels and motels. Regional papers include the *Miami Herald* and *Orlando Sentinel*, which are available in coin-operated machines.

Police In an emergency call *911*. For theft, file a report at the local police station.

Post Offices See mail p. 42.

Safety see p. 22.

Smoking Smoking is not permitted on public transport, including taxis, or in public buildings. Nor can you smoke anywhere that serves food, although many restaurants will have an outside smoking area. Hotel rooms are either 'smoking' or 'non-smoking', so make sure you ask for a smoking room when making a reservation. At the theme parks smoking is only allowed in designated areas.

Taxes A sales tax of up to 7% is added on to everything you buy in Florida. Hotels will also often add a resort tax on to your bill, see p. 37.

Taxis It is not the norm to hail cabs in Florida. Ask your hotel reception for a recommended taxi company or look in Yellow Pages. Larger hotels sometimes have taxis waiting outside, which the bell hops call over for you.

Telephones The majority of accommodation options will have at least one telephone in their rooms. All local calls are free and area codes *800, 888, 866,* and *877* are all freephone numbers; however, some hotels will charge to call these numbers from your room (check when making a reservation).

Coin-operated public telephones are widely available and calls cost a minimum of 50¢ (25p). Phones accept 25¢, 10¢ and 5¢ coins and a voice message will let you know when you need to put in more money.

For reversed charge or collect calls, dial 0 followed by the number and let the operator know that you're calling collect. If you need to make an international reverse charge call, ask the operator for the overseas operator. And for directory assistance within the US dial *411*.

Telephone Cards Prepaid phone cards can be bought in US$5, US$10 and US$20 (£2.50, £5 and £10) denominations at most convenience stores and in shops such as Walgreens. Each card has a phone and PIN number on the back. Call the number, enter the PIN number when asked then dial the number you want.

Time Zones Florida has two zones. The Florida peninsula operates under Eastern Standard Time – 5 hours behind BST – and west of the Apalachicola River in the Panhandle, the state operates under Central Standard Time, which is another hour behind.

Tipping: Tipping is an important part of American culture and it's standard to leave a 15–20 per cent tip at a bar or restaurant. Some will include a gratuity as part of your total bill, so make sure you don't pay twice. In hotels the norm is a US$1 (50p) tip for each item of luggage carried up to your room, US$2 (£1)for the valet who delivers your car and US$1–US$2 (50p–£1) for housekeeping for each night of your stay. Many also tip the guide or driver of sightseeing tours if they have been informative and/or helpful.

Toilets & Baby-Changing Facilities Just about every attraction, public building, restaurant and shopping mall will have public toilets with baby-changing facilities.

Water Florida's tap water is safe to drink although many prefer bottled water, which is readily available and inexpensive in large supermarkets.

Weather For up-to-date weather information, watch the Weather Channel on cable TV or check ***www.weather.com***. For more information on hurricanes, see p. 22.

3 The Major Attractions

Cinderella Castle © Disney

MAJOR ATTRACTIONS

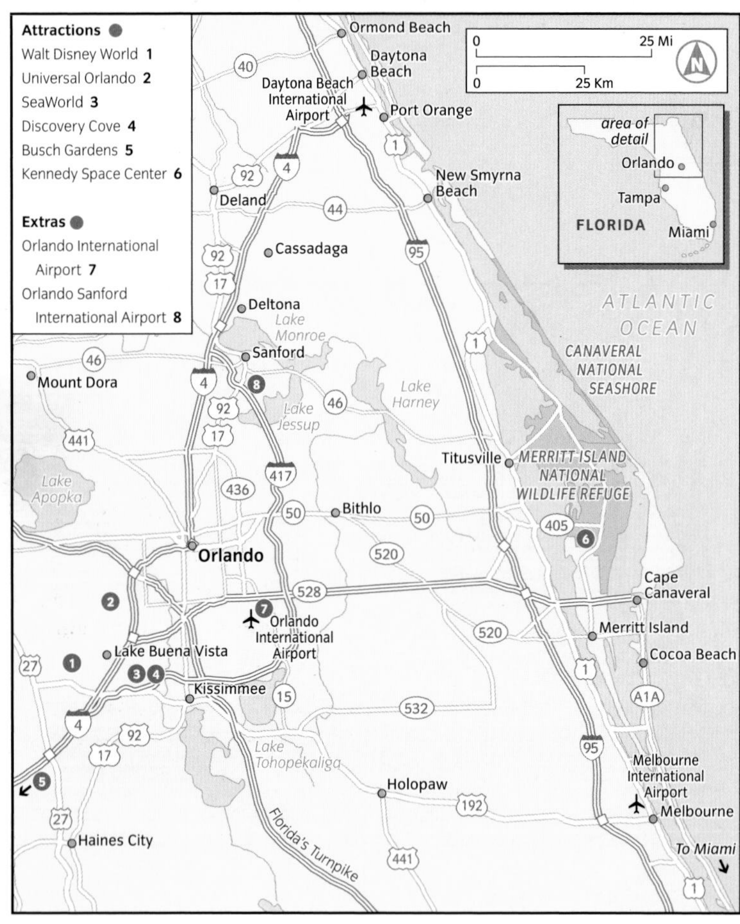

For many families the main reason to visit Florida is to indulge in all the escapist entertainment that its major attractions promise, and millions flock here every year to do just that. At the centre of the state, and at the top of many lists of 'must sees', is the enormous Walt Disney World, a complex the size of a small city containing four very different theme parks – Magic Kingdom, Epcot, MGM Studios and Animal Kingdom – where, if you believe Disney, dreams can come true. Also dominating central Florida is Universal Orlando, which, although much smaller than Walt Disney World, is equally as popular with families and its two large theme parks – Universal Studios and Islands of Adventure – take visitors deep into the make-believe worlds of the movies and fantasy realms respectively.

Two marine parks – SeaWorld and Discovery Cove – make up central Florida's other major attractions and are both places where visitors can get up close to the beauty of some of Florida's glorious marine animals. Over on the south west coast, Tampa's Busch Gardens is the place to view all kinds of native and exotic wildlife, while also enjoying some of the greatest thrill rides Florida has to offer. And on the east coast, the Kennedy Space Center, with its feet firmly planted in the real world of space exploration, is the odd one out of the major attractions, but no less exciting than those based on fantasy. Don't expect to do or see everything all of these attractions offer in one visit. They are constantly updating themselves with new rides, new shows and even whole new theme parks, all of which pull some families back year upon year. And while some of these attractions have a more general appeal to certain age groups, all of them cater in some way for children of all ages, not to mention the child in all of us.

Children's Top 10 Attractions

1. **MGM Studios'** superb end-of-night spectacular Fantasmic! show; p. 57.
2. **Getting** up close to the animals on Animal Kingdom's Kilimanjaro Safari; p. 59.
3. **SheiKra** at Busch Gardens, Florida's latest and greatest roller coaster; p. 72.
4. **Kennedy Space Center's** all new Shuttle Launch Experience; p. 74.
5. **Seuss Landing** at Universal's Islands of Adventure, excellent for pre-school-age children; p. 66.
6. **Shamu's (the killer whale)** dazzling performance at SeaWorld; p. 68.
7. **Universal Studios'** speedy and scary Revenge of the Mummy ride; p. 63.
8. **Lunch** at MGM Studios' quirky Sci-Fi Dine-In Theater themed restaurant; p. 80.
9. **Monsters Inc.** Laugh Floor, Magic Kingdom's newest show; p. 53.
10. **Epcot's** The Seas With Nemo and Friends, a brilliant adventure ride for small children; p. 56.

ESSENTIALS

Getting There

Information on Disney and Universal holiday packages for UK travellers can be found on their UK websites: ***www.disneyworld.co.uk*** and ***www.universalorlando.co.uk***. Both companies send out free holiday-planning DVDs on request through these sites. For more general information on package tour operators and flights to Florida see p. 28.

INSIDER TIP

Virgin Holidays is the only UK package tour operator to have check-in facilities at Walt Disney World, allowing you an extra day in their theme parks and no long waits at the airport. They also hold twice weekly receptions in Downtown Disney (see p. 60).

VISITOR INFORMATION

For details of the main tourist offices in central Florida, see p. 86. Each of the theme parks hosts its own Guest Services Desk, where staff can help with specific enquiries.

INSIDER TIP

For useful unofficial information on Walt Disney World, see *www.allearsnet.com*.

Orientation

I-4 runs through Orlando and central Florida and is a useful landmark from which to locate the major attractions. Walt Disney World is south west of Orlando and west of I-4 from exits 64–68. Universal is north of Walt Disney World and west of I-4 at exit 75A. Halfway between the two, SeaWorld and Discovery Cove are east of I-4 at exit 72 if you're driving from Orlando, and exit 71 if coming from Tampa.

To reach Busch Gardens on the outskirts of Tampa from Orlando, travel west on I-4 until the junction with I-75. Take I-75 north to exit 265 onto Fowler Avenue (also signposted to the University of South Florida). Bear left on to Fowler Avenue and then turn left on to McKinley Drive. Drive south until the left-hand turn into Busch Gardens's car park.

For the Kennedy Space Center, drive east from Orlando along SR-528 (the Bee Line Expressway) to the junction with SR-407. Exit on to SR-407 and travel north until it ends. Turn east on to SR-405, which leads directly to the Space Center.

INSIDER TIP

Rush hour on the I-4 is from 7–9am and 4–6pm. If you're travelling to and from the parks at these times, avoid this road.

When to Visit

During peak times, tens of thousands flock to Florida's theme parks every day. These times are: Christmas and New Year, the two weeks of Easter, Thanksgiving weekend (fourth Thursday in November), Martin Luther King Jr. holiday weekend (third Monday in January), college spring break (see p. 21) and the summer months. In between these dates the parks are somewhat quieter, with the periods from the end of Easter until early June and September being the best times to visit.

Getting Around

The most convenient way to reach the major parks is by car (for details on car hire, see p. 29), but there are limited options to getting around without driving. Most hotels in the Orlando area offer free shuttle buses to Disney, Universal and SeaWorld (there's a free shuttle between SeaWorld and Discovery Cove). Mears Transportation *www.mearstransportation.com* operates the shuttles and also runs a daily express service to Busch Gardens from some hotels in central Florida. Check the 'park information' section of Busch Gardens's website (see p. 72) for details or call 1 800 221 1339.

Some hotels offer complimentary transport on this shuttle service, which is also free with an Orlando Flexi ticket (see p. 62). Otherwise tickets cost US$10 (£5) per person.

Mears Transportation also operates a shuttle service to Kennedy Space Center on Mondays, Wednesdays and Fridays. Tickets are US$30 (£15) per person 407 423 5566 for 24-hour reservations.

For details of Orlando's bus service, see p. 88 and for the I-Ride Trolley, a frequent tourist trolley service that covers International Drive, see p. 94.

Child-friendly Festivals & Events

Mardi Gras at Universal Studios ★★

www.universalorlando.com/mardigras

Top entertainers from New Orleans's famous Mardi Gras recreate their spectacular parades and concerts at Universal Studios each March. The dates vary each year (check the website for information) and entrance to all Mardi Gras events is included in Universal's admission price.

Epcot International Flower & Garden Festival ★★

From April to early June, Epcot transforms itself with a stunning themed festival of fantastic floral displays and sculptures. A programme of supporting events includes 'Flower Power' concerts and parties featuring Disney favourites, all for the normal admission price.

INSIDER TIP

The Epcot International Flower and Garden Festival is a good time to visit with grandparents, as the park runs regular behind-the-scenes horticultural tours (adults US$10 – £5, children US$8 – £4).

Space Shuttle launch from Cape Canaveral ★★★

Space shuttles take off from Cape Canaveral on a relatively

Spaceship Earth, Epcot © Disney

frequent basis and witnessing one of these iconic events will provide your children with a memory of a lifetime. Visit 'Experiencing a launch at KSC' on their website (see p. 74) to view a launch timetable. This timetable can change at the last minute, so keep checking if you're planning your holiday around a launch. Tickets go on sale online five days before take off and you'll need to be quick to get one. Parts of the Space Center close on launch day, so you'll get to see a launch but not all the other attractions.

Most of the theme parks host special events at Halloween, Christmas and New Year. All of Walt Disney World's attractions and resorts are decorated throughout December and there's a multitude of seasonal events.

WHAT TO SEE & DO

> **INSIDER TIP**
> Most parks offer photograph packages – have your picture taken around the park by professional photographers and pick up the ones you like when you leave. They're not cheap, but it's worth splashing out for that special picture if you don't want to carry a camera around.

The Big Theme Parks

Walt Disney World

407 824 4321
www.disneyworld.com

'I only hope that we don't lose sight of one thing – that it was all started by a mouse.' Walt Disney.

When it comes to theme parks, no one can match the panache, attention to detail and magic touch of Walt Disney World, which originally consisted of the Magic Kingdom and two hotels when it opened in 1971. Since then, Epcot, MGM Studios and Animal Kingdom have joined the list of major attractions along with another 21 resorts – and Disney just keeps on growing. Everything about Disney is overwhelming, from orientating yourself within its 47 square miles to working out which ticket deal to go for. Walt Disney World is one of the most expensive attractions in Florida, so take time to research ticket deals (see box p. 54) and find out exactly what each member of your family wants to get out of the four very different parks before you get there.

Magic Kingdom ★

This granddaddy of theme parks' iconic status makes Magic Kingdom a Florida must see for anyone into theme parks. Despite it being a bit dated, and having little to please thrill-seeking teens for whom the fab five (Mickey, Minnie, Donald, Pluto and Goofy) aren't as cool as they used to be, you really can't claim to have done Disney without experiencing this park's most famous rides. Magic Kingdom is

WALT DISNEY WORLD

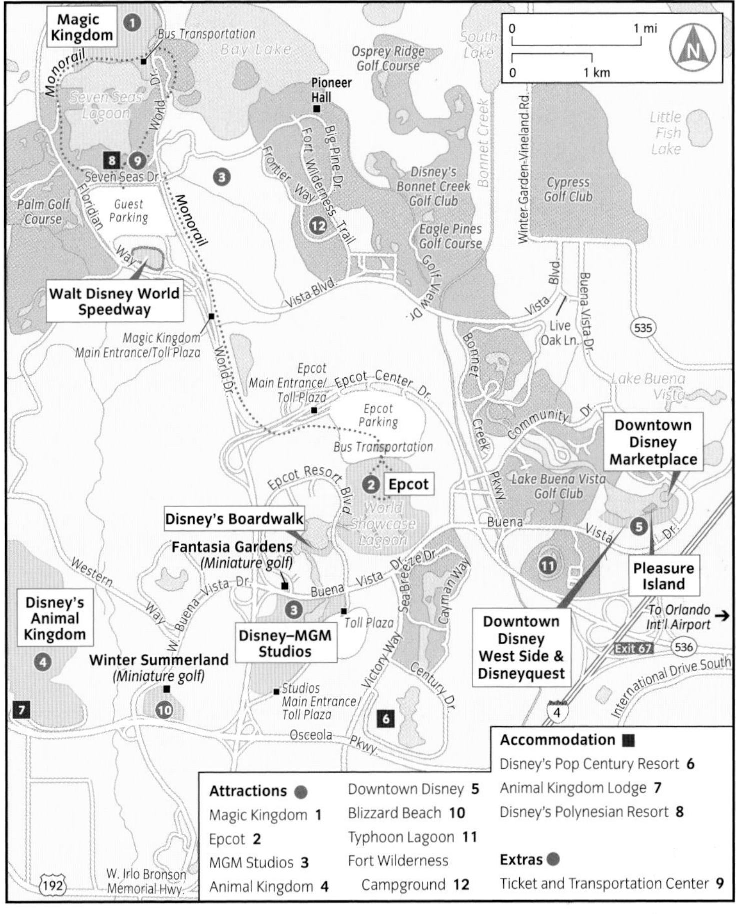

easily reached via a short monorail journey from the Ticket and Transportation Center and it's impossible not to get caught up in young children's excitement when entering, as many dress up as princesses or their favourite Disney character just for the occasion. And with its infectious fun-filled atmosphere, abundance of all things shaped like mouse ears and wacky street performers, this is the ideal starting point for Florida's main attractions if you're visiting with small children.

On arrival, visitors stream through Main Street USA, a bustling thoroughfare styled around early 20th century small-town America and packed with themed shops and eating options.

The Theme Parks – A Family Survival Guide

The sheer size and scale of Florida's major attractions takes British families some getting used to. Visits involve long days starting with a sugar-rush of excitement and ending in a crash of exhaustion, with lots of walking and queuing in between in high temperatures. Here's some practical advice to help you stay sane: Don't promise your children that you can see everything in one day. Pick what's important, do that first, and then see what else you've time for.

- Most young children flag around 3–4pm, when the parks are at their hottest and busiest. If you can, take a break for a couple of hours and come back later.
- Don't over-estimate your family's staying power. To avoid burnout, alternate between a day at a theme park and the next relaxing by the pool or taking in some light shopping.
- Organise a place to meet in case you get separated and make sure young children have identification details with them.
- Take a plastic bag to put your camera in, as some seating areas for the shows in the marine parks and *all* water rides will drench you.
- Make a note of where you park. Theme park car parks are enormous. Take a sunshade for the windscreen.
- Wear sunscreen and comfortable shoes and drink lots of fluids.
- Don't put your children on rides if they are upset.
- Bring a change of clothes for children who won't like wearing wet clothes after the water rides or playing in the splash areas.

INSIDER TIP

VMK (Virtual Magic Kingdom) Central on Main Street USA is a good place to head when it's raining. Here you can play games and answer trivia questions about the park online.

Main Street USA leads to Cinderella's Castle, a fairytale structure at the heart of Magic Kingdom, around which six other lands fan out. And there are over 40 attractions to experience, with different age groups getting more out of some areas than others; however, all have a more general appeal to young children.

Of the rides that are aimed at all age groups, don't miss Pirates of the Caribbean ★★ (updated to feature Captain Jack Sparrow) in Adventureland, the runaway Big Thunder Mountain Railroad ★★ in Frontierland and the twilight world of the Haunted Mansion in Liberty Square.

Highlights for small children include the sugar sweet It's a Small World in Fantasyland and cute Mickey's Toontown Fair, an interactive play area and favourite haunt of Disney characters which pre-school children love. But if you don't have small

FUN FACT **Cinderella's Castle**

Due to forced perspective, Cinderella's Castle appears larger than it is.

children, steer clear of this area because the number of buggies and children make it impossible to navigate.

Older children should gravitate towards Space Mountain ★ in Tomorrowland (a roller coaster ride to the stars in pitch black) and Magic Kingdom's vertiginous flume ride Splash Mountain ★ in Frontierland (you'll get very wet).

This venerable park consistently adds new attractions, including a growing number of shows that appeal to older children. Successful recent additions include Mickey's PhilharMagic 3-D movie in Fantasyland and interactive Monsters Inc. Laugh Floor ★ in Tomorrowland, which incorporates jokes texted from the audience into the action.

Every afternoon the Magic Kingdom's Dreams Come True parade winds its colourful way through Frontierland, past Cinderella's Castle and up Main Street USA. This spectacle is aimed at, and loved by, the under-eights, and if you're not interested, don't get caught in Frontierland while it's on. This is a good time to snatch a go on the most popular rides, as the queues are shorter.

While Magic Kingdom doesn't always have an end of day show, when it does, they are excellent. Check the website, or the daily schedule to see if SpectroMagic ★★, a dazzling illuminated parade, or Disney Wishes ★★★, an inspiring fireworks and pyrotechnic spectacular, is being shown when you are there and make sure you see it!

Epcot ★★

Epcot – an acronym for Experimental Prototype Community of Tomorrow – is the most spacious of Disney's parks and is split into two distinct sections: the World Showcase is a circle of striking pavilions from 11 nations settled around a lagoon (open around 11am); and Future World is a collection of attractions and rides around Epcot's famous giant white geocentric dome. This is the largest of Disney's theme parks, so allow a day and a half to see everything.

Height Restrictions at Magic Kingdom

Tomorrowland Indy Speedway – 52"

Space Mountain – 44"

Splash Mountain, Big Thunder Mountain Railroad and Stitch's Great escape – 40"

Essential Walt Disney World Information

What Things Cost Tickets: Disney's ticketing structure is organised to allow you to customise your visit. It starts with a **Magic Your Way Base Ticket**, which gives individual entry to one park a day (either Magic Kingdom, Epcot, MGM Studios or Animal Kingdom) for up to seven days in a 14-day period. These tickets start at: one day US$67 (£33.50) adults, US$56 (£28) children aged 3—9, under 3s free, and get cheaper per day the more days you buy, ending at 7 days costing US$210 (£105) adults, US$173 (£86.50) children.

For an additional fee of US$10–US$90 (£5–45) depending on the number of days, you can buy a **'No Expiration'** add-on, which means there's no time limit to when you can use your days. Other 'add-ons' are a **'Park Hopper'** option for US$45 (£22.50), which allows you to move around between parks on each of your days. This is worth buying if you qualify for **Extra Magic Hours** (see p. 54). Finally, the **'Water Park Fun & More'** option for US$50 (£25) includes entry to Disney's other attractions, including Typhoon Lagoon (see p. 93) and Blizzard Beach (see p. 92).

Parking: US$10 (£5) per day (free if you are staying in a Disney hotel)
Buggy rental: single US$10 (£5), double US$18 (£9)
Wheelchair rental: US$10 (£5)
Lockers: US$7 (£3.50) – US$2 (£1) of which is a returnable deposit
Mouse ears: US$9 (£4.50)

Disney accepts all major credit cards.

Getting Around All Disney parks, resorts and attractions are connected by free shuttle buses and some by monorail and ferry, so if you're staying at a Disney-owned hotel you can easily move around between all the attractions.

If you're not staying at Disney and arrive via the free shuttle service provided by your accommodation, you'll be dropped off at the **Ticket and Transportation Center** near Magic Kingdom (see the map on p. 51), which is also where you'll find bus stops for the public transportation system (for details on central Florida's bus service, known as Lynx buses, see p. 88). Use Disney transport from here to get to the theme parks, but allow plenty of time for the return journey to the Ticket and Transportation Center (on average buses depart every 20 minutes), as buses can be frustratingly slow if there's a lot of traffic.

If you're driving to Disney as a day visitor, park at any of the theme parks and use Disney transport to get around.

Opening Times All four Disney theme parks open at 9am, but their closing times vary between 6pm and midnight. Guests at Disney resorts can take advantage of the **Extra Magic Hours** programme that allows an extra hour before opening time and up to 3 hours after closing time in one of the theme or water parks each day at no extra cost.

Details of the opening and closing times of all Disney's theme and water parks and the Extra Magic Hours schedule for up to six months in advance can be found on Disney's website.

Park Maps and Schedules Disney print a **'Times and Information'** leaflet that contains details of all the parks' operating hours and parade, show and fireworks times over a two-week period. Specific park maps and daily schedules can be picked up at the entrances.

Fast Pass This free service eases wait times at the most popular attractions. All you have to do is insert your entry ticket into the Fast Pass ticket slot of any ride that offers this service and you'll be allocated a time when you can return to this attraction and go to the front of the line. Return times vary depending on how busy the park is and rides can run out of time slots on very busy days. You can only have one Fast Pass for one attraction at any one time.

Families With Little Ones All Disney parks have themed play areas, changing facilities in the toilets and baby-care centres to warm bottles, feed, change nappies and buy baby supplies, all of which are clearly indicated on the park maps, which you'll pick up on arrival.

Most attractions offer a **Rider Switch** service, where one parent waits with the children while the other rides and then you switch roles. Pick up an **'Every Little Detail'** leaflet (available at all of the parks). It's filled with advice on how to get the most out of your visit to Disney if you have pre-school age children.

Disney has identified September and October as months when the parks are generally quieter and therefore ideal times for families with children under 5 to visit. Disney has called this time **Little Ones' Travel Time**, and lays on special events for young ones to encourage families to come to the parks during these quiet periods. See ***www.disneyworld.com/PreK*** for more details and an online planning kit for travelling with toddlers.

Eating at Disney Walt Disney World has around 400 dining options. Many families prefer fast food to sit-down dining and most outlets have a 'kids picks' selection for children under 10. Disney does attempt to provide healthy options and each theme park contains stalls selling fruit. If you're looking for something special, each park also has fantastic themed restaurants – for highlights see Family-friendly Dining on p. 80. Book these restaurants in advance during busy periods (for all dining reservations ☎ *407 939 3463*). If you don't book in advance, the information centres at the parks have details on availability and can make reservations. There are also many opportunities for your children to dine with their favourite Disney character; for more information call the number above.

Additional Amenities Disabled access. ATMs.

Epcot appeals to older children – families with pre-school age children might struggle to keep their youngsters entertained. To address this, Disney has introduced Kidcot stations around the park, with activities to keep youngsters amused. Visit the Kidcots around the World Showcase, where children are given blank masks and invited to decorate them with artefacts collected from each country's pavilion, providing an incentive to visit them all. Some pavilions have rides and films with a family focus, of which the El Rio del Tiempo ★, a boat ride through time in the Mexico Pavilion, is the most entertaining.

INSIDER TIP

Most people ride Spaceship Earth – a ride through the past, present and future of the earth – as soon as they enter Epcot, so leave this ride until later in the day when the wait times are often shorter.

The World Showcase is an excellent place to shop, with each pavilion selling crafts, clothes and food native to the country it represents – don't miss the superb food market in Japan. If your children are missing their favourite chocolate, visit the shop in the United Kingdom pavilion, which sells English confectionery, biscuits and, naturally, tea.

Although the futuristic theme of Future World hasn't stood the test of time and its attractions are more educational than adrenaline-fuelled, children get more out of this section of Epcot. It is a great place for families to enjoy together, so allow plenty of time to experience everything. Favourites here include the interactive ImageWorks ★, where children learn about photography and send their friends virtual postcards, and Innovations ★★, an excellent learning environment in which you crawl through bug tunnels, build molecules and operate industrial robots. Young children should not miss the Seas with Nemo and Friends ★★ ride; climb aboard a 'clamobile' on an underwater search for Nemo. If your children are looking for thrills, head for the high-speed, race track simulator Test Track, Mission: Space, an inter-galactic adventure, and Soarin', a simulated flight over California.

Every day at Epcot ends with IllumiNations ★★, a stunning 30-minute firework, fountain and laser light display at the World Showcase lagoon. Not to be missed if your children aren't too tired. (check daily park schedule for closing and show times).

Height Restrictions in Epcot

Mission: Space – 44"

Test Track and Soarin – 40"

FUN FACT The Earffel Tower

Keep your eyes open for MGM's distinctive water tower – known as 'The Earffel Tower' because it supports a pair of 5000 lb giant mouse ears.

MGM Studios ★★

It'll take a day to explore this 1950s-style park, the smallest of Disney's theme parks, which celebrates the golden age of Hollywood, or, as Disney's chairman described it, 'the Hollywood that never was and always will be'. Most age groups enjoy the movies and there's something to appeal to everyone here. Look out for the impromptu outdoor entertainment, provided by the likes of Power Rangers and phoney movie producers, which make this one of the most enjoyable parks to wander around.

After arriving in the park through the Art Deco entrance, stroll down Hollywood Boulevard towards the enormous model of Mickey's Sorcerer's Hat from *Fantasia* at the centre of the park. MGM's themed areas, all named with films in mind, circle around this hat, while behind it sits a full-scale replica of Hollywood's famous Chinese Theater – home to the Great Movie Ride ★. This is a must for film fans of school age and above (little ones might be scared by the *Aliens*). While queuing, you file past glass cases filled with film memorabilia, including a carousel horse from *Mary Poppins* and the ruby slippers from *The Wizard of Oz*.

MGM is a working production studio and a visit also involves discovering the backstage world of film, via attractions like the Disney-MGM Studios Backlot Tour and the Magic of Disney Animation. Shows are an important feature of this park and the Indiana Jones Epic Stunt Spectacular ★, Beauty and the Beast musical and Voyage of the Little Mermaid ★ show are all fantastically popular. Plan your day around their start times detailed in the park schedule, which you'll pick up along with a map on arrival.

Parents with small children should be wary of the Muppet Vision 3-D film, whose loud noises at the end might upset tots, but do allow time for the enormous playground at Honey I Shrunk the Kids Movie Set Adventure ★. Older children will love some of Disney's best rides for teenagers, including Star Tours ★ a flight-simulation ride based on the original *Star Wars* film, and the Rock 'n' Roller Coaster ★, an indoor high-speed roller coaster featuring the music of Aerosmith. Scariest of all is the legendary Twilight Zone Tower of Terror ★★★, a ride that is never the same twice but always truly terrifying – if you don't believe me, just listen to the screams.

Height Restrictions at MGM Studios

Rock 'n' Roller Coaster Starring Aerosmith – 48"

Star Tours and The Twilight Zone Tower of Terror – 40"

At the entrance to MGM is my favourite theme park shop – Sid Cahuenga's One of a Kind. A must for the serious (and rich) film fan, here you can buy a range of original movie memorabilia such as a signed photograph of Liz Taylor for US$1,400 (£700) or the stripy jacket worn by Dick Van Dyke in *Mary Poppins* for a cool US$65,000 (£32,500).

Each afternoon the Stars and Motor Cars parade, a procession of custom cars ridden by Disney characters, rides along Hollywood Boulevard. And a day at MGM ends with Fantasmic! ★★★ a 25-minute show based on the much-loved Disney classic *Fantasia*. This features around 50 performers in a water, laser and fireworks extravaganza. It has nearly 7,000 seats and 3,000 standing room places that fill up every night, so arrive early to get a place.

The Twilight Zone Tower of Terror™ © Disney

The Twilight Zone™ is a registered trademark of CBS, Inc. and is used pursuant to a licence from CBS, Inc.

INSIDER TIP

The Fantasmic! dinner package is available at either the Hollywood Brown Derby, Mama Melrose's Ristorante Italiano or the Hollywood and Vine restaurants and includes dinner and seat reservations at Fantasmic! (adults US$23–36 - £11.50–18; children US$11 - £5.50). Book in advance via the dining reservation number on p. 55.

Animal Kingdom ★★★

With its abundance of shade and lack of high-octane rides, Animal Kingdom is unlike any other major attraction. The sheer number of animals in this park (around 1,700) makes Animal Kingdom an instant hit with all children, and it's worth arriving early to beat the crowds and to view the animals before it gets too hot and they get less active.

The park's entrance leads to Oasis, one of six lands surrounding Discovery Island and the Tree of Life. With around 300 animals carved into its massive trunk, the Tree of Life forms

Tree of Life® Attraction © Disney

Animal Kingdom's focal point and is one of its most fascinating creations for children.

Popular with most visitors, the Kilimanjaro Safari ★★ is an open-air jeep ride through a large savannah, where you'll spy roaming elephants, giraffes, lions, rhinos and gazelles. If you don't arrive early for this ride, expect a long wait. However, you can take as much time as you like watching the different species on Animal Kingdom's walking tours. My favourite is the Maharajah Jungle Trek, a walk through the recreated ruins of an ancient palace where you'll encounter tigers, tapirs, Komodo dragons and surprisingly adorable giant fruit bats. Pick up a brochure at the start of this walk to find out more about the animals and the best places to see them.

Parents of young children should pick up *Kid's Discovery Club Guide,* a small booklet of activities for children to complete as they go around the park. There's plenty to keep toddlers entertained in DinoLand USA, with dinosaur-themed carnival games and a crazy maze made of prehistoric bones. Children also enjoy the Conservation Station and Affection Section in Rafiki's Planet Watch, where they can interact with farmyard animals and learn about their care.

Older children should head to the Primeval Whirl ★ coaster and DINOSAUR ★ ride in DinoLand USA, while next door in Asia is Animal Kingdom's newest and best thrill ride. Expedition Everest – Legend of the Forbidden Mountain ★★★ is a perilous high-speed train ride into the unknown. You'll also find two of Disney's best family shows here: the hugely popular Festival of the Lion King ★ in Camp Minnie–Mickey (look out for the bird boxes with mouse-ear-shaped holes) is an explosion of colour, music and acrobatics. Finding Nemo – The Musical ★ in DinoLand USA fuses puppets

FUN FACT Ancient Legends & Mickey Mouse

Although the murals decorating the Maharajah Jungle Trek's crumbling palace represent ancient legends, look closely and you'll see that the hunter in the turban is wearing a Mickey Mouse earring.

Height Restrictions at Animal Kingdom

Primeval Whirl – 48"

Expedition Everest – 44"

Dinosaur – 40"

Kali River Rapids – 38"

and performers in an underwater spectacular – check show times on the park schedule when you arrive.

Every afternoon the Jammin' Jungle Parade rocks its way from the Kilimanjaro Safari in Africa around Discovery Island and back again.

Downtown Disney

As with everything Disney, the scale and scope of its downtown entertainment, dining and shopping complex is huge. This vast area is open to all and split into three distinct areas – Marketplace, Pleasure Island and West Side – each with its own style and age-group appeal.

Marketplace, with its LEGO Imagination Center, toy shops, interactive fountains and casual dining, is better suited to families with small children. Older children prefer the West Side because of Disney Quest, an enormous indoor interactive game centre (open 11.30am–11pm Sun–Thur, until midnight Fri and Sat, US$36 (£18) adults, US$30 (£15) children aged 3—9, who must be accompanied by someone over 16 years old, under 3s are free) featuring bumper cars that fire asteroids and a human pinball game. The West Side also features a 24-screen cinema and a giant Planet Hollywood (booking advisable) and is the perfect destination for

Downtown Disney® West Side. © Disney

Cirque du Soleil

Downtown Disney's West Side is home to a giant Cirque du Soleil theatre, whose stunning *La Nouba* ★★★ show, with its acrobats, sublime performers and sheer spectacle, wows audiences of all ages. Performed Wed–Sun at 6pm and 9pm, this is one of the most expensive attractions in Walt Disney World, costing US$67–US$120 (£33.50–60) for adults and US$53–US$96 (£26.50–48) for children, but it's also one of its most memorable. Tickets should be booked in advance 📞 *407 939 7600*.

teenagers on a rainy day. Pleasure Island stands at the centre of Downtown Disney and is designed for adults, with numerous clubs and bars.

Universal Orlando Resort

1000 Universal Studios Plaza, Orlando 📞 407 363 8000 ***www.universalorlando.com***

Universal has rapidly grown from one theme park – Universal Studios – to an entire resort complex whose size, scale and excitement competes with Disney. Day visitors arrive via moving walkways from the car parks into City Walk, an entertainment complex that comes into its own at night. During the day it is a busy thoroughfare for Universal's two theme parks – Universal Studios and Islands of Adventure – which sit at either end of City Walk. Universal's three hotels also lead off this area; the Hard Rock and Portofino Bay hotels are close to Universal Studios and the Royal Pacific Resort by Islands of Adventure. Each park deserves a whole day and although both parks have much to offer young children, the overall appeal of Universal, with its slew of action-packed rides and shows, has more appeal to older children.

Universal Studios ★★

From the moment you walk past Universal's enormous, iconic spinning globe and through the massive movie studio style gates into the park, you're catapulted into the make-believe world of the movies. The shop-lined Plaza of the Stars leads from the park's jazzy entrance to Production Central, the first of six themed areas – most of which circle around a large lake on the east side of the park.

Parents of young toddlers should head to Woody Woodpecker's Kidzone, with its two interactive playgrounds, a children's roller coaster and two children's shows performed regularly throughout the day. Also great for this age group and above is the E.T. Adventure ride – board your flying bicycles to help E.T. save his planet.

The rest of Universal Studios, from its disaster-movie simulators such as Twister...Ride it Out and Earthquake, to the futuristic thrills of Terminator 2: 3-D ★★

UNIVERSAL ORLANDO RESORT

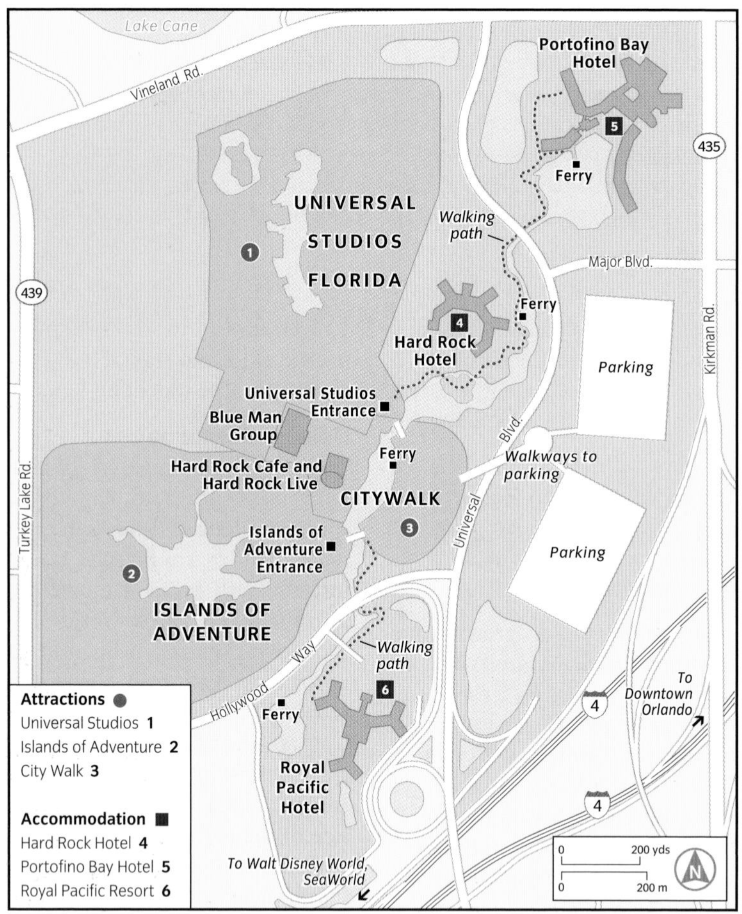

The Orlando Flexi Ticket

A cheaper option than buying individual park entry is the four-park **Orlando Flexi ticket**, which offers unlimited access over a 14-day period to Universal Studios, Islands of Adventure, SeaWorld and Wet 'n' Wild water park (see p. 94) (US$208/£104 adults, US$172/£86 children aged 3–9). A five-park Orlando Flexi ticket adds Busch Gardens to the deal, including free transport (US$256/£128 adults, US$214/£107 children aged 3–9). Flexi tickets can be bought at any of the participating attractions – also see the Ticket Deals box on p. 54.

The Jaws Ride. © 2007 Universal Orlando Resort. Alll Rights Reserved.

and Men In Black Alien Attack ★★★, is a theme park of stunts and sci-fi orientated towards older children and adults.

The park has a good balance between brand new thrills, such as the horrifically fast Revenge of the Mummy ★★★, where riders are plunged into darkness to face fireballs, scarab beetles and mummies, and long-time favourites like Jaws. Even though you know it's coming, that great white shark makes you jump every time it lunges out of the water. While Shrek 4-D, a 20-minute film presented through the miracle of 'Ogre Vision', provides welcome comic relief.

Universal's painted backlot sets and fleet of 1950s cars aren't just for show; the park is also a working studio. This fact is reflected in the Horror Make Up Show, which reveals how some of film's special effects are created. And the star-struck in your family have the chance to be part of the action in Fear Factor Live, where willing contestants are made to face their fears live on stage – brave hopefuls should turn up 75 minutes prior to show time for casting.

Height Restrictions at Universal Studios

For all rides, children under 48" must be accompanied by an adult and able to sit upright on their own.

Revenge of the Mummy – 48"

Men in Black: Alien Attack – 42"

Woody Woodpecker's Nuthouse Coaster – 36"

Children under 40" must also use the stationary seats in Jimmy Neutron's Nicktoon Blast.

Essential Universal Orlando Information

What Things Cost

Tickets: one park, one day US$63 (£31.50) adults, US$52 (£26) children aged 3–9, under 3s free; two-park, two-day ticket, with unlimited access to both parks over the two days, US$112 (£56) adults, US$102 (£51) children aged 3–9.

Parking: US$9 (£4.50), free after 6pm.

Buggy rental: single US$11 (£5.50), double US$17 (£8.50)

Wheelchair rental: US$10 (£5)

Lockers: US$5 (£2.50)

Universal accepts all major credit cards.

Getting Around

Although large, the whole Universal complex can be easily explored by foot. Day visitors can walk through City Walk to reach both Universal Studios and Islands of Adventure. Universal's hotels are reached via landscaped walkways and there's a frequent free water taxi service for guests from their hotels to City Walk.

Opening Times

Universal opens at 9am and closes at between 6pm and 10pm, depending on the time of year. Details of opening hours for six months in advance can be found on Universal's website (see p. 61).

Park Maps and Schedules

Both of these are available at the entrance to each park.

Express Passes

Universal sells a limited number of Express Passes for each park every day. The passes are bought in addition to entry tickets and allow visitors into Express Access lines with short waiting times. Buy them in advance or on the day. A one-day ticket valid for either Universal Studios or Islands of Adventure costs US$46 (£23) per person and a one-day ticket valid for both parks costs US$56 (£28). If you're staying at any of the Universal hotels you'll receive free Express Access with your room key.

Families With Little Ones

Both theme parks have baby-change facilities in all toilets as well as play areas. There are nursing facilities in the Family Services area of Universal Studios and in the first-aid area of Islands of Adventure. Universal operates a Child Swap programme, which allows parents of small children to take it in turns to ride while one of them looks after the children.

Additional Amenities

Disabled access. Currency exchange. ATMs.

INSIDER TIP

Both Universal parks offer the chance for children to meet and have their photographs taken with Shrek and Donkey, SpongeBob SquarePants and Spider-Man. Check the park maps for a schedule of where and when they'll appear.

Islands of Adventure ★★★

The coolest theme park in Orlando for families with older children and teenagers, Islands of Adventure delivers thrilling roller coasters and exciting water rides like no other attraction in Florida. From the moment you walk through its atmospheric Port of Entry, clustered with shops and eateries themed after the far east, you know this imaginative park, which boasts Steven Spielberg as one of its creative consultants, will be completely different in style and ambience to Universal Studios.

The park's five themed lands form a circle from the Port of Entry. Teenagers will head straight in an anti-clockwise direction towards Marvel Super Hero Island to experience its amazing collection of adrenaline-fuelled rides. These include the outstanding Amazing Adventures of Spider-Man 3-D ★★★, the great green Incredible Hulk Coaster ★★, which catapults its riders at a G-force equivalent to that of a jet fighter, and the stomach-churning Doctor Doom's Fearfall, which shoots riders up a 150-foot tower only to plummet them back down again.

Directly opposite Marvel Super Hero Island is The Lost Continent, the Islands of Adventure's other land with a direct appeal to older children. Here you'll find The Dueling Dragons ★★, a double roller coaster where you choose to ride either the ice or fire dragon and whose riders narrowly miss each other as they hurtle around. Nearby, Poseidon's Fury engulfs you in a battle between the god of the sea and an evil sorcerer in a water-and-pyrotechnic filled adventure in the dark.

There are three excellent water rides at this park. Jurassic Park River Adventure ★★, which whirls its way through a recreated primeval forest complete with T-Rex and an 85 ft plunge in complete darkness, is definitely not for young ones. With merely a 75 ft drop, the wacky Dudley Do-Right's Ripsaw Falls flume ride is more fun than scary, while Popeye and Bluto's Bilge-Rat Barges river rapids ride gets every rider totally drenched.

FUN FACT **Fast Rides**

Doctor Doom's Fearfall accelerates riders upwards faster than a launching space shuttle.

Height Restrictions at Islands of Adventure

Dueling Dragons and The Incredible Hulk Coaster – 54"

Doctor Doom's Fearfall – 52"

Dudley Do-Right's Ripsaw Falls – 44"

Jurassic Park River Adventure and Popeye and Bluto's Bilge-Rat Barges – 42"

The Amazing Adventures of Spider-Man – 40"

The Flying Unicorn – 36"

The High in the Sky Seuss Trolley Train Ride – 34"

Pregnant women are also requested not to ride on 11 of Islands of Adventure's rides.

Although the focus of this fantasy-filled park isn't on small children, it provides some excellent entertainment for them. Families with toddlers should head in a clockwise direction from the Port of Entry to colourful Seuss Landing ★★★, where the best-loved characters from Dr Seuss's stories come to life. Here you'll find a number of rides for small children, including the fabulous Caro-Seuss-el merry-go-round created out of Seussian characters, and you can pick up a green eggs and ham sandwich from the Green Eggs and Ham Takeaway stand.

Other attractions for youngsters include the gentle Flying Unicorn ride in The Lost Continent and the Pteranodon Flyers and Camp Jurassic playground in Jurassic Park.

There's only one show to catch in Islands of Adventure, the swashbuckling Eighth Voyage of Sinbad Stunt Show.

Jurassic Park River Adventure, Islands of Adventure.

Emeril's Restaurant.

Good for all age groups, performances take place at regular intervals throughout the day. And any child who loves dinosaurs can learn all about these prehistoric giants via interactive displays at the Jurassic Park Discovery Center.

The Wizarding World of Harry Potter is currently being built inside Islands of Adventure. This theme park within a theme park is scheduled to open in 2009.

City Walk

407 363 8000 ***www.citywalkorlando.com***

City Walk, with its collection of themed restaurants, clubs, shops and 20-screen multiplex cinema, is Universal's equivalent to Downtown Disney and, with none of Disney's squeaky-clean image to uphold, a much trendier place for older children and teenagers to hang out. City Walk is home to the world's largest Hard Rock Café, a huge NBC City restaurant, and the upmarket Emeril's for a more sophisticated (and expensive) dinner.

INSIDER TIP

If you're missing an all-important footie match while you're away, head over to the NBA City restaurant in City Walk – chances are, if there's no basketball on, they'll be screening football on its big-screen TVs instead. If you don't want to eat here, listen to the match on the speakers outside.

A great place to eat in City Walk is the popular Jimmy Buffet's Margaritaville ***www.margaritavilleorlando.com***, a lively Key West-style restaurant with an open-air deck for families to dine during the day. However, City Walk is a serious party place and a much more adult affair in the evening, with cover charges coming into force at many venues. You can purchase a City Walk Party Pass (US$12/£6), which allows unlimited entry into all the attractions at night (this pass is free with Universal's multi-day, multi-park ticket deals, see p. 62); some establishments only allow over 21s entry after a certain time.

Florida's Other Major Theme Parks

SeaWorld ★

7007 SeaWorld Drive, Orlando ☎ *407 351 3600* ***www.seaworld.com***

One of the world's largest marine parks and extremely popular with British families, SeaWorld, with its shady landscaped grounds and large lake, is a less frantic experience than some of the other parks.

> **INSIDER TIP**
> The I-Ride Trolley (see p. 94) makes frequent stops at SeaWorld throughout the day. If you're staying on International Drive, travelling here by trolley is cheaper than paying for parking.

Visitors flock to SeaWorld to watch dolphins, sea lions, otters, penguins and tropical birds perform in its shows. There's even a show for young children called Pets Ahoy! featuring dogs, cats and pot-bellied pigs. However, the star show for all age groups is Believe, SeaWorld's memorable killer whale show staring Shamu – an awesome 8,000-pound killer whale – and friends. These incredible animals amaze audiences with their stunningly choreographed acrobatics and drench those sitting in the first 14 rows of the stadium.

Its sheer number of shows, including the fairytale-themed Blue Horizons performed by a troupe of beautiful dolphins and tropical birds, makes SeaWorld excellent for children on a very hot day, as they'll sit in the shade of the stages for much of a visit. The predominance of shows means you'll need to plan your day carefully around start times in order to fit everything in – pick up a park map and schedule at the entrance to the park as you arrive.

SeaWorld's other big draw for children is the chance to get up close to its animals, including penguins, manatees, alligators, sharks and the magnificent Clydesdale horses, all housed in various landscaped areas where you can learn all about these amazing creatures. Be sure to see the dolphin nursery, where you can watch expectant mothers and new-born calves at play, and, for those brave enough, there is the chance to pet sting rays in open tanks.

Older children will find plenty of attractions to keep them entertained, including two excellent thrillers: Kraken ★★, the steepest roller coaster in Orlando, and Journey to Atlantis ★, a water ride and roller coaster combination. Catch these rides when one of the shows is in full swing and the wait time is reduced. Also popular is the exhilarating Wild Arctic, where you experience

INTERNATIONAL DRIVE

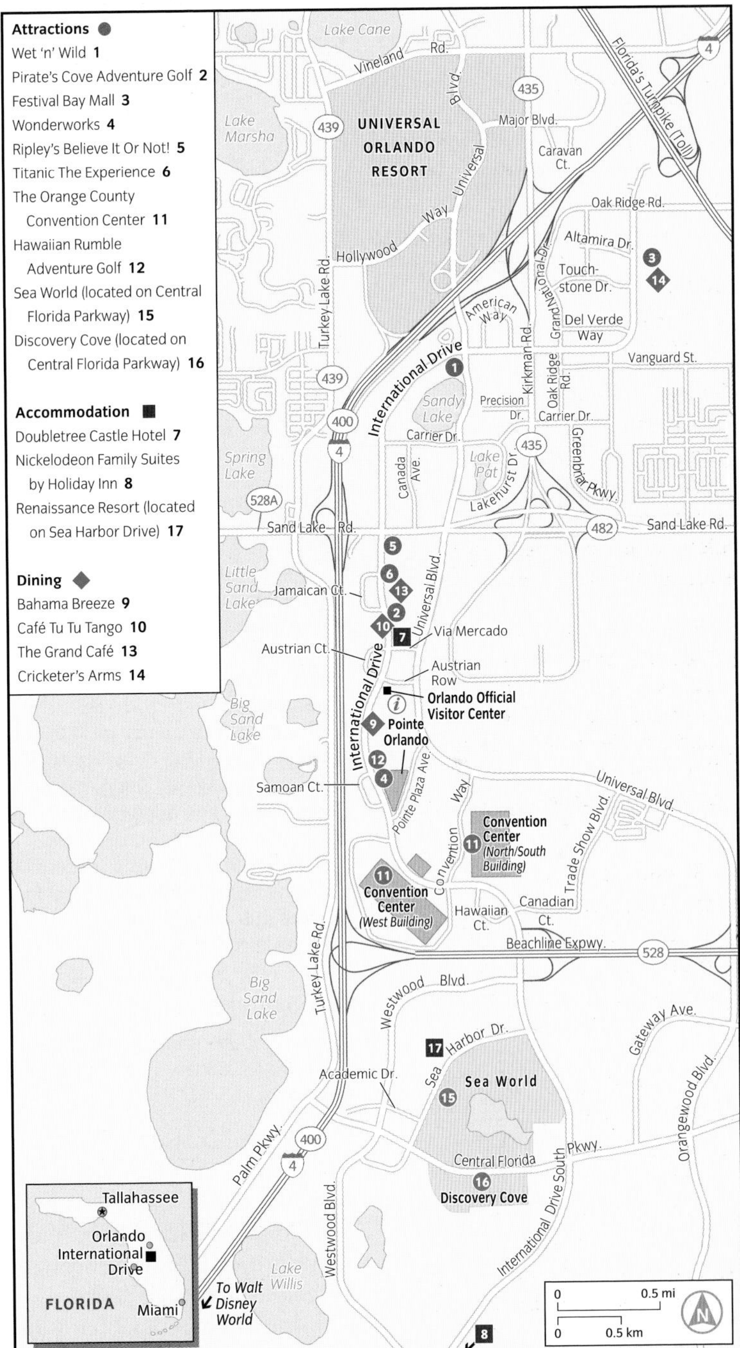

Height Restrictions at SeaWorld

Paddle Boats – 56" or accompanied by a supervising companion but no hand-held infants

Kraken – 54"

Sky Tower – 48" or accompanied by a supervising companion

Jazzy Jellies – 42" or accompanied by a supervising companion but no hand-held infants

Journey to Atlantis – 42" but 42" – 48" must be accompanied by a supervising companion

Shamu Express – 38" but 38" – 41" must be accompanied by a supervising companion

Swishy Fishes – 36" or accompanied by a supervising companion but no hand-held infants

breathtaking simulations of the frozen north (be warned, young children may suffer from motion sickness on this ride).

There's a range of small attractions at a nominal extra cost, including the Sky Tower (US$3/£1.50) a 400 ft scenic aerial ride above the park, plus the Xtreme Zone, where children can try their hand at rock climbing (US$6/£3).

INSIDER TIP

Parents with older children who want to wander off can keep in touch with them via rented walkie talkies.

Shamu's Happy Harbour, to the right of the whale's stadium, is a three-acre play area with net jungles, water cannon and fountains for small children to let off steam in and includes a baby-care centre. For an extra cost there's a range of tours and animal encounters for adults and children that can be booked on arrival or online – check SeaWorld's website for full details.

Open *9am–7pm and until 10pm in winter.* ***Admission*** *US$65 (£32.50) adults, US$55 (£27.50) children 3–9, under 3s free.* ***Credit*** *AmEx, MC, V.* ***Amenities*** *Parking US$10 (£5) or US$15 (£7.50) for priority parking. Lockers US$1 (50p). Restaurants, cafés and takeaways. Buggy rental: single US$10 (£5), double US$17 (£8.50). Wheelchair rental US$10 (£5). Shops. ATM. Disabled access. Currency exchange. Baby-changing facilities and nursing area for mothers. Identification wrist bands.*

Discovery Cove

Central Florida Parkway, Orlando, ☎ *407 370 1280* ***www.discoverycove.com***

With a distinct absence of rides and shows, Discovery Cove is the odd one out of Orlando's parks. You'll find 30 acres of lush, landscaped tropical gardens, tiny by Florida standards, all designed with relaxation in mind but with a high price tag attached.

Guests are limited to 1,000 per day, so book as far in advance as possible, as Discovery Cove gets full most days. Once inside, laze on the sandy beach or snorkel around the coral reef, complete with underwater shipwreck and teeming with tropical fish (the sharks and barracudas are kept safely behind glass). You can also pet sting rays in a separate lagoon and hand-feed exotic birds in large aviaries. If that sounds like hard work, simply float down the tropical river as it winds its way around the park.

INSIDER TIP

Don't put on any of your own sunscreen before coming here, Discovery Cove provides its own fish-friendly version for free.

Although snorkelling the recreated reef is popular, the main draw to this intimate park is the chance to interact with one of its 20 dolphins (for an extra US$100/£50). Anyone over six can undertake a 30-minute session – plus a 10-minute orientation programme – during which you get up close to a dolphin under the supervision of its trainer. The session includes the chance to hold on to the animal's dorsal fin and be whizzed back to shore or, if your child is nervous, they can cradle the dolphin in shallow waters.

Whether you partake in a dolphin encounter or not, this chilled-out park is a challenge for families with children who have lots of energy and want more in the way of entertainment. However, it's a good, if expensive, break from the more exhausting attractions.

Discovery Cove also offers Trainer for a Day programmes (US$459/£229.50), an opportunity for children to spend a day working behind the scenes with one of the park's trainers. During the summer, a maximum of 150 guests a night can enjoy an evening of fine food and animal interaction through their Twilight Discovery Packages. For

Discovery Cove

FUN FACT **Dolphins**

Dolphins don't have a sense of smell.

families who can't get enough of dolphins, Dolphin Lovers' Sleepovers give you the chance to camp for the night on Discovery Cove's beach.

Open *9am–5.30pm, check in opens at 8am.* ***Admission*** *12th Nov – 11th March US$159 (£79.50), with dolphin swim US$259 (£129.50), 12th March – 11th Nov US$179 (£89.50), with dolphin swim US$279 (£139.50), no reductions for children, under 2s free. Admission includes complimentary food and drink, a free group photograph, use of wet suits, snorkel equipment and towels and a seven-day unlimited pass to either SeaWorld or Busch Gardens.* ***Credit*** *AmEx, MC, V.* ***Amenities*** *Free parking. Free lockers. Free shuttle bus to SeaWorld. ATM. Disabled access. Baby-change facilities. Restaurant and takeaways. Shops.*

Busch Gardens

3000 E. Busch Boulevard, Tampa *813 987 5283* ***www.buschgardens.com***

Situated on the outskirts of Tampa and an easy day trip from Orlando, Busch Gardens is one of Florida's oldest attractions. The 335 acres of this veteran theme park are divided into eight lands, each depicting a different aspect of colonial Africa and each with its own style of attractions, shopping and dining, although none featuring any great display of enchantment.

It will take planning to fit everything Busch Gardens has on offer into one day, particularly as there's no fast-track system to reduce waiting times, so pick up a map and schedule of show times when you arrive and plan your day. However, this park's maps and signposting system are not that easy to follow, so allow plenty of time to reach show venues.

The main draw to Busch Gardens is its collection of roller coaster rides. Fast, furious and not for the faint-hearted, these rides are unmatched by any other theme park for their thrill factor. It's perfect for teenagers who love high-speed rides.

Busch Gardens is also one of America's largest zoos and there are various opportunities to get up close to the animals. On the 65 acres of Serengeti Plain you will encounter around 800 animals, including giraffes, zebras, rhinos, elephants, buffaloes, flamingos and antelopes. Look down on them from the Skyride monorail or, closer still, via an open-sided train.

The most family-friendly attractions at Busch Gardens are its flume rides; the Congo River Rapids is the most thrilling and the Tanganyika Tidal Wave gets you the wettest. And small children are not forgotten, with rides such as Cheetah Chase, a children's roller coaster in Timbuktu, Rhino Rally's Off Road Adventure in Nairobi and

SheiKra, Busch Gardens

the Land of Dragons themed play area.

There are two shows to experience: KaTonga, a 35-minute celebration of animal folklore at the Moroccan Palace Theatre, and Pirates 4-D, a 15-minute comedy adventure film staring Leslie Nielsen and Eric Idle at the Timbuktu Theatre, both of which are aimed at all age groups.

For those addicted to thrill rides, the latest and most terrifying is SheiKra ★★★, Florida's tallest roller coaster, which, now floorless, hurtles riders down a 200ft drop at a 90-degree angle. Other high-adrenaline attractions are Gwazi, a wooden roller coaster that reaches speeds of 100mph and Kumba ★, with a large vertical loop giving riders a full three seconds of weightlessness. Queuing for these rides can take as long as 90 minutes during busy periods. The only way to avoid them is to arrive early.

Families with animal-loving children should check the park's schedule for Meet the Keeper times. There's also a programme of educational and behind-the-scenes tours starting at US$34 (£17) per person. For details on both of these, visit the information point near the Desert Grill restaurant in Timbuktu.

INSIDER TIP

A number of rides are closed in Busch Gardens if it rains. If rain has ruined your visit, stop by Guest Services (to the left of the main tram stop) on your way out to be issued with a complimentary ticket valid for 7 days.

Height and Age Restrictions at Busch Gardens

Kumba, Montu and SheiKra – 54" minimum

Gwazi, Phoenix and Tanganyika Tidal Wave – 48" minimum

Stanley Falls Log Flume – 46" or 2 years of age accompanied by an adult minimum

Cheetah Chase – 46" and 6 years old minimum

Congo River Rapids, Scorpion, Sandstorm and (accompanied by an adult) bumper cars – 42" minimum

Serengeti Safari and Animal Adventure Tour – 5 years old (accompanied by an adult) minimum

Open *between 9am–10am and closes between 5pm–10pm depending on time of year, car park opens half an hour before the park.* ***Admission*** *US$62 (£31) adults, US$52 (£26) children aged 3–9, under 3s free.* ***Credit*** *AmEx, MC, V.* ***Amenities*** *Parking US$9 (£4.50), or US$14 (£7) for priority parking. Restaurant and takeaways. Buggy rental: single US$10 (£5), double US$15 (£7.50). Wheelchair rental: US$10 (£5). Lockers US$5 (£2.50). Shops. ATM. Disabled access. Baby-change facilities and nursing area for babies. Child identification wristbands.*

Kennedy Space Center ★★

NASA Parkway (SR-405) 📞 321 449 444 ***www.kennedyspacecenter.com***

A family highlight, whether your children are smitten with the space bug or not, the Kennedy Space Center sits on the east coast parallel with, and about a 45-minute drive from, Orlando. The centre is set up in a theme-park style that makes learning about America's space programme fun and interactive. However, the subject matter and attractions are a bit much for pre-school age children, although the centre tries to cater for all age groups by providing areas such as the Children's Play Dome.

Visiting the Space Center is a two-part experience. The first, and more entertaining for children, is the Visitor Complex, situated a short walking distance from the car park. Don't miss the amazing IMAX theatre shows featuring a shuttle launch and breathtaking views of the earth from space, or the brand new Shuttle Launch Experience ★★★ (48" height restriction), where you're strapped into a simulated shuttle to experience take off. Children love the life-size replica of the Space Shuttle Explorer; peer into the cockpit to see just how small it is. And my favourite are the actual old Mercury Mission Controls, which look disturbingly like a set from Thunderbirds.

The second part of a visit consists of a 2-to-3-hour-long bus tour of NASA's inner workings. These tours depart every 15 minutes from the Visitor Complex from 10am to 2.45pm; do the tour first, as waiting times

FUN FACT **Moon & Beyond**

In 2010 NASA plans to retire the Space Shuttle and replace it with the Orion, which will take people to the moon and beyond.

get longer as the day goes on. The tour passes the enormous Vehicle Assembly Building, where space shuttles are built and rolled out onto the launch pad. You'll get to view these pads from a distance, but better still is getting close up to a 363 ft-long Saturn V rocket and stepping back in time to the nail-biting excitement of the Apollo missions. Not the most thrilling, but perhaps the most nostalgic, part of the tour for adults is the Lunar Theater and its depiction of the first moon landing.

INSIDER TIP

Make sure your children go to the lavatory before embarking on the bus tour; there's only one set of toilets along the way.

Also included in the centre's admission price is entry to the Astronaut Hall of Fame (open 9am–7pm), situated 6 miles west of the main visitor complex on SR-405. Here, space fanatics can explore a collection of astronaut artefacts and experience two great simulations: G-Force Trainer and a ride across the moon's rocky terrain – both are popular with children.

***Open** 9am–6pm. **Admission** US$38 (£19) adults, US$28 (£14) children aged 3–11, under 3s free. **Credit** AmEx, MC, V. **Amenities** Free parking. Free buggy and wheelchair rental. Shop. Restaurants and cafés. ATM. Disabled access. Baby-change facilities.*

US Astronaut Hall of Fame® at Kennedy Space Center

FAMILY-FRIENDLY ACCOMMODATION

There are 23 Disney resorts to choose from, all of them family friendly. For an overview of the options, see this section of Walt Disney World's website: ***http://disneyworld.disney.go.com/wdw/resorts/resortOverview***

If you plan to stay near Downtown Disney, there are another seven 'official' hotels that are endorsed but not owned by Disney. Check ***www.downtowndisneyhotels.com*** for details. Information on the three Universal resorts can be found on Universal's website ***www.universalorlando.com***. Listed here are a selection of my favourite family-friendly accommodation options linked to the major attractions.

EXPENSIVE/VERY EXPENSIVE

Animal Kingdom Lodge ★★★

2901 Osceola Parkway, Bay Lake, Orlando ☎ *407 934 7639* ***www.disneyworld.com***

This sumptuous hotel tucked away in the far south-western corner of Walt Disney World, close to Animal Kingdom, is a firm favourite with families. Furnished in the style of an African game reserve lodge, with thatched roofs, dark mahogany furnishings, rich tapestries and warm colours, the highlight of Animal Kingdom Lodge is its 33-acre savannah, where giraffes, zebra, wildebeest and exotic birds flourish. The theme extends to the hotel's restaurants, with two of its three dining options serving African-influenced cuisine. There's a varied range of children's activities from safaris to storytelling and, best of all, night-vision goggles through which they can watch the animals as darkness falls. The only downside is that you're away from most of Disney's theme parks and other attractions, but they're all reachable via Disney's frequent and free bus service.

Rooms *1,293.* ***Rates*** *Standard rooms (sleep up to four) US$215–US$310 (£108–155), deluxe rooms (sleep up to five) US$300–US$350 (£150–175), suites (sleep between six and eight) US$675–US$2,585 (£338–1,293) (children under 17 stay free in parents' room).* ***Credit*** *AmEx, MC, V.* ***Amenities*** *Three restaurants. Lounge. Heated outdoor pool. Children's pool. Health club. Children's centre. Arcade. Shops. Babysitting (for a fee). Guest laundry service* ***In room*** *A/C. Cable TV. Safe. High-speed Internet. Fridge and cot on request (free).*

Disney's Polynesian Resort ★

1600 Seven Seas Drive, Lake Buena Vista ☎ *407 824 2000* ***www.disneyworld.com***

Close to Magic Kingdom (there's a boat service to this park across the Seven Seas Lagoon), the Polynesian is styled after a South Seas tropical island resort. The beach area is superb and features two heated outdoor pools, one with a volcano theme and grotto slide, children's play area and hammocks. There's a real focus on outdoor recreation, as guests can rent pontoon boats, play

Disney's Animal Kingdom Lodge. © Disney.

volleyball, go fishing and enjoy a scenic jogging trail. The big draw for families is its excellent Neverland childcare club for children aged 4–12, which provides supervised evening activities, leaving parents free to enjoy evenings out alone. The resort's family-friendly Ohana (Hawaiian for family) restaurant serves an excellent Polynesian buffet. This is the best Disney resort to stay in if you want to explore further afield but don't want to rent a car, as the Ticket and Transportation Center, where the buses pull in (see p. 54), is next door.

Rooms *853.* ***Rates*** *Standard rooms (sleep up to five) US$329–US$455 (£165–228), suites (sleep between five and nine) US$750–US$1,955 (£375–978) (children under 17 stay free in parents' room).* ***Credit*** *AmEx, MC, V.* ***Amenities*** *Restaurant. Café. Two lounges. Two heated outdoor pools. Children's pool. Water sports equipment. Children's club. Arcade. Shops. Babysitting service. Guest laundry service.* ***In room*** *A/C. Cable TV. High-speed Internet. Safe. Fridge and cot on request (free).*

Hard Rock Hotel ★★

5800 Universal Boulevard, Orlando
407 503 7625 ***www.universalorlando.com***

One of the most stylish places to stay in Florida for any family with school-age children, and a must if your youngsters are into certain kinds of music, the Hard Rock Hotel, with its priceless collection of rock memorabilia – yes my favourite is the Elvis outfit – is one of Orlando's funkiest hotels. It's worth staying here for the enormous pool alone, with its white sand beach, 260 ft-long water slide and amazing underwater sound system. There's plenty of evening activities for families, including DJ nights and films, a supervised children's play area, programme of children's activities and evening childcare available for a fee until 11pm Sunday–Thursday and until midnight Friday and Saturday. You can choose between cheaper room-style accommodation or more expensive suites that provide separate sleeping areas for children, complete with their own TV and video games.

Rooms *650 rooms, 29 suites.* ***Rates*** *rooms US$239–US$479 (£120–240), suites US$479–US$789 (£240–395), Graceland Suite US$1,520–US$2,020 (£760–1010) (children 18 and under stay free in the same room).* ***Credit*** *AmEx, MC, V.* ***Amenities*** *Parking US$12 (£6) per day. Three restaurants. Two bars. Café and ice cream bar. Outdoor heated pool. Games rooms. Cinema. Workout room US$8 (£4) daily fee. Children's activities. Evening childcare US$12 (£6) per hour per child. Guest laundry service. Shops. Free shuttle to SeaWorld.* ***In room*** *A/C. Cable TV. DVD/CD (some rooms). Video games (for a fee). Safe. High-speed Internet. Cots on request (free). Fridges and microwaves on request (fee).*

MODERATE

Renaissance Orlando Resort at SeaWorld

6677 Sea Harbour Drive, Orlando
407 351 5555 ***www.renaissanceseaworld.com***

Situated just minutes from the buzz of International Drive and a short walk from SeaWorld and Discovery Cove, the Renaissance Orlando is a simple stylish hotel that's well located for getting to all of the major attractions. Like the hotel as a whole, the rooms are airy and spacious and I particularly like the oversized bathrooms. There are numerous recreation opportunities including the tropically landscaped pool – a perfect place to recover from a day at a theme park – and

Hard Rock Hotel. © 2007 Universal Orlando Resort. All rights reserved.

Additional Accommodation

There is a host of chain motels in Tampa around Busch Gardens. The closest is the Safari Lodge at Busch Gardens Maingate 4139 E. Busch Boulevard ☎ *813 988 9191* rooms around US$99 (£50). Also recommended, though slightly further away, are the Best Western 3001 University Center Drive ☎ *8139718930* rooms around US$90 (£45) and La Quinta Inn 9202 N. 30th Street ☎ *813 930 6900* rooms around US$75 (£37.50), and the cheaper Days Inn Busch Gardens 2901 E. Busch Boulevard ☎ *813 933 64 71* rooms around US$60 (£30). See p. 128 for additional accommodation in the Tampa area. For accommodation close to the Kennedy Space Center, see the Family-friendly Accommodation section of the East Coast chapter on p. 157; for more on accommodation in central Florida not linked to the main attractions, see p. 100.

children's pool, play area and games room.

***Rooms** 714 rooms, 64 suites. **Rates** US$179–US$419 (£90–210) (children under 17 stay free in parents' room). **Credit** AmEx, MC, V. **Amenities** Parking US$12 (£6) per day. Three restaurants. Three lounges. Outdoor heated pool. Children's pool. Four tennis courts. Basketball. Volleyball. Health club. Spa. Two jacuzzis. Sauna. Play area. Arcade. Shops. Babysitting. Guest laundry service. **In room** A/C. Cable TV. High-speed Internet. Safe. Sofa bed. Fridge (some rooms). Cot on request.*

BUDGET/MODERATE

Disney's Pop Century Resort

VALUE

1050 Century Drive, Lake Buena Vista ☎ 407 938 4000 ***www.disneyworld.com***

Themed around 20th century popular culture and featuring a giant tub of Play Doh and an enormous Rubik's Cube, the Pop Century Resort is one of Disney's four value resorts – the others are styled around music, Disney films and sport. Although this resort has none of the frills of many Disney hotels, I like it because its low prices enable families on restricted budgets to stay at Walt Disney World and enjoy the related benefits. Despite its basic nature, there's plenty to keep children entertained, such as poolside water fountains, games rooms and play areas. This hotel's only limitation is its dining. The main option is a colourful food court serving fast food, but there's also a food shop with healthier items to take away. The rooms are on the small side compared with other Disney resorts, but still maintain a high standard.

***Rooms** 2,880. **Rates** Standard rooms (sleep up to four) from US$82 (£41). **Credit** AmEx, MC, V. **Amenities** Food court. Shop. Three pools. Children's pool. Arcade. Babysitting service. Guest laundry service. **In room** A/C. Cable TV. Safe.Cot on request (free). Fridge on request (fee).*

FAMILY-FRIENDLY DINING

Magic Kingdom

Aloha Isle in Adventureland serves vegetarian options and has the best shaded eating area. For a sit- down meal of soups and sandwiches, try the peaceful Plaza Restaurant tucked away off Main Street USA, which is easier to get a booking at than other places. And the ultimate treat for the princess in your family is a meal at Cinderella's Royal Table in the heart of her castle. Here you can dine with Cinderella and a princess at breakfast and lunch (mains US$30/£15 adults, US$20/£10 children) or with Cinderella and her fairy godmother for dinner (mains US$40/£20 adults, US$30/£15 children). This experience of a lifetime should be booked well in advance via the reservations number on p. 55 or call from 6am on the day of your visit to see if there have been any cancellations.

Epcot

Each of the World Showcase's pavilions has an excellent selection of dining options. Modelled after a 1692 hacienda, complete with its own smoking volcano, the San Angel Inn in Mexico is my family favourite (lunch and dinner mains US$15–US$29/£7.50–14.50) – book a table as soon as you arrive. The Rose & Crown pub in the United Kingdom pavilion is a honey pot for Brits desperate for a (rather expensive) pint of beer and traditional pub grub including fish and chips (US$15/£7.50). Reservations are advised for the Garden Grille inside The Land section of Future World, whose rotating booths are super popular with small children (mains US$20/£10 adults, US$12/£6 children). There's also an excellent Seasons food court offering a variety that will appeal to families who can't agree on what to eat.

MGM

It's not surprising that a theme park celebrating entertainment is where you'll find some of the most inventive family dining in Florida. The Sci-Fi Dine-In ★★★ is modelled after a 1950s drive-in movie theatre. Here you'll dine under starlight inside model vintage cars, while watching clips from classic B movies on a huge movie screen (mains US$11–US$18/£5.50–9 adults, US$7.50/£3.75 children). Everyone is treated like a child at the Prime Time Café ★★, a 50s style kitchen where mom makes you clean your plate and old sitcoms play on retro TVs – their excellent milkshakes come with or without alcohol (mains US$12–US$16/£6–8 adults, US$7.50/£3.75 children).

Animal Kingdom

Although at the time of writing a new table service restaurant – the Anandadur Yak and Yeti – is scheduled to open in Animal Kingdom, the emphasis in this park is on casual dining and takeaway stands. The most entertaining place to eat is the Rainbow Café near the entrance. Featuring a large fish tank, waterfalls and even the occasional thunderstorm, this restaurant also has an entrance outside of the park and opens for breakfast from 8.30am (mains, US$9—28/£4.50–14 adults, US$8/£4 children).

Universal Studios & Islands of Adventure

In Universal Studios, table service is available at Finnegan's Bar and Grille in New York and Lombard's Seafood Grille in San Francisco, the latter has a picturesque waterfront setting and vegetarian options (mains US$12/£6, children's menu for the under 9s). Monster's Café in Production Central, easily identified by Frankenstein on its roof, is popular with children and serves pasta and pizzas for around US$7/£3.50. While Mel's Drive-In, a 50s style diner in Hollywood, is a cool place for teens to hang out, listen to live music and keep their eyes open for the Marilyn Monroe look-a-like who often cruises by.

In Islands of Adventure the Mythos restaurant is themed to look as though it has been carved from rock and is claimed by many families to be the best restaurant in any theme park (mains around US$12/£6, children's menu for the under 9s). However, for pre-schoolage children, the Circus McGurkus Café Stoo-pendous in Seuss Landing, with its burgers, pizza and chicken dishes for around US$7/£3.50, is the only place to eat.

Also see City Walk p. 67 for more eating options at Universal Orlando.

INSIDER TIP

Universal operates a Meal Deal system that allows you to eat as much as you want at certain restaurants inside its two parks. A one-park meal deal costs US$20 (£10) adults, US$10 (£5) children under 9 and a two-park meal deal ticket costs US$25 (£12.50) adults, US$13 (£6.50) children under 9. For an extra US$9 (£4.50) for all ages, an additional Sipper Cup deal can be purchased, allowing unlimited soft drinks.

SeaWorld

There are numerous restaurants, cafés and takeaway stands throughout SeaWorld, plus a picnic area near the entrance. Most venues serve children's meals with Mama's Kitchen being the only healthy option (veggie chilli US$9/£4.50) and I like Spice Mill with its range of sandwiches (from US$12/£6) and pleasant views of SeaWorld's large lake. The only table service restaurant is Sharks Underwater Grill (mains US$22–US$29/ £11–14.50, children's menu for the under 12s), where you'll eat surrounded by water tanks containing 30 sharks. This restaurant opens for reservations at 10am; get there as soon as possible to book a table. However, SeaWorld's ultimate restaurant experience for many children is dining with Shamu (US$37/£18.50 adults, US$19/ £9.50 children aged 3–9), a buffet-style evening meal served alongside the killer whale tank with close-up views of behind-the-scenes training exercises. Prior reservations to this and SeaWorld's other themed dining experiences can be made through the park's website – ***www.seaworld.com***.

Busch Gardens

Busch Gardens's eating options are the most limited of all the major attractions, being, on the whole, fast, fried and overpriced. The main options are the Zaragosa takeaway near the entrance in Morocco; the Desert Grille fast food restaurant in Timbuktu – whose dark-themed hall is a welcome relief from the midday heat and whose stage provides regular entertainment – and the Crown Colony House Restaurant, which has a good view of the Serengeti Plain and whose menu features some salads and fruit options for US$10 (£5) and sandwiches for US$9 (£4.50) – there's a table service with the same menu upstairs. Wherever you eat, the children's menu features hot dogs, fries and chicken strips for around US$6.50 (£3.25).

Kennedy Space Center

The most popular dining option is the Orbit Food Court situated in the Visitor Complex, which serves a range of fast food including pizza, sandwiches and veggie wraps for around US$8 (£4) and children's meals for US$5 (£2.50). The nearby, but more expensive, Mila's retro-style diner provides table service. Or families can have lunch with an astronaut (US$23/£11.50 adults, US$15/£7.50 children), during which you can chat, have your photographs taken with and get autographs from one of the few people who've been into space. Make a reservation for this at the ticket plaza when you arrive or ☎ *321 449 4400* to book in advance.

Also see the Family-friendly Dining section of the Central Florida chapter on p. 104.

4 Central Florida

CENTRAL FLORIDA

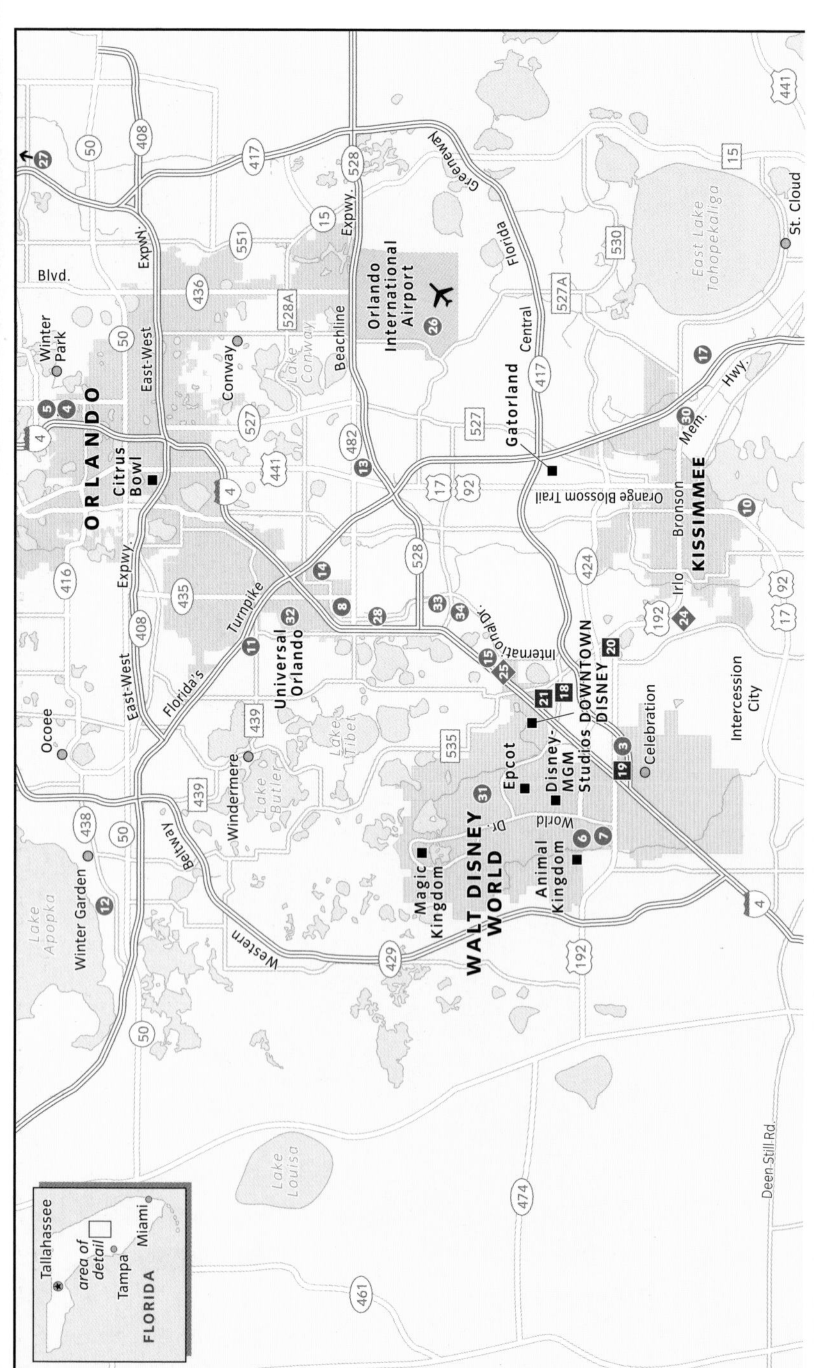

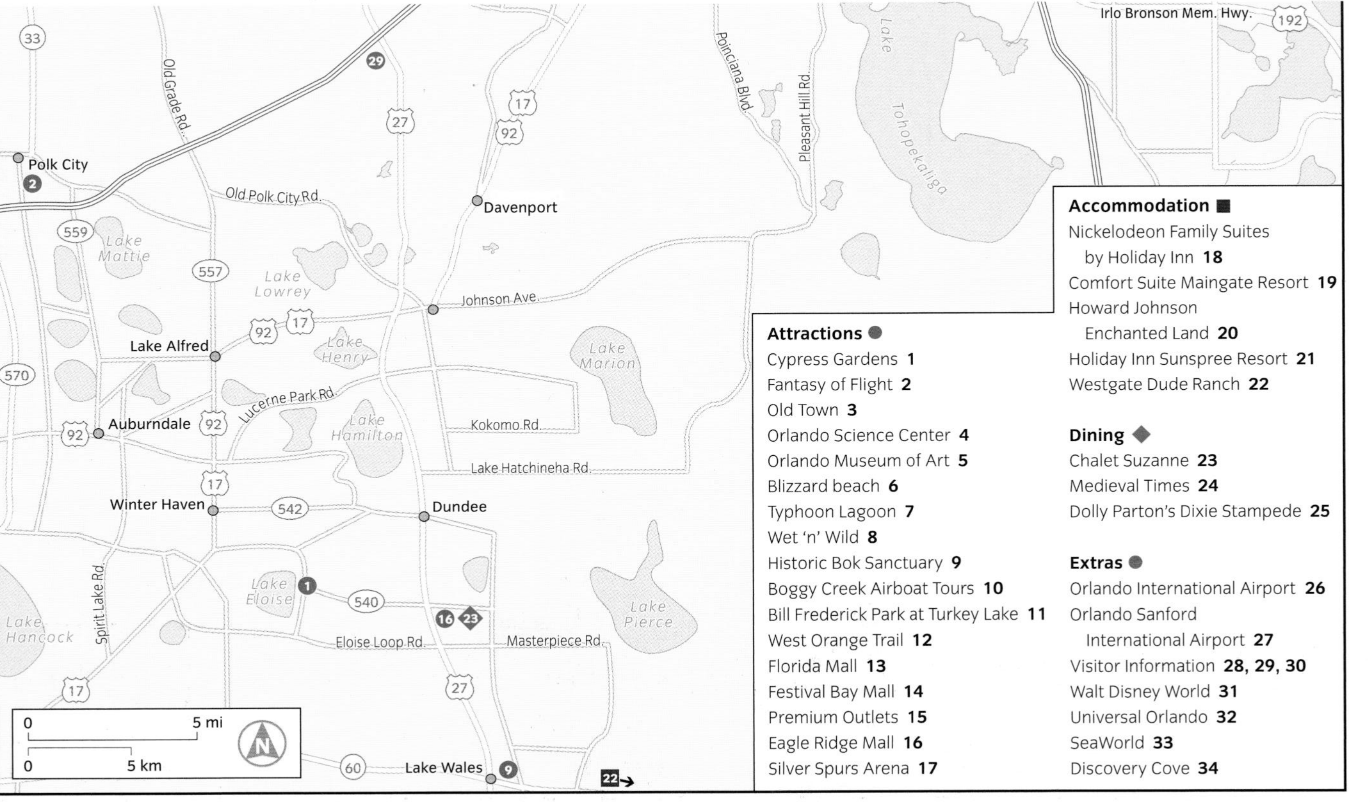
Irlo Bronson Mem. Hwy.
Polk City
Old Grade Rd.
Old Polk City Rd.
Davenport
Lake Mattie
Lake Lowrey
Johnson Ave.
Lake Alfred
Lake Henry
Lake Marion
Lucerne Park Rd.
Auburndale
Lake Hamilton
Kokomo Rd.
Lake Hatchineha Rd.
Winter Haven
Dundee
Lake Eloise
Lake Pierce
Lake Hancock
Spirit Lake Rd.
Eloise Loop Rd.
Masterpiece Rd.
Lake Wales
Poinciana Blvd.
Pleasant Hill Rd.
Lake Tohopekaliga
0 5 mi
0 5 km
N
Attractions
Cypress Gardens 1
Fantasy of Flight 2
Old Town 3
Orlando Science Center 4
Orlando Museum of Art 5
Blizzard beach 6
Typhoon Lagoon 7
Wet 'n' Wild 8
Historic Bok Sanctuary 9
Boggy Creek Airboat Tours 10
Bill Frederick Park at Turkey Lake 11
West Orange Trail 12
Florida Mall 13
Festival Bay Mall 14
Premium Outlets 15
Eagle Ridge Mall 16
Silver Spurs Arena 17
Accommodation
Nickelodeon Family Suites by Holiday Inn 18
Comfort Suite Maingate Resort 19
Howard Johnson Enchanted Land 20
Holiday Inn Sunspree Resort 21
Westgate Dude Ranch 22
Dining
Chalet Suzanne 23
Medieval Times 24
Dolly Parton's Dixie Stampede 25
Extras
Orlando International Airport 26
Orlando Sanford International Airport 27
Visitor Information 28, 29, 30
Walt Disney World 31
Universal Orlando 32
SeaWorld 33
Discovery Cove 34

Ever since Walt Disney bought land and opened up theme parks in central Florida, a deluge of further tourist attractions, from the tasteful to the tacky, and thousands of new hotels and restaurants have transformed this region. For the first-time family this area can be confusing, as it consists of a number of areas each with their own distinct personalities and appeal. Standing in the middle of them all is the modern city of Orlando, whose glittering high rises most visitors never see, as the bulk of the tourist-focused entertainment clusters around the likes of Walt Disney World and Orlando Universal on the city's outskirts. Those not interested in the big thrill buzz of these attraction-soaked areas soon discover a quieter side to central Florida in the laid-back small towns that lie further afield. And it's surprising just how quickly Orlando's network of built-up highways gives way to empty countryside, dotted with less glitzy attractions and a multitude of ways of getting back to nature.

ESSENTIALS

Getting There

By Plane Central Florida's main airport, Orlando International Airport ☎ *407 825 2001* ***www.orlandoairports.net***, is situated nine miles south east of Orlando, while Orlando Sanford International Airport ☎ *407 585 4000* ***www.orlandosanfordairport.com***, located 18 miles north east of Orlando, is a growing favourite with package-tour operators.

Both airports are served by Mears Transportation ☎ *407 432 5566*, who operate taxi and shuttle bus services to any accommodation in the Orlando area. They have a desk at Orlando International Airport and you can book in advance online at ***www.mearstransportation.com***. At the time of writing, online reservations for Orlando Sanford International Airport are not available: call the Mears number to book transport.

For details of package tours and flights to Florida, see p. 28.

By Car Two of Florida's major roads – I-4 and the Florida Turnpike – cross on the south-western outskirts of Orlando. If you're driving from the south east or north west you'll arrive via the Florida Turnpike and from the north east or south west via I-4. Those travelling directly east arrive via SR-528 – the Bee Line Expressway.

VISITOR INFORMATION

Orlando's Official Visitor Center, 8723 International Drive ☎ *407 363 5872* ***www.orlandoinfo.com/uk*** is open daily 8am–7pm. The ticket desk shuts at 6pm. Pick up information on all of Orlando's attractions, accommodation and dining, and book discounted tickets here. You can also order a holiday planning kit in advance from their website or by calling the UK freephone number 0800 018 6760.

INSIDER TIP
Orlando's Official Visitor Center is hard to find if you're driving, as it's tucked away off International Drive and poorly signposted. Try parking at Titanic – The Experience (see p. 95), which is easy to spot, and walking back to the centre.

Central Florida's Visitor Center – Polk Outpost 27 – is located south west of Orlando on Hwy-27, half a mile south of Exit 55 off I-4 800 828 7655 ***www.visitcentralflorida.org*** and is open daily 9am–6pm. At this excellent and interactive centre you can take a virtual balloon ride over the local area, email family and friends for free, visit their Discovery Dock to find out about the region's nature-orientated activities and pick up plenty of information on, and discounts to, central Florida's attractions.

The Kissimmee-St Cloud Visitors' Bureau, 1925 E Hwy-92 407 847 5000 ***www.floridakiss.com***, open Mon–Fri 8am–5pm, is a good source of information and discounts for the south of the region.

INSIDER TIP
For family-friendly advice on holidaying in central Florida, see ***www.travel-insights.com***

Orientation

Central Florida consists of a number of distinct regions, most of which are clustered around Orlando.

Focused around Hwy-192 (Irlo Bronson Memorial Highway) to the south of Orlando is the small town of Kissimmee.

Walt Disney World is located south west of Orlando.

To the north east of Walt Disney World and skirted by SR-535 is Lake Buena Vista.

And running parallel with, and east of, I-4 from Hwy-192 to Universal Orlando is International Drive (Hwy-536).

Further afield, Hwy-27 runs through the centre of Polk County to the south west of Walt Disney World, where a number of attractions are located.

Getting Around

The most convenient way to travel around central Florida is by car, but the traffic can be heavy, so allow plenty of time for your journey – especially during peak periods. For details of car hire see p. 29.

INSIDER TIP
The Orange County Convention Center, sprawled across both sides of International Drive at the junction with SR-528, hosts massive conventions. At these times, sections of the road are impossible to drive. Take Universal Boulevard instead.

If you're in Florida for the theme parks and staying in a hotel, there's little reason to rent a car – see p. 54 for alternatives.

Discount Cards

Of the mind-blowing array of ticket deals and discounts available in central Florida, two cards are really useful. The free **Orlando Magicard** is available from the Official Visitor Center (see above) or can be downloaded and printed from their website ***www.orlandoinfo.com/uk/magicard*** and offers discounts to numerous regional attractions, shops and restaurants. The **Go Orlando Card** ***www.goorlandocard.com*** permits entry to many attractions, tours and dinner shows in central Florida – including the Kennedy Space Center – and can be purchased in denominations of between 1 and 7 days. All days purchased must be used over a 2-week period and prices range from US$59 (£29.50) adult, US$49 (£24.50) child under 12 for 1 day to US$249 (£124.50) adult, US$199 (£99.50) child under 12 for 7 days. Go Orlando Cards can be purchased through the website above or at the Hawaiian Rumble Adventure Golf, 8969 International Drive (next door to WonderWorks) open daily 9am–10pm. For more information on ticket deals, see p. 54.

Orlando's public bus service is operated by Lynx Buses *407 841 5969* ***www.golynx.com*** and the Official Visitor Center (see p. 86) has information on how to get to all the major attractions by bus. The I-Ride Trolley (see p. 94) is the easiest way to get up and down International Drive.

Child-friendly Festivals & Events

The Great American Pie Festival

Celebration 407 644 2636 www.piecouncil.org

Founded in 1994, the small town of Celebration, to the west of Kissimmee off Hwy-192, is the result of Disney-led research into how to create the ideal community. Every April (check website for exact dates) Lakeside Park in this pseudo-Utopian community, which has all the feel of small-town southern America in the 1930s, hosts The Great American Pie Festival – two days of pie tasting, pie-eating contests and children's games and pie making. Winning pies feature in the festival's Never Ending Pie Buffet. Admission is free, tickets to the buffet are US$8 (£4) adults, US$4 (£2) children aged 5–10.

FUN FACT **A Lot of Pies**

If all the pies sold in the US at Thanksgiving were lined up, they would stretch over halfway around the world.

Silver Spurs Rodeo

Silver Spurs Arena, Osceola Heritage Park, 1875 Silver Spur Lane, off Hwy-192, Kissimmee ☎ 407 677 6336 ***www.silverspursrodeo.com***

Founded in 1944, the Silver Spurs Rodeo is one of the US's top 20 rodeos. Silver Spurs features afternoon and evening events when America's best professional rodeo cowboys pit their wits and reflexes against bucking bulls and bareback horses.

There are also barrel racing and cowboy clowns to entertain all ages. Tickets can be bought on the gate or in advance by phone. Silver Spurs is held twice yearly in February and October (check website for dates and times).

Admission *US$15 (£7.50), children under 10 free with a paying adult.* ***Credit*** *MC, V.*

For Child-friendly festivals and events in the theme parks, see p. 49.

WHAT TO SEE & DO

Children's Top Five Attractions

1. A flight in a vintage biplane at Fantasy of Flight; p. 90.
2. Splashing around in Typhoon Lagoon's enormous wave pool; p. 93.
3. Lunch at Chalet Suzanne; p. 105.
4. A night out at Disney's Hoop de doo Review; p. 106.
5. Staying at Westgate River Ranch and watching the Saturday night rodeo; p. 103.

Top Family Attractions

Cypress Gardens

Cypress Gardens Boulevard, Winter Haven, ☎ 863 324 2111 ***www.cypressgardens.com***

A 45-minute drive from Orlando and famous for its

Cypress Gardens

water-ski shows and Southern Belles, Cypress Gardens opened in 1936, making it Florida's very first theme park. A firm favourite with local families (for whom the annual passport ticket is a better deal than the expensive daily rate) the emphasis of this charming, old-fashioned park is placed on the whole family having a day out together. Although not as glitzy as its main competitors, there's something for all age groups and its 40 rides include thrills such as the all-new Starliner, a traditional-style roller coaster, and Thunderbolt, a white-knuckle high-speed freefall ride. The lively and colourful Splash Island water park is popular with young and old (bring swimming costumes), while the tranquil botanical gardens are a haven for adults seeking time out. The animal draws include the Wings of Wonder butterfly arboretum and Nature's Way, a small zoo area which youngsters love. Of the numerous shows, the water ski spectacular is fun for older children and adults, and the comedy pirate and animals shows are aimed at young children. There are lots of cafés and restaurants throughout.

Open *10am daily, closing times vary between 5pm and midnight.* ***Admission*** *US$45 (£22.50) adults, US$40 (£20) children aged 3–9, under 3s free.* ***Credit*** *AmEx, MC, V.* ***Amenities*** *Cafés. Disabled access. Baby-change facilities. Parking US$10 (£5). Restaurant. Shops. ATM. Lockers US$1–US$6 (50p–£3), deposit US$5 (£2.50). Buggy rental US$10 single (£5), US$15 double (£7.50). Wheelchair rental US$9 (£4.50). Tube rental US$5 (£2.50).*

INSIDER TIP

When purchasing day tickets to Cypress Gardens, you can get a second day with free entry, which must be used within 6 days.

Fantasy of Flight ★★

1400 Broadway Blvd. S.E. Polk City *☎ 863 984 3500* ***www.fanasyofflight.com***

Enter Fantasy of Flight's enormous hangers, home to the world's largest private collection of vintage aircraft, through a themed recreation of aviation history up until WW2. Clambering into a WW2 B26 bomber is the best bit! Once inside you are surrounded by historic and famous planes, including ones that featured in *Indiana Jones and the Temple of Doom* and *Rocket Boy*. The interactive education centre is filled with games and simulators that teach the science of flight. You don't have to be an aviation

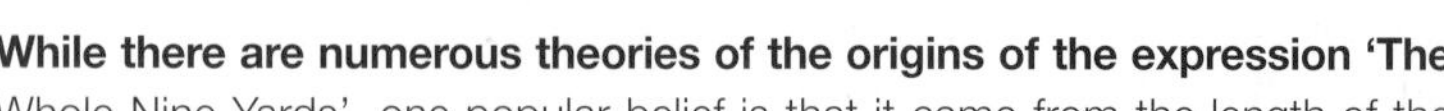

FUN FACT **Whole Nine Yards**

While there are numerous theories of the origins of the expression 'The Whole Nine Yards', one popular belief is that it came from the length of the ammunition belts on WW2 bombers. The 50 calibre machine guns took belts 27 ft (9 yards) long, so if a gunner fired all his ammo at a target, he gave it 'the whole nine yards'. An example of the whole 9 yards can be found at Fantasy of Flight.

Fantasy of Flight

enthusiast to enjoy this museum, but the undoubted highlight of a visit is a shared flight in a vintage biplane that seats up to four (US$60/£30 per person, helmets and goggles included!).

***Open** 10am–5pm daily. **Admission** US$27 (£13.50) adult, US$14 (£7) children aged 6–15, under 6s free. **Credit** AmEx, MC, V. **Amenities** Café. Disabled access. Baby-change facilities. Free parking. Shop.*

Old Town

Hwy-192 (Marker No.9) Kissimmee
*📞 407 396 4888 **www.old-town.com***

Situated on Hwy-192, 3 miles east of Walt Disney World and easily identified by its large Ferris wheel, Old Town is a great place to while away a couple of hours without forking out for any entrance fees. At the front of this old-fashioned attraction is a collection of rides for older children and teens, such as fun track go-carts, while at the back, away from the road, you'll find a cluster of gentle rides for youngsters including the ever-popular tea cups. Linking the two is an old southern USA style street filled with quirky shops, amusement arcades and restaurants, including a British shop where you can pick up UK newspapers,

Old Town's vintage car parade.

magazines and good old British chocolate. Or you can just sit on a bench and watch classic old 1950s cars cruise by.

***Open** 10am–11pm daily, rides 12 noon–11pm. **Admission** Old Town is free to enter, rides cost US$1–US$6 (50p–£3). **Amenities** Free parking. Disabled access.*

INSIDER TIP

Sunday is Family Day at Old Town and cheap ticket deals are available for the rides.

Orlando Science Center ★★

*777 East Princeton Street, Orlando ☎ 407 514 2000 **www.osc.org***

Although the Orlando Science Center is a good rainy-day family option, don't wait for bad weather to bring your children to this entertaining and educational attraction. Located on the edge of the attractive Loch Haven Park, three miles north of downtown Orlando, you'll need half a day to explore the 10 interactive exhibition areas that make up the centre. The exhibits delve into the realms of science, agriculture and astronomy and can be as much fun for adults as children; become scientists in Dr Dare's Laboratory, explore the human body in BodyZone and learn about Florida's ecosystems in NatureWorks. Kid's Town is strictly for children under 48"; they can learn to build, climb trees, play in miniature shops and turn oranges into orange juice. CineDome, aimed at adults and older children, is an eight-storey-high domed cinema showing science and nature films (about 30–40 minutes long) on its massive screen with supporting digital sound.

***Open** 10am–6pm Sun–Thurs, 10am–9pm Fri and Sat. **Admission** US$15 (£7.50) adults, US$10 (£5) children aged 3–11, under 3s free. **Credit** AmEx, MC, V. **Amenities** Café. Disabled access. Parking US$4 (£2). Baby-change facilities. Free buggy and wheelchair rental. Shop.*

INSIDER TIP

Also on the edge of Loch Haven Park is the Orlando Museum of Art (2416 N Mills Avenue ☎ *407 896 4231* ***www.omart.org*** 10am–4pm Tues–Fri, noon – 4pm Sat and Sun; US$8/£4 adults, US$5/£2.50 children aged 6–18, under 6s free) where you'll find collections and changing exhibitions of ancient and modern American and African art. The first Saturday of the month is Family Day, when, for US$5 (£2.50) per family, you can take part in a workshop from 10am to 12noon during which parents and children aged 3–5 explore art, music and stories together (no reservations required).

INSIDER TIP

The Café Grande next to Titanic – The Experience opens at 6am and serves good coffee, ice cream and smoothies. It also has Internet access for US$4 (£2) for 15mins and US$10 (£5) per hour.

Top Water Parks

Blizzard Beach ★★

*Walt Disney World ☎ 407 560 3400 **www.disneyworld.com***

Disney legend claims that once, during a cold winter, an entrepreneur tried to open a ski resort in Florida. The snow

Water Parks – The Top Tips

- You can take picnics into all of the water parks listed below, but no glass containers or alcohol are allowed.
- After a thunderstorm, most water parks are very quiet, even during peak holiday periods.
- One-piece swimming costumes are less likely to come off on water slides than bikinis.
- All the parks have height restrictions on some rides.
- During busy periods, Disney's water parks can be full by mid-morning. Either arrive early or sometime after mid-afternoon when visitors start to leave.

melted, leaving behind a mountain, alpine lodge and ski lift. It's nonsense of course, but makes for an inventive theme for an incredibly popular water park where sand and fake snow sit side by side. The 'ski jump' Summit Plummet ★★, which at 120 ft is America's tallest water slide, forms the park's focal point and gives riders panoramic views of Walt Disney World from the top. There are two other large-scale thrill rides – Slush Gusher and Downhill Double Dipper – and a range of less high-energy options. Ski Patrol Training Camp is an area specially created for pre-teens and features tunnel slides and iceberg walks, while very young children are catered for at Tike's Peak; here you'll find small rides and a fountain play area. However, one of the best ways for families to spend time together at Blizzard Beach is to float around Cross Country Creek in an inner tube as it winds its lazy way around the whole park or simply splash around in Melt-Away Bay, a huge waterfall-fed pool.

Open *between 9–10am daily, closing times vary from 5–8pm.* ***Admission*** *US$42 (£21) adults, US$36 (£18) children aged 3–9, under 3s free (see p. 54 for Disney ticket deals).* ***Credit*** *AmEx, MC, V.* ***Amenities*** *Café. Disabled access. Baby-change facilities. Parking US$10 (£5). Locker, life jacket and towel rental. No buggy rental. Limited number of complimentary water wheelchairs available.*

Typhoon Lagoon ★★★

Walt Disney World ☎ 407 560 4141
www.disneyworld.com

Themed around a tropical island, Typhoon Lagoon is the place to head if you fancy a day at the beach but don't want to drive to the coast – yes, Disney thinks of everything! This park's big thrills are the Crush 'n' Gusher ★ water coaster and the speed slide Humunga Kowabunga ★★, while Gangplank Falls white-water rafting ride is one for all the family. Young children love the Ketchakiddee Creek play area and Bay Slides. Shark Reef comes complete with tropical fish and is

International Drive

www.internationaldriveorlando.com

Stretching from SR-536 and running north parallel with I-4, International Drive is a busy and tourist-focused strip crammed with hotels, restaurants, museums, galleries, tourist attractions and shops. There's something on I-Drive for all ages and many are within easy (and often tree-lined) walking distance. For those attractions a little further away, the **I-Ride Trolley** (***www.iridetrolley.com***) runs frequently and is a fun, hassle-free and cheap (single fare US$1/50p, daily pass US$3/£1.50, children under 12 free) way to get around.

These are a selection of the family-friendly attractions on International Drive. For shopping, see p. 98, and for dining options, see p. 104.

WonderWorks, 9067 International Drive ☎ *407 351 8800* ***www.wonderworksonline.com***, open daily 9am–midnight, US$20 (£10) adults, US$15 (£7.50) children aged 4–12, under 4s free, housed in an unmissable upside-down mansion, this mad attraction is full of interactive science-based displays and an energetic laser tag where you enter a large maze for a virtual shootout.

a safe place for children to try snorkelling for the first time.

Typhoon Lagoon's rides are tucked away around the edge of a vast fake beach that forms the central focus of this park. Around this runs a charming creek where you get to float through grottos and rainforests. And this is the best water park to visit with youngsters, as playing on the sand is given equal prominence to shooting down the water slides.

Open *between 9–10am daily, closing times vary from 5–8pm.* ***Admission*** *US$42 (£21) adults, US$36 (£18) children aged 3–9, under 3s free (see p. 54 for Disney ticket deals).* ***Credit*** *AmEx, MC, V.* ***Amenities*** *Café. Disabled access. Baby-change facilities. Parking US$10 (£5). Locker, life jacket and towel rental. No buggy rental. Limited number of complimentary water wheelchairs available.*

I-Ride Trolley

Wet 'n' Wild ★

6200 International Drive ☎ 407 351 1800 ***www.wetnwild.com***

Ripley's Believe It Or Not Odditorium, 8201 International Drive ☎ *407 363 4418* ***www.ripleysorlando.com*** open 9am–1am daily, US$19 (£9.50) adults, US$12 (£6) children aged 4–12, under 4s free, is a mad collection of weird, bizarre and barely believable artefacts from around the world. (There are also 'odditoriums' in Panama City Beach, St Augustine and Key West. See ***www.ripleys.com*** for details of these locations).

According to the ticket office, **Titanic – The Experience**, The Mercado, 8445 International Drive ☎ *407 248 1166* ***www.titanictheexperience.com*** open 9am–9pm daily, US$20 (£10) adults, US$15 (£7.50) children aged 4–12, under 4s free, is more popular with women than men. Here you can wander through recreations of the interior of the famous but doomed 'ship of dreams' and get up close to movie memorabilia from James Cameron's equally famous film.

And for older children and adults, **SkyVenture**, 6805 Visitors Circle (just off International Drive) ☎ *407 903 1150* ***www.skyventureorlando.com,*** open Sun–Thurs 10am–10pm, Sat and Sun 10am–11pm, US$45 (£22.50) per person, family packages available, is a thrilling freefall sky-diving simulator where you get to 'fly' on a column of air.

Located on a busy junction of International Drive and surrounded by railings, Wet 'n' Wild is not as secluded or slick as Disney's water parks, but it offers more rides and bigger thrills. Whole families can enjoy The Flyer, The Bubba Tub and Disco H2O ★ together. Older children seeking to pump up their adrenaline levels should head to The Brain Wash ★★, featuring a 53 ft vertical drop, and The Storm ★, where riders spin around a giant bowl before plunging into the water below. For small children, the Kids Park contains miniature versions of the thrill rides and the brilliant Bubble Up, a large water-covered inflatable bubble to bounce around on. Chill out on The Lazy River, float in the large wave pool, enjoy a game of volleyball or just lie back and sunbathe.

Keep a firm eye on little ones when Wet 'n' Wild is busy, because it's easy to lose sight of them.

Open *between 9–10am daily, closing times vary from 5–11pm.* ***Admission*** *US$37 (£18.50) adults, US$31 (£15.50) children aged 3–9, under 3s free, afternoon discount sessions available from 2–5pm depending on the closing time (Wet 'n' Wild is part of the Orlando Flexi Ticket deal* *see p. 62**).* ***Credit*** *AmEx, MC, V.* ***Amenities*** *Café. Wheelchairs can be brought into the park but there's limited disabled access to the rides. Parking US$9 (£4.50). Baby-change facilities. Shop. Picnic area. Tube rental US$4 (£2), towel rental US$2 (£1), locker rental US$5 (£2.50), all with a US$2 (£1) deposit.*

Two new water parks are scheduled to open in 2008: Aquatica **www.aquaticabyseaworld.com**, SeaWorld's water park, is due to open in March (for SeaWorld, see p. 68) and Ron Jon's surf park, in the Festival Bay Mall on International Drive, **www.ronjonsurfpark.com** mid way through the year.

Historic Gardens

Historic Bok Sanctuary

1151 Tower Boulevard, Lake Wales *863 676 1408* ***www.boksanctuary.org***

Head for Historic Bok Sanctuary to the south of Orlando if you have small children and want to escape full-on central Florida for a few hours. Following his grandmother's credo to make the world 'a bit more beautiful because you lived in it', author Edward W. Bok created this beautiful, landscaped sanctuary filled with trees, flowers, wild birds and butterflies, which he dedicated to the American people in 1929. Most beautiful of all is a 205 ft Art Deco carillon tower made from pink marble and coquina stone (a soft limestone made up of shell fragments), which forms the focal point of the gardens and houses 60 bells – the largest weighing 12 tonnes – whose recitals chime out daily at 1pm and 3pm. You can't go in the tower, but you can spend time wandering around the sanctuary's beautiful trails and gardens. A number of activities have been created to keep children entertained; pick up the free booklet at the visitor centre located at the entrance to the sanctuary. Make sure your children stand on the human sundial and let their shadow tell the time. No food or drink is allowed into the main gardens but there's a family-friendly garden and lovely picnic area just off the car park.

Open *8am–6pm daily, last admission 5pm.* ***Admission*** *US$10 (£5) adults, US$3 (£1.50) children aged 5–12, under 5s free.* ***Credit*** *AmEx, MC, V.* ***Amenities*** *Café. Disabled access. Baby-change facilities. Free parking. Picnic area. Shop.*

INSIDER TIP

Families wanting to explore the great outdoors in central Florida can pick up a copy of the *Celebrate Nature* leaflet from Central Florida's Visitor Center (see p. 87), which is crammed with information on the region's parks, nature centres and trails.

Child-friendly Tours

Boggy Creek Airboat Rides

2001 E. Southport Road, and 3702 Big Bass Road, Kissimmee *407 344 9550* ***www.bcairboats.com***

Historic Bok Sanctuary

Spook Hill at Lake Wales

Just south of Bok Sanctuary is the small, charming town of Lake Wales, whose historic downtown district is home to several quaint gift and antique shops and restaurants. Just a few blocks from this district on North Wales Drive (5th Street) you'll find mysterious Spook Hill. If you park your car at the bottom of this hill and leave it in neutral, for some inexplicable reason it rolls uphill. Legend blames a fight between a Seminole Indian Chief and large bull alligator for this gravity-defying incline, but whatever the explanation is, thousands flock here each year to witness Spook Hill in action.

It's easy to forget when immersed in central Florida's theme parks and highways that the flat wetland landscape, known generically as the Everglades, starts just a few miles south of Orlando. Boggy Creek Airboat Tours are a safe and educational way to introduce your children to this peaceful landscape teeming with native wildlife including eagles, ospreys, turtles and, of course, alligators. No reservations are required for the half-hour airboat tours that run at 30-minute intervals throughout the day from both Kissimmee locations. From there you will be whizzed at speed into the swampy landscape, which, just like the horizons, seems to stretch on forever. Prior reservations are required for the popular 60-minute night-time tours, which are a wonderful way to discover the other side of Florida.

Open *9am–5pm daily (weather permitting).* ***Tickets*** *half-hour tours US$22 (£11) adults, US$16 (£8) children aged 3–12, under 3s free. Night tours US$35 (£17.50) adults, US$30 (£15) children. Discount tickets can be printed from their website listed above.* ***Credit*** *AmEx, MC, V.* ***Amenities*** *Both locations are wheelchair accessible, but the boats are not.*

For Active Families

Bill Frederick Park at Turkey Lake

3401 S. Hiawassee Rd, ☎ 407 299 5581

Located next to the Florida Turnpike north of Universal, Turkey Lake Park is Orlando's largest park, where children can let off steam and enjoy the outdoors without parents having to drive too far from the main attractions. There's plenty to do in this attractive park, which is also a popular camp site, including swimming, hiking and picnicking, and the large playground is terrific for small children.

Open *Nov–March 8am–5pm, April–Oct 8am–7pm daily.* ***Admission*** *US$4 (£2) per car.* ***Amenities*** *Disabled access. Parking. Picnic area. Toilets.*

INSIDER TIP

If you fail to see any gators on a Boggy Creek tour, head over to Gatorland theme park to the north of Orlando (*407 855 5496* ***www.gatorland.com*** open 9am–5pm daily. US$23/£11.50 adults, US$15/£7.50 children aged 3–12, under 3s free). At this self-proclaimed Alligator Capital of the World you can get up close to hundreds of these and other scary reptiles.

West Orange Trail

County Line Station: From Orlando take SR50 past Winter Garden, this access station is on the right after the Florida Turnpike.

Winter Garden: From Orlando take SR50 west to 9th Street in Winter Garden, turn right (north) to CR43 (Plant Street), then head left (west) to the station

Running along the south-eastern shore of Lake Apopka to the west of Orlando is the 19-mile-long, paved West Orange Trail. Hire bikes to explore the trail at its western end from Bikes & Blades, 17914 State Road 438, Winter Garden *407 877 0600* ***www.orlandobikerental.com*** for US$6 (£3) per hour or US$30 (£15) a day. Bikes & Blades also organises a number of cycling tours along the West Orange Trail and around the historic area of downtown Orlando. If you want to explore on your own, the company delivers rented bikes to your hotel along with a free rack to transport them on your car.

INSIDER TIP

Guests at Walt Disney World can hire bikes from a number of their resorts, including the Bike Barn *407 824 2742* at the Fort Wilderness Resort and Campground. Bikes cost US$8 (£4) per hour and US$22 (£11) per day to hire (no extra cost for a child's seat) and can be used to explore the roads and trails of Walt Disney World.

Shopping

The shopaholic will be in heaven in central Florida, and with a favourable exchange rate for UK travellers especially, there are plenty of good bargains to be had. A number of large malls are dotted around the outskirts of Orlando, of which the **Florida Mall** on Sand Lake Road close to Orlando's International Airport is the largest. The mall, open 10am–9pm Mon–Sat, 12noon–6pm Sun, has famous shops, large department stores including Sears and Macy's and plenty of teen and children's fashion shops.

Easier to reach if you're staying on International Drive is the **Festival Bay Mall** at the far north of I-Drive. Open 10am–9pm Mon–Sat, 11am–7pm Sun, this is the place to bring teenagers, as there's a large branch of Ron Jon's Surf Shop and a multiplex cinema.

Those seeking designer brands such as Gucci, Levi's and Dior, should head for the **Premium Outlets** outdoor shopping mall on Vineland Avenue between Walt Disney World and

Adventure Golf

When the theme parks get too much for your children, a round of adventure golf is an entertaining way of spending a couple of hours together. There are lots of wild and wacky themed courses dotted around to choose from. Pirate's Cove Adventure Golf, 8501 International Drive ☎ *407 352 7378*, ***www.piratescove.net*** is tucked away off the main road and shaded by lots of trees just south of Titanic – The Experience. The course opens daily 9am–11.30pm, and 18 holes costs US$10 (£5) adults, US$9 (£4.50) children under 12, under 3s free. A second round costs US$7 (£3.50) for both adults and children.

Universal, open 10am–11pm Mon–Sat, 10am–9pm Sun.

Anyone staying in a holiday villa around SR-27 looking to shop but avoid traffic can head to the **Eagle Ridge Mall** in Lake Wales (see p. 97), which features an antique carousel, a 12-screen cinema and around 90 shops (open 10am–9pm Mon–Sat, noon–6pm Sun).

For families in search of tacky souvenirs, a cruise along Hwy-192 is a must. Here you'll find enormous, often themed, souvenir factory outlets, such as Orange World located inside the world's largest orange, where prices (and quality) are a fraction of those in the theme parks' shops and worth a wander around for the experience alone.

INSIDER TIP

If you need new memory cards or batteries for your digital camera, ignore the large photography factory outlets along Hwy-192 and the I-Drive and head for cheaper chain stores like Circuit City, Best Buy or Radio Shack, located in the malls.

Festival Bay Mall

FAMILY-FRIENDLY ACCOMMODATION

Most of central Florida's accommodation options are geared up for families, but from basic chain motels to luxury resorts, there's an incredible amount of choice and price ranges, and finding the right option to suit your needs and budget can be confusing. The best way to start is by working out what you want to do here and if you'll be hiring a car. Then search for accommodation options in the area that's convenient for you, bearing in mind that most hotels offer free transport to Disney, Universal and SeaWorld.

One area recommended if you don't want to drive is the tree-lined section of International Drive between the Orange County Convention Center and Sand Lake Road. This area is convenient for Universal Orlando, and many sights and restaurants are within walking distance. You can use the I-Ride Trolley (see p. 94) for those that are not.

Families on a budget wanting to be close to Disney often choose to stay on Hwy-192, which is far less tacky than it used to be, but still stick with the reputable chains when picking a resort or motel in this area. Lake Buena Vista, to the north of I-4 and Walt Disney World, is home to a number of Disney-affiliated hotels (see p. 76) and is one of the quieter tourist areas that's still convenient for most parks.

INSIDER TIP

Two useful websites for researching accommodation in the Orlando area are ***www.orlando.com*** and ***www.justorlandohotels.com***

International Drive Area

MODERATE/EXPENSIVE

Nickelodeon Family Suites by Holiday Inn ★

14500 Continental Gateway ☎ *866 462 6425* ***www.nickhotel.com***

Families staying here won't have any problem persuading their children that a day at the hotel swimming pool is a good alternative to going to a theme park. This resort's large pool areas feature an interactive water tower complete with huge water slides, sandy play area and whirlpool tubs. Families stay in two- or three-bedroom suites themed after cartoon characters like SpongeBob Square Pants and fitted with full kitchens and family areas. I like this resort because children are its main focus, there's even a Sparkle Kids Spa where children can have manicures, hair wraps and temporary tattoos, and every night the resort's Nick Studio hosts family-friendly entertainment. A range of on-site eating options includes a food court, and children eat free with paying adults at all of the hotel's restaurants. Alternatively, evening childcare is available if parents want a night out alone.

Rooms *777.* ***Rates*** *US$140–US$535 (£70–268).* ***Credit*** *AmEx, MC, V.* ***Amenities*** *Shuttle to Disney,*

Universal, SeaWorld and Wet 'n' Wild. Children's games room. Two pool complexes. Laundry facilities. Basketball court. Mini golf. Shops. Snack bar. Five restaurants. Cocktail lounge. ***In Room*** *A/C. Cable TV. Video Games. CD player. Fridge. Microwave. High-speed Internet.*

MODERATE

Doubletree Castle Hotel ★★

8629 International Drive ☎ *407 345 1511* ***www.doubletreecastle.com***

If your children don't want the fairy tale to end when they leave the theme parks, then this large resort styled after a European medieval castle is the place to stay. Lavish purple dominates the themed décor and I particularly love the gold throne-like chairs in the opulent dining room and romantic roof-top bar nestled amongst fake turrets. The large swimming pool is one of the best features of this hotel, which offers families luxury minus a high price tag. Its spacious rooms sleep up to four and feature Sony Playstations to keep children occupied, and young guests are entertained by a court jester most mornings at breakfast in the Castle Café. The hotel is located in a pleasant area of International Drive and a number of restaurants, including Café Tu Tu Tango (see p. 104), are right on its doorstep.

Rooms *216.* ***Rates*** *US$130– US$150 (£65–75).* ***Credit*** *AmEx, MC, V.* ***Amenities*** *Free shuttle to Disney, Universal and SeaWorld. Bar. Restaurant. Pool. Fitness centre. Games arcade. Gift shop. Laundry facilities.* ***In room*** *A/C. Cable TV. Sony Playstation. Microwave (some rooms). Fridge. Safe. Wi-Fi Internet (fee).*

Hwy-192

BUDGET

Comfort Suites Maingate Resort

2775 Florida Plaza Boulevard, Kissimmee ☎ *407 397 7848* ***www.comfortsuitesfl.com***

With Walt Disney World only two miles down the road, Comfort Suites Maingate is one of the better value resorts within easy travelling distance of the big theme parks. I like it as a family choice because it's set back off the busy Hwy-192 and the spacious one- and two- bedroom suites are tastefully decorated, not themed. The pool area is large and well set up to keep children entertained while adults sunbathe, and Old Town (see p. 91), with its restaurants and shops, is right next door.

Rooms *198.* ***Rates*** *from US$90 (£45).* ***Credit*** *AmEx, MC, V.* ***Amenities*** *Free shuttle to Disney, Universal, SeaWorld and Wet 'n' Wild. Complimentary continental breakfast. Pool. Children's pool. Whirlpool. Bar. Games arcade. Gift shop. Fitness centre. Laundry facilities. ATM.* ***In room*** *A/C. Cable TV. Fridge. Microwave. Safe. Internet access.*

Howard Johnson Enchanted Land

4985 Hwy-192, Kissimmee ☎ *407 396 4343* ***www.hojo.com***

One of my favourite budget options on Hwy-192, Howard Johnson Enchanted Land is well placed for all the major attractions and offers basic, no frills attached, value for money accommodation. Family rooms include themed sleeping areas for children, partitioned off from the rest of the room, providing some privacy for adults. Every evening the motel hosts an ice cream party for children. The on-site Indian restaurant serves excellent food and there's a large supermarket and some decent chain restaurants within walking distance.

***Rooms** 160. **Rates** US$75–US$90 (£37.50–45). **Credit** AmEx, MC, V. **Amenities** Free shuttle to Disney, Universal and SeaWorld. Pool. Whirlpool. Restaurant. Laundry facilities. Fitness room. Bar. **In room** A/C. Cable TV. Safe. Fridge. Microwave. Wi-Fi Internet. VCR (some rooms).*

Lake Buena Vista

MODERATE

Holiday Inn Sunspree Resort ★

13351 SR-535, Lake Buena Vista
*407 239 4500 **www.kidssuites.com***

From the moment families arrive at this colourful hotel right on Disney's doorstep, where children have their own check-in area and free welcome goodie bag, you know this is a resort where young guests are as important as adults. Families have a choice of two types of accommodation: basic rooms with two queen-size beds or, if your budget allows, Kidsuites. The latter include separate themed sleeping areas for up to four pre-teenage children complete with their own TV and VCR, CD player and Nintendo games. There's a range of activities to keep children entertained throughout the day, including a Kiddie Camp Holiday for 4–12-year-olds and a small children's cinema that screens free children's films all day. There's no on-site evening childcare, but there is a range of family-friendly entertainment and children under 12 eat free with a paying adult in the resort's restaurant. Parents can hire pagers for US$5 (£2.50) when leaving their children in the Kiddie Camp Holiday if they want time off alone.

***Rooms** 507. **Rates** Rooms from US$110 (£55), suites from US$159 (£79.50). **Credit** AmEx, MC, V. **Amenities** Free shuttle to Disney. Two pools. Basketball court. Fitness centre. Shop. Bar. Restaurant. Laundry facilities. **In room** A/C.*

Villas

A number of families choose to rent villas in the Orlando area rather than stay in hotels. This can work out much cheaper if you self cater but it can be harder to meet other families and for your children to make friends. The Central Florida Visitor Information Center's website, ***www.visitcentralflorida.org*** (see p. 87) has details of a range of villa-hire companies, of which AAA SunState Management is recommended *352 242 0351 **www.sunstate-rentals.com***.

Cable TV. Free cots. Safe. Fridge. Microwave. Internet access.

Out of Town

MODERATE

Westgate Dude Ranch ★★

3200 River Ranch Blvd., River Ranch, Nr Lake Wales ☎ 863 692 0727 ***www.wgriveranch.com***

An hour's drive but a million miles away from Orlando, Westgate Dude Ranch is an authentic American family experience that's not to be missed by families who want to get back to nature and enjoy the outdoors. There are three types of accommodation, from basic rooms to suites, all of which have cooking facilities and can sleep up to four. The family-focused activities on offer, such as hayrides, country cookouts, barrel racing and pony riding, are ones you just won't find at the tourist resorts, and visitors can also hire bikes and canoes, go on airboat rides and explore nature trails. Evening entertainment includes movie nights for children at the Kiddie Corral and karaoke and line dancing at the saloon. An absolute must is the Saturday night rodeo, where the patriotism takes some getting used to for a British audience, but the skill of the riders will wow all ages – expect your daughters to fall in love with the cowboys and your sons to want to be one.

Rooms *100.* ***Rates*** *Rooms US$89–US$119 (£45–60), one-bedroomed cottages US$159–US$179 (£80–90), two-bedroomed cottages US$279–US$299 (£140–150).* ***Credit*** *AmEx, MC, V.* ***Amenities*** *Outdoor pool. Hot tub. Golf course. Petting zoo. Fitness centre. Tennis and basketball courts. Games arcade. Food shop. Bakery. Restaurant. Bar.* ***In room*** *A/C. Kitchen or kitchenette. Cable TV. Screened patio. High-speed Internet (fee).*

Westgate Dude Ranch Rodeo

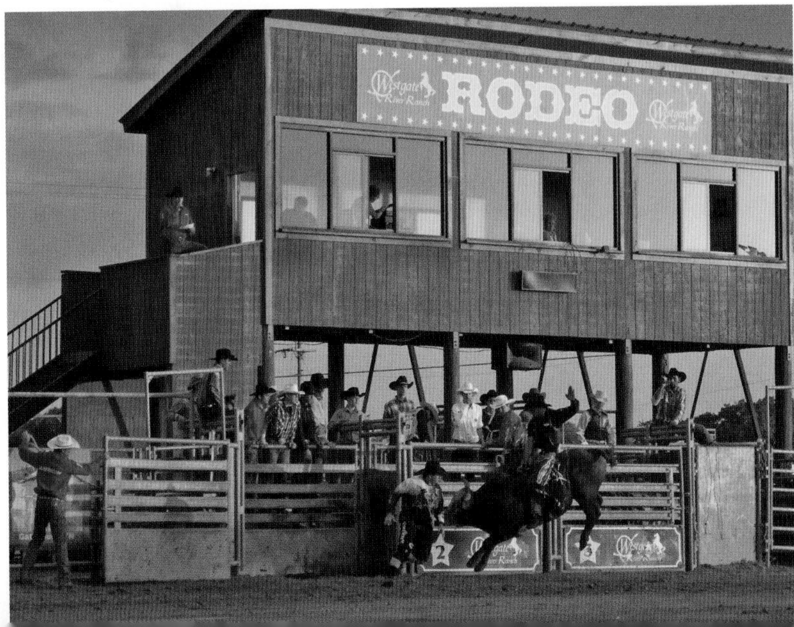

INSIDER TIP
Westgate River Ranch is also a good family day out.

Also see accommodation options at the major attractions in central Florida on p. 76.

FAMILY-FRIENDLY DINING

With Orlando boasting over 5,000 places to eat, there's an overwhelming choice of dining options. Both Downtown Disney (see p. 60) and Universal's City Walk (see p. 67) are home to a large range of themed restaurants. However, if you want to get away from the bustle, International Drive has a selection of family-friendly dining options. Try The Mercado, a Mediterranean-styled courtyard adjacent to Titanic – The Experience (see p. 95), which is home to a number of family-friendly restaurants.

Hwy-192 features chain restaurants and all-you-can-eat buffets, while Restaurant Row is handy for Lake Buena Vista at the junction of Sand Lake Road and Dr Phillips Boulevard west of I-4. This stretch of highway features around 20 upmarket restaurants within a mile. Look out for restaurant discount vouchers in the visitor information centres (see p. 86).

INSIDER TIP
The Spice Garden restaurant 📞 407 690 8821 located within Howard Johnson Enchanted Land on Hwy-192 at the junction with SR-535 (see p. 101) is the best place in the Orlando area for an Indian takeaway. The restaurant is open daily from 5–11pm.

International Drive

MODERATE

Bahama Breeze ★

8849 International Drive 📞 407 248 2499 ***www.bahamabreeze.com***

Bahama Breeze is one of America's better chain restaurants and hugely popular with families – make sure you book for dinner. A dark wood décor adds warmth to the laid-back atmosphere but it's the excellent Caribbean-influenced food that people flock here for. I especially like the large range of tropical drinks and selection of non-alcoholic options on the children's menu. The menu features a varied selection of inexpensive soups, salads and sandwiches and plenty of Caribbean dishes such as West Indies Patties and superb Coconut Shrimp. There's also a branch of Bahama Breeze at 8735 Vineland Avenue, Lake Buena Vista *📞 407 938 9010.*

Open *11am–1am Sun–Thurs, 11am–1.30am Fri and Sat.* ***Main Courses*** *US$9–US$35 (£4.50–17.50).* ***Credit*** *AmEx, MC, V.* ***Amenities*** *Children's menu for under 12s. Highchair. Disabled access.*

Café Tu Tu Tango ★★

8625 International Drive 📞 407 248 2222 ***www.cafetututango.com/orlando***

Café Tu Tu Tango is a casual and eclectic eatery styled around a bohemian Spanish artists' loft and is a good choice for families who want to experience something a bit different in terms of atmosphere. The imaginative interior is decorated by the work of local artists and the Mediterranean and Latin American influenced food, full of strong flavours and served tapas style, is meant to be shared. The less imaginative children's menu features spaghetti and pizza options but young diners can always eat tapas too and everyone can enjoy regular entertainment, which features acrobats, magicians and live music.

Open *11.30am–11pm Sun–Thurs, 11.30am–1am Fri and Sat.* ***Main Courses*** *US$4–US$20 (£2–10).* ***Credit*** *AmEx, MC, V.* ***Amenities*** *Children's menu for under 12s. Entertainment. Highchairs.*

Cricketer's Arms Pub

5250 International Drive at Festival Bay Mall 📞 *407 354 0686* ***www.cricketersarmspub.com***

With all the ambience of a British local, this pub in the middle of Orlando is the place to head if you're pining for inexpensive British pub grub. Wooden beams, a large fireplace and TV screen showing all the latest footie and rugby matches add to the atmosphere and the array of imported British beer and ales features the likes of London Pride, Fullers' ESB and Old Speckled Hen on tap. Just like pubs at home, this is a family-friendly eatery and the children's menu includes fish, bangers or chicken and chips.

Open *noon–2am daily.* ***Main Courses*** *US$7–US$19 (£3.50–9.50).* ***Credit*** *MC, V.* ***Amenities*** *Children's menu. Highchair.*

Out of Town

EXPENSIVE

Chalet Suzanne ★★

3800 Chalet Suzanne Drive, Lake Wales 📞 *863 676 6011* ***www.chaletsuzanne.com***

Set in a pink fairytale, Swiss-style building, crammed with antiques from around the world, Chalet Suzanne is one of central Florida's top restaurants. Open for breakfast, lunch and dinner, the gourmet food is well worth the half hour's drive from Orlando to experience – their soup has nourished NASA astronauts when in space – and children love to watch small planes fly in and out of the tiny airstrip. Although on the formal side in the evening, there's plenty of garden space for children to play in, however, this is also my favourite romantic restaurant in this region and perfect for a special parents-only night out. Chalet Suzanne is also a quirky place to stay (rates US$169–US$229/£85–115)) and features a lovely lake in its grounds, which all ages enjoy exploring.

Open *8am–9pm daily.* ***Main Courses*** *breakfast US$16–US$18 (£8–9), lunch US$29–US$39 (£14.50–19.50), dinner US$59–US$79 (£29.50–39.50).* ***Credit*** *AmEx, MC, V.* ***Amenities*** *Children's menu. Highchair. Disabled access. Reservations requested for dinner.*

Dinner Shows

A prominent feature of Orlando's evening entertainment is its multitude of dinner shows. From the spirit of Polynesian to murder mystery, there are plenty of themes to choose from, and audience participation is an essential feature of all of them. Tickets costs around US$50 (£25) adult and US$30 (£15) children and families should expect good entertainment rather than fine dining. The most popular show is Disney's **Hoop de Doo Review** ★★ (☎ *407 939 3463* ***www.disneyworld.com*** – book well in advance) held at Fort Wilderness Campground. This vaudeville-style show was described by a Disney employee as being 'so bad it's good' – even the strawberry shortcake dessert is a production number in its own right.

Of the remaining shows, those involving horses are popular with children. **Medieval Times** (4510 Hwy-192 ☎ *1 888 935 6878* ***www.medievaltimes.com***) transports audiences back to the age of chivalry and jousting, **Arabian Nights** (6225 Hwy-192 ☎ *407 239 9223* ***www.arabian-nights.com***) is set in the world's largest indoor equestrian ring and stars 60 handsome horses. The patriotic **Dolly Parton's Dixie Stampede** (8251 Vineland Avenue ☎ *866 443 4943* ***www.dixiestampede.com***) transports diners back to Dolly's childhood family life.

If you want to know what you're letting yourself in for before buying tickets, there are plenty of clips of Orlando's dinner shows on ***www.youtube.com***.

INSIDER TIP

Garfield's restaurant and pub at the Eagle Ride shopping mall on SR-27 at Lake Wales, runs special meal-and-movie deals with the multiplex cinema in the same mall. If you're staying in a villa around this area, this is a good option for a family night out without having to drive into the busy tourist areas.

For more information on family-friendly dining in the central Florida region, see the Family-friendly Dining section of the Major Attractions chapter on p. 80.

5 Tampa Bay & the South West Coast

TAMPA BAY & THE SOUTH WEST COAST

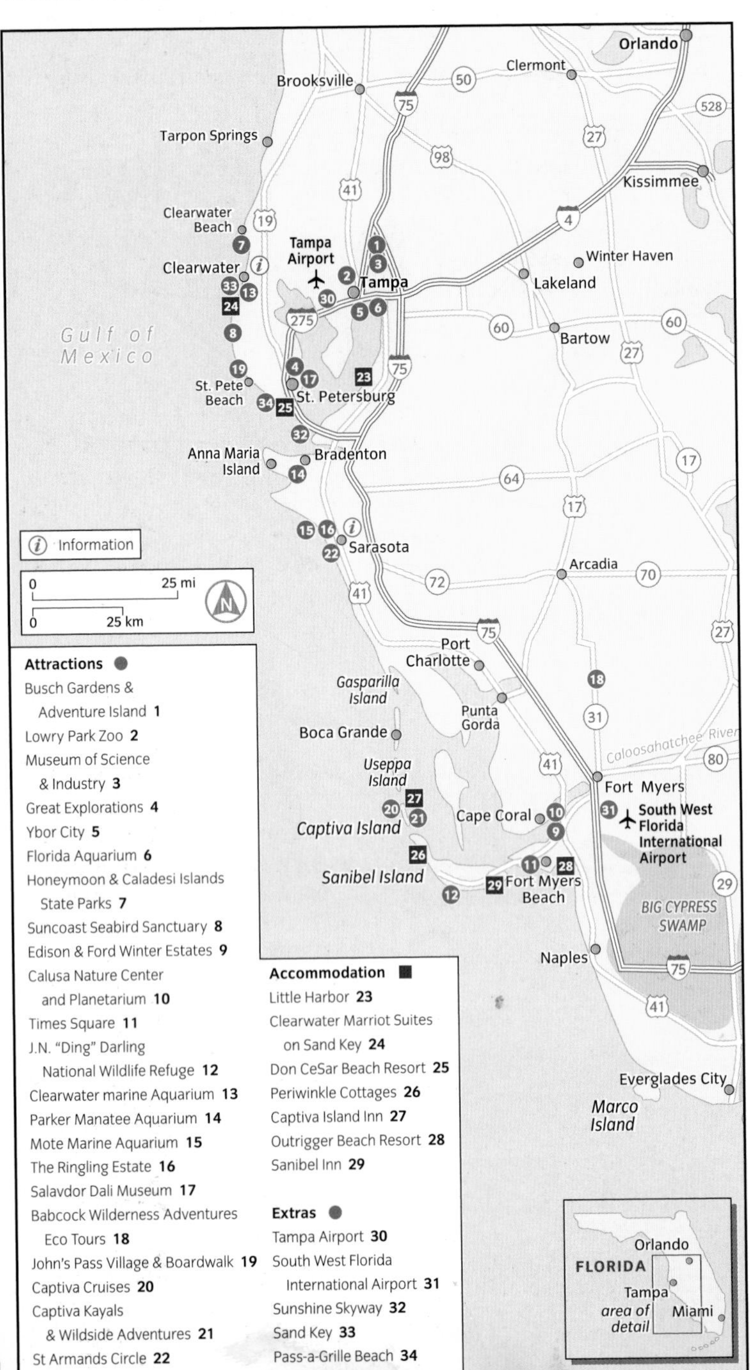

Fringed by the Big Bend's coastal wetlands to the north and the subtropical wilderness of the Everglades to the south, the long stretch of glorious beaches this region is famous for has been attracting holidaying families for decades. This part of Florida is made up of two distinct areas. The central area, which contains the cities of Tampa and St Petersburg, beaches from Honeymoon Island to Fort de Soto and a large natural harbour, is known generically as Tampa Bay. Many British families spilt their time in Florida between the big theme parks in the centre of the state and the Tampa Bay beaches, which claim an average of 361 days of sunshine a year. South of Tampa Bay, from Bradenton to Marco Island, is the south west coast, which is becoming increasingly popular with those venturing away from the main tourist regions and has much to offer visitors who want a more authentic experience of the Sunshine State. Any family seeking a good beach will find one to suit their taste, budget and lifestyle in this region. All are lapped by the Gulf of Mexico's warm waters and while some are known for their water sports, paragliding, pirate cruises and beach bars, others are equally celebrated for their remoteness. Far removed from its beaches, the cities of south west Florida are rich in history, culture and child-friendly attractions, many of which will take first-time families pleasantly by surprise.

ESSENTIALS

Getting There

By Plane Located five miles west of downtown, Tampa Airport ☎ *813 870 8770* ***www.tampairport.com*** is the region's main airport. British Airways operates a regular service from London Gatwick and numerous American airlines schedule internal flights from Miami, Fort Lauderdale, Fort Myers, Key West, Pensacola and Tallahassee.

Serving the south of the region, the South West Florida International Airport ☎ *239 768 1000* ***www.flylcpa.com*** is three miles east of I-75 near Fort Myers and welcomes internal flights from Miami, Tampa, Key West and Orlando.

For details of package tours, see p. 28.

By Car Tampa is approximately 85 miles south west of Orlando. The I-4 connects the two cities and ends in Tampa at I-275, which then continues across the north of Tampa Bay to St Petersburg. Once over the bay, join SR-688 to the beaches. If you want to avoid Tampa Bay on your journey south, leave I-4 at its junction with I-75 east of Tampa.

Hwy-17, which joins I-75 at Punta Gorda, is a more direct route from Orlando to Fort Myers.

By Ferry The Key West Express ferry travels between Fort Myers Beach and Key West. High-speed boats leave at 9am from

Tampa Bay

the Fisherman's Wharf and Salty Sam's Marina on Fort Myers Beach and take approximately three-and-a-half hours to reach Key West, from where they depart for the return journey to Fort Myers Beach at 6pm. Adult singles cost US$73 (£36.50); round trips US$128 (£64). Children aged 6–12 will pay US$35 single, US$68 round trip; under 5s with a fee-paying adult only pay port fees. For further information ☎ *1 888 539 2628* ***www.seakeywestexpress.com***. This ferry service also connects Key West with Miami; see p. 168 for details.

VISITOR INFORMATION

Tampa's Visitor Information Center is located in the Channelside Entertainment complex near the cruise ship port and Florida Aquarium at 615 Channelside Drive ☎ *813 223 2752* ***www.visittampabay.com***. Open 9.30am–5pm Mon–Sat, 11am–5pm Sun.

For information on St Petersburg and Clearwater, visit the booth at Clearwater's Pier 60, see p. 117 – ☎ *727 726 1547* ***www.floridasbeach.com***. Open 9am–5pm Mon–Sat, 10am–5pm Sun.

Sarasota's Visitor Bureau is located on Hwy-41 north of the junction to St Armands Circle – ☎ *941 957 1877* ***www.sarasotafl.org***. Open 10am–4pm Mon–Sat, noon–3pm Sun.

Fort Myers has visitor information points at Times Square on its beach (see p. 118) and downtown at the Edison and Ford Winter Estates (see p. 121). The visitor center for the islands of Sanibel and Captiva is located on Sanibel by the causeway from the mainland. ☎ *239 472 1080*. Open 9am–7pm Mon–Sat, 10am–5pm Sun. The official website for this region is ***www.fortmyerssanibel.com*** and ☎ *01273 832 832* is the UK telephone number to call for more information.

Orientation

Various roads, including I-275, SR-60 and SR-580, link Tampa with the beaches of Tampa Bay. Alt-19 is the quickest route through the beach communities, while the slower SR-699 travels the length of St Pete's beaches along the coast. I-75 is the fastest way to travel through south west Florida, with Hwy-41 – also known as the Tamiami Trail – running parallel to the interstate.

Getting Around

With limited public transport options, the only feasible way to travel around Tampa Bay and the south west coast with children is by car. For details of car hire, see p. 29.

Child-friendly Festivals

American Sandsculpting Championship Festival
Every November, artists from all over North America gather on Fort Myers Beach between the Outrigger (see p. 132) and Holiday Inn resorts to create amazing artwork out of sand. The creations could be anything from intricate castles to people and animals. If you're inspired by the master sculptures, test your own skills by entering the amateur contest. The event attracts thousands of visitors who come to watch the artists at work and chill out in the Sand Magic Village, filled with food and craft stalls.

Free admission ☎ *239 454 7500* ***www.sandfestival.com****. Check website for exact dates each year.*

Cinco de Mayo Fiesta
Each 5th May, in recognition of the Mexican celebration Cinco de Mayo, a Mexican restaurant in Dunedin (see p. 115) called Casa Tina's throws a street party. The festivities, which run from 11am–11pm, take place on Main Street outside the restaurant and include live music, dance lessons, costume and dance contests and plenty of Mexican food and drink.

Free admission ☎ *722 734 9226.*

The Sunshine Skyway

Crossing the south of Tampa Bay and linking St Petersburg with the rest of the south west coast, the Sunshine Skyway (toll US$1/50p), built by the American Bridge Company, is one of the world's most spectacular bridges. Opening to traffic in 1987, the bridge is five and a half miles long and provides panoramic views of Tampa Bay and the Gulf of Mexico. The rest stops stationed at either end of the bridge are memorable places to take a break.

WHAT TO SEE & DO

Children's Top 10 Attractions

❶ **Discovering** the waters around Captiva island with Captiva Kayak and Wildside Adventures; p. 126.

❷ **Seeing** circus history come to life at The Ringling Estate; p. 123.

❸ **Learning** about Florida's aquatic environments at Tampa's Florida Aquarium; p. 122.

❹ **Getting** up close and personal with nature at the J.N. 'Ding' Darling National Wildlife Refuge; p. 127.

❺ **Kite flying** on Honeymoon Island; p. 116.

❻ **Viewing** surrealist masterpieces at the Salvador Dalí Museum; p. 124.

❼ **Searching** the shores of Sanibel for shells; p. 120.

❽ **Witnessing** 'nature unscripted' on a Babcock Wilderness Adventure; p. 125.

❾ **Blowing** your spending money at St Armands Circle's shops; p. 127.

❿ **Tackling** an enormous, sticky dessert at Captiva's Bubble Room restaurant; p. 136.

Towns & Cities

Tampa

With the arrival of the railway in the 1880s and the dredging of its harbour to accommodate large ships, Tampa's status rapidly developed from fishing village into the commercial heart of south west Florida. Today the city sprawls along the banks of the Hillsborough river as it flows into Tampa Bay and its downtown skyscrapers dominate the bay's skyline.

Most visitors fail to venture further than Busch Gardens (see p. 72) or its seasonal adjacent water park Adventure Island ***www.adventureisland.com***. However, Tampa's other family-friendly attractions are some of the best in the region and if your children are not ready for the beach, the sights are worth navigating the city's confusing road system to explore.

INSIDER TIP

Tampa's big-city status comes along with big-city problems, so stick to the major roads when driving around and don't be tempted to take short cuts.

FUN FACT **Lightning Capital**

Tampa Bay is known as the lightning capital of the US and afternoon thunderstorms are common during the summer.

Tampa's Family-friendly Attractions

In addition to Busch Gardens (see p. 72) and the Florida Aquarium (see p. 122), Tampa has two other large family-friendly attractions. Six miles north of downtown, **Lowry Park Zoo** ★ (1101 West Sligh Avenue ☎ *813 935 8552 **www.lowryparkzoo.com***. Open 9.30am–5pm daily. US$15/£7.50 adults, US$11/£5.50 children aged 3–11, under 3s free) offers six landscaped areas featuring native and foreign species. **Primate World**, with its collection of monkeys, orang-utans, chimpanzees and baboons, is entertaining and educational and children can feed animals and interact with kangaroos and wallabies at Wallaroo Station. There are some rides and a water playground for small children (bring bathing suits) and manatee lovers can view these endangered animals in the Aquatic Center and learn about conservation efforts to protect them. For an extra fee (US$14/£7 adults, US$10/£5 children), you can join a nature cruise along the Hillsborough River and view native wildlife in its natural habitat.

With its three floors housing 450 hands-on displays, the **Museum of Science and Industry** ★★ (4801 East Fowler Avenue, Tampa ☎ *813 987 6000 **www.mosi.org***. Open 9am–5pm daily. US$10/£5 adults, US$8/£4 children aged 2–12, under 2s free) is one of America's largest science centres. Developed under the guidance of children, the Kids in Charge area targets the under 12s and provides a multitude of opportunities for learning through play. Tour the human body, experience hurricane-force winds, ride on a high-wire bicycle and view an enormous dinosaur skeleton. A giant IMAX cinema screens impressive education-based films throughout the day.

INSIDER TIP

If you can't get to Tampa's Museum of Science and Industry, Great Explorations in St Petersburg (1925 4th Street North ☎ *727 821 8992 **www.greatex.org***. Open 10am–4.30pm Mon–Sat, noon–4.30pm Sun. Admission US$9/£4.50) has a similar theme.

Tampa's most fascinating and tourist-friendly area is the Cuban district of Ybor City. In 1886, Don Vincente Martinez Ybor moved his cigar-making business from Key West to Tampa, attracting a migrant workforce of around 20,000 to the region. Despite the decline in the cigar industry, Ybor maintains its vibrancy and many of its old cigar factories and workers' cottages have been transformed into pavement cafés and trendy shops.

Ybor's small, historic grid of streets is cluttered with red-brick Victorian buildings and Cuban-influenced architecture, some decorated with colourful murals. Centro Ybor, a dining and shopping complex with a streetcar

FUN FACT **That's a Lot!**

There are over 5,000 known species of sponge.

stop (see p. 114) outside, stands at its heart and is a good starting point from which to explore. Ybor is easily covered on foot and walking tours can be picked up from the Visitor Information Center on East 8th Ave ☎ *813 241 8838* ***www.ybor.org***, where you can also watch a film on Ybor's history and pick up discount tokens to attractions including a museum and restored cigar worker's house. Best of all are the old Cuban cafés, where the coffee is fabulous and you can watch cigars being hand rolled. Teenagers who enjoy poking around retro second-hand clothes stores will love Ybor, but there isn't much here to hold the attention of younger children.

INSIDER TIP

If you want to visit Ybor City and the Florida Aquarium, you can park at either and catch the streetcar ***www.tescolinestreetcar.org***, a vintage trolley service connecting the two. One-way trips cost US$2 (£1) and day passes US$4 (£2). You'll need exact change if you buy tickets on board, or passes can be purchased from the Visitor Information Center near the Aquarium (see p. 110).

Tarpon Springs

www.tarponsprings.com

Known as the Sponge Capital of the World, the small town of Tarpon Springs, 30 miles north of St Petersburg, attracted an influx of Greek immigrants in

Tarpon Springs Harbour

the early 20th century, who came to harvest the natural sponges growing in the surrounding waters. It's their influence on the town, and its working harbour, which now attracts droves of tourists who come to stroll along Dodecanese Boulevard, the town's waterfront, stuffed with souvenir shops and Greek restaurants.

The town's Spongeorama museum (510 Dodecanese Boulevard, 10am–5pm daily. Free) and Aquarium (850 Dodecanese Blvd, ☎ *727 938 5378.* 10am–5pm Mon–Sat, noon–5pm Sun. US$6/£3 adults, US$4/£2 children aged 3–11, under 3s free) are both disappointing. However, it's the Mediterranean-influenced atmosphere whose upbeat nature appeals to children that visitors flock here to enjoy. Explore away from the main tourist drag, which can be uncharacteristically aggressive for laid-back Florida. A free self-guided walking tour is available from the harbourside visitor centre, or take the trolley that loops around the main sights (US$1/50p for a round trip).

INSIDER TIP

If the intensity of Tarpon Springs's harbour becomes too much, seek refuge in St Nicholas Greek Orthodox Cathedral, a peaceful and beautiful haven from the heat and crowds.

Greek food is a big draw to Tarpon Springs and there are numerous authentic restaurants to choose from, most offering at least one refreshing alternative to burgers and hot dogs on their children's menu. Hellas on Dodecanese Boulevard ☎ *727 934 8400* ***www.hellas-restaurant.com*** specialises in Greek pastries, however, popular with locals is Mama Maria's on North Pinellas Avenue (Alt-19) ☎ *727 934 5678* ***www.theoriginalmamamarias.com***. Located away from the main tourist area and looking like little more than a fast food joint, this restaurant's reasonably priced Greek food is fabulous and you can choose to eat in or take away – *spanakopita* from heaven!

Dunedin ★★ FIND

www.dunedin-fl.com

I stumbled across Dunedin late one night while trying to find a place to stay and was delighted to discover the attractive, friendly, waterfront community tucked away from the region's tourist hot spots and largely ignored by foreign visitors. Families can easily spend half a day exploring the shops, cafés and restaurants of its quaint downtown. Recommended are Cappuccino's Bakery Café (open 8am Mon–Fri, and 10am Sat until early evening and 1–5pm Sun), for its speciality coffees and scrumptious cakes, and the Children's Art Museum located inside Dunedin's Fine Art Center (1143 Michigan Boulevard, ☎ *727 298 3322* ***www.dfac.org***. Open 10am–5pm Mon–Fri, 10am–2pm Sat, 1–4pm Sun) where interactive displays help small children understand the artwork on display in the main galleries.

FUN FACT **Highland Fun**

Dunedin's sister city is Sterling in Scotland, and each spring the town hosts its own highland games.

There's no beach at Dunedin, instead at its pleasant waterfront you'll find a small fishing pier, children's park and oceanside walkway. Active families can hire bikes to explore the Pinellas Trail (see p. 127), which passes through the town.

INSIDER TIP

Ales brewed at the Dunedin Brewery can be sampled at the Snug Pub, 937 Douglas Ave, open from 4pm until late Tues–Sat.

Best Beaches & Beach Communities

Honeymoon & Caladesi Islands State Parks ★★

www.romantichoneymoonisland.com

Anyone who enjoys kite flying should bring one to Honeymoon Island State Park (open 8am–sunset, US$5/£2.50 per car), a large island north of Dunedin where seagulls take food from your hand. The glorious undeveloped seashell-strewn sandy beach is surrounded by mangrove swamps and a pine forest, and is a favourite with local families. There are plenty of activities to keep all ages occupied including beach volleyball, kayak hire, nature trails, snorkelling, a lively café and new Nature Center (9am–5pm) filled with information on the island's wildlife and history.

Visitors can spend up to four hours on the glorious Caladesi Island State Park ★★, which lies a 20-minute ferry ride away from Honeymoon Island (round trip US$9/£4.50 adults, US$5.50/£2.75 children aged 4–12, under 4s free) where the 3-mile beach is fringed with gentle sand dunes leading to mangrove woods. It's considered to be one of the best beaches in North America.

Clearwater & Sand Key

www.visitclearwaterflorida.com

Dominated by large resorts, Clearwater's wide beach is one of the most developed in south west Florida and popular with young people and European tourists, making its sands an attractive option for families with older children who are seeking a lively party beach.

INSIDER TIP

The main causeway to Clearwater Beach from the mainland (SR-60) is crammed with traffic during rush hour and at the weekends.

FUN FACT **Marry Me?**

Many couples get married on Honeymoon Island.

Clearwater's marina and Pier 60 form the beach's energetic hub and are situated at the point where the causeway from the mainland joins the coast. Numerous tour operators are found here, offering everything from dolphin spotting to pirate cruises; jet ski and paragliding operators jostle for your attention.

South of Clearwater and far better suited for families with small children, is Sand Key Park ★★. Parking is metered (US$1.25/63p per hour – bring plenty of quarters) and plentiful, and even when the beach is busy you'll find a quiet spot on this vast expanse of crystal-white sand. The park also features a large play area, shaded picnic tables, changing facilities and toilets, but you'll need to bring your own food and drink.

INSIDER TIP

The Suncoast Beach Trolley serves the length of the coast from Clearwater to Pass-a-Grille. The route has frequent stops and trolleys run every 30 minutes from 5.15am–7.30pm daily. Fares US$1.25 (63p) per ride or US$3.50 (£1.75) for a day pass. Exact change required.

St Pete's Beaches

Stretching from Belleair Shore in the north to Pass-a-Grille in the south, this collection of beaches, known generically as St Pete's Beaches, attract thousands of tourists every year. Each beach varies in character, with some residential and others overdeveloped.

Drive along SR-699 to explore them all; if you're into water sports, aim for Treasure Island, and the best shopping

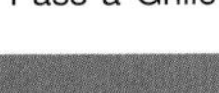

Pass-a-Grille

Suncoast Seabird Sanctuary

18328 Gulf Blvd, Indian Shores *727 391 6211* ***www.seabirdsanctuary.org***

Open daily from 9am to sunset, this free sanctuary is accessed from either the beach or main road and is the largest wild-bird hospital and rehabilitation centre in the US. Hundreds of rescue birds can be viewed, including pelicans, owls, gannets, falcons and hawks, and more nest in the surrounding trees or hang out on the beach outside.

option is John's Pass at Madeira Beach (see p. 127). Here, an array of water-based activities is also on offer, including parasailing, dolphin-watching tours and, best of all for children, a Pirate Ship Cruise complete with water-gun battles, face painting and treasure hunts (*727 423 7824* ***www.thepirateshipatjohnspass.com***. Cruises depart 11am, 2pm and sunset Tues–Sun. US$30/£15 adults, US$20/£10 children aged 2–20, under 2s free.)

Lively but low-key Pass-a-Grille was named by French fishermen who once grilled their catch here. Nestled among the yachts of a nearby marina, Pass-a-Grille's The Wharf *727 367 9469* is a gem where families can dine on inexpensive clam chowder (US$3/£1.50) or blackened fish (US$12/£6).

Holmes Beach ★

If you want to slip away from European tourists to a beach where Floridian families come to enjoy themselves, Holmes Beach on Anna Marie Island, just north of Sarasota, is an easy-to-reach option. Situated at the end of SR-64 from the mainland, Holmes Beach is a busy stretch of sand with a number of beachside shops and a popular café that opens early for breakfast and provides live entertainment in the evening. This beach is full of life but hasn't sold its soul to big developers.

Fort Myers, Sanibel & Captiva Islands ★★★

A three-and-a-half hour drive from Orlando, the stretch of the south west region incorporating the town and beach of Fort Myers and islands of Sanibel and Captiva is one of the best areas in Florida for families, whatever age your children. The beaches are consistently near perfect with some, such as Bowman's Beach on Sanibel, maintaining an aura of remote paradise even when busy with sunbathing visitors. Others, including Lovers Key State Park to the south of Fort Myers, are a haven for kayaking, cruises and fishing charters to supplement the sunbathing and swimming. There's an abundance of opportunities to get up close to nature on these unspoilt islands, while in contrast Fort Myers Beach is a place to mingle with other tourists and enjoy fun on the sand.

INSIDER TIP

The height of the Fort Myers, Sanibel and Captiva tourist season is January to April. Visitors can save up to 60% on accommodation during the summer and autumn.

Known as the 'City of Palms', Fort Myers has an old-fashioned charm despite its modern office buildings, and if you have older children, take time off the beach to wander around downtown – don't miss Noel's (229 Main Street), a large and quirky second-hand store filled with all things retro and kitsch. The Edison and Ford Winter Estates, the one-time winter residences of inventor Thomas Edison and founder of the Ford Motor Company Henry Ford, is the most popular attraction in town (see p. 121).

Other attractions include the Calusa Nature Center and Planetarium (3450 Ortiz Ave ☎ *239 275 3435 www.calusanature.com*. Open 9am–5pm Mon–Sat, 11am–5pm Sun. US$8/£4 adults, US$5/£2.50 children aged 3–12, under 3s free) where you can experience the area's natural history and the Imaginarium Hands-On Museum (2000 Cranford Ave ☎ *239 337 3332*. Open 10am–5pm Mon–Sat, noon–5pm Sun. US$8/£4 adults, US$5/£2.50 children aged 3–12, under 3s free) which invites visitors to interact with the world of science and nature.

Stretching along Estero Boulevard, 15 miles south of downtown, Fort Myers's long beach is lined with hotels and low-key resorts with a laid-back, family-friendly atmosphere. At the north end of Estero Boulevard, bordering the busiest part of the beach, is the bustling Times Square, a favourite with teenagers and older children. Here you'll find a play area,

Fort Myers

numerous souvenir and beachwear shops and plenty of inexpensive dining options, most with outdoor seating – try the outdoor deck of the Beach Pierside Grill (☎ *239 765 7800*), where parents can relax while keeping an eye on their children playing on the sand. If you're looking to dine somewhere a bit more formal, but still on the child-friendly side, try Snug Harbor ☎ *237 463 8077* ***www.snugharborrestaurant.com*** at the adjacent Fisherman's Wharf, where the seafood comes straight out of the sea on to your plate.

INSIDER TIP

Parking can be hard at Times Square. If you're staying on Estero Boulevard, catch the hourly tram service that runs the length of Fort Myers Beach – including a stop at Lovers Key State Park – from 6am–9pm. The fare is 25¢ (12.5p).

A short drive from Fort Myers Beach, and reached via a mile-long causeway, the islands of Sanibel and Captiva are hailed as paradise by many visitors and claim a history rich with Calusa Indians, pirates and Pulitzer-Prize-winning political cartoonists.

Sanibel is dominated by the J.N. 'Ding' Darling National Wildlife Refuge (see p. 127) named after the cartoonist and conservation activist Jay Norwood Darling. There are four beautiful public access beaches on this island, and the most popular, especially at sunset, is Bowman's to the west. If you're looking for supplies for a beach picnic, head for Bailey's General Store (Periwinkle Way and Tarpon Bay Road. Open 7am–9pm daily). If you'd rather eat away from the sand, the Sanibel Café ★ (2007 Periwinkle Way ☎ *239 472 53323*) opens at 7am for speciality breakfasts and serves a range of inexpensive omelettes, burgers and fantastic sandwiches for lunch until 3pm.

Shelling

Sanibel and Captiva are famous for shells and you'll see all ages combing the sands for samples of the hundreds of species found here. Shelling is a good way to keep restless children entertained, although by law you can't remove any shell with a living creature inside from the beach, and it's better to take a few favourite samples rather than bucketsful. Sanibel's Shell Museum (3075 Sanibel–Captiva Road ☎ *239 395 2233* ***www.shellmuseum.org***. Open 10am–5pm daily. US$7/£3.50 adults, US$4/£2 children aged 5–16, under 5s free) displays shells from all over the world and includes information on what species to look out for on the islands. For some serious shell shopping, head to the Shell Factory (2787 Tamiami Trail (Hwy-41) ☎ *239 995 21 41* ***www.shellfactory.com***. Open 9am–9pm daily), a large store selling all kinds of shell-related gifts, with an adjacent nature park.

FUN FACT **Palm Trees**

It's illegal to build higher than the tallest palm tree on Sanibel.

INSIDER TIP
Parking is limited on Sanibel and a good way to get around is to park and then cycle. A range of bikes and accompanying baby trailers can be hired from Billy's Rentals (1470 Periwinkle Way *239 472 5248* ***www.billysrentals.com***) or Finnimore's Cycle (2353 Periwinkle Way *239 472 5577* ***www.finnimores.com***).

Travel west from Sanibel across Blind Pass and you'll reach the tiny Captiva Island. Visitors travel here to indulge in a remote island paradise, but there are plenty of activities to keep children entertained and a much livelier nightlife than on Sanibel. Tourist activities are focused around the art galleries, cafés and restaurants of Andy Rosse Lane, and the stretch of beach outside the Mucky Duck Pub *239 472 3434* ***www.muckyduck.com*** (closed Sundays) at the end of this lane is the busiest on the island. Founded in the 70s by an ex London bobby, The Mucky Duck is a popular, family-friendly gastro pub where you can dine on the edge of the beach, and any Brit missing their local can pop in for a quick game of darts. At the other end of Andy Rosse Lane, you'll find McCarthy's Marina, where a number of cruise operators (see Captiva Cruises p. 125) and kayak tour and rental companies (see Captiva Kayaks and Wildside Adventures p. 126) are based.

Top Family Attractions

Edison and Ford Winter Estates ★

2350 McGregor Boulevard, Fort Myers *239 334 7419* ***www.efwefla.org***

Thomas Edison, one of the world's most prolific inventors, created an idyllic winter retreat in Fort Myers, which his wife dedicated to the town after his death. The estate straddles two sides of McGregor Boulevard. One side, with a spectacular waterfront setting, features Edison's charming Victorian home and guest house, both decorated with original furnishings, and beautiful landscaped gardens complete with a fabulous swimming pool (no longer in use). Better for children is the other side of the estate,

FUN FACT **Treasure Ghosts**

According to legend, Spanish pirate José Gaspar based himself in the Sanibel/Captiva area. The small island of Cayo Pelau to the north of Captiva is reputedly haunted by the ghosts of his fellow pirates, still protecting the treasure they buried there.

South West Coast Aquariums

A number of aquariums are dotted along Florida's south west coast. The largest is downtown Tampa's **Florida Aquarium** ★★ (701 Channelside Drive, Tampa ☎ *813 273 4000* ***www.flaquarium.org***. Open 9.30am–5pm daily. Admission US$18/£9 adults, US$13/£6.50 children aged 3–12, under 3s free. Parking US$5/£2.50). This impressive attraction features thousands of aquatic plants and animals and takes visitors through the journey of a drop of water from the Florida wetlands to a coral reef. **Explore A Shore** aquatic discovery zone is an educational play area designed for 3–13-year-olds and children love the impressive shark exhibit. The aquarium runs 90-minute catamaran eco trips into Tampa Bay, where visitors view aquatic animals in the wild. (US$20/£10 adults, US$15/£7.50 children. Admission and boat tours combination tickets US$33/£16.50 adult, US$23/£11.50 children).

Admission to the **Clearwater Marine Aquarium** (249 Windward Passage, Clearwater Beach ☎ *727 441 1790* ***www.cmaquarium.org***. Open 9am–5pm Mon–Sat, 10am–5pm Sun. Admission US$9/£4.50 adults, US$6.50/£3.25 children aged 3–12, under 3s free) lasts all day. Come and go as you please to view the sealife in pools and watch animal presentations throughout the day. Regular behind the scenes tours highlight the aquarium's rescue work and the Sea Life Safari cruises take visitors out to sea with a marine biologist. Both of these tours are extra and combination tickets are available.

Born in captivity in 1948, Snooty the Manatee lives at the **Parker Manatee Aquarium** in Bradenton and shares his pool with young manatees being readied for release. The aquarium forms part of the South Florida Museum (201 10th Street, Bradenton ☎ *941 746 41 31* ***www.southfloridamuseum.org***. Open 10am–5pm Tues–Sat, noon–5pm Sun. Admission US$16/£8 adults, US$12/£6 children aged 4–12, under 4s free).

Admission to Sarasota's **Mote Marine Aquarium** (600 Ken Thomas Parkway, City Island ☎ *941 388 4441* ***www.mote.org***. Open 10am–5pm daily. Admission US$15/£7.50 adults, US$10/£5 children aged 4–12, under 4s free) includes an interactive shark movie at the Immersion Cinema, sting ray touch pools and access to the rehabilitation centre.

where you'll find Edison's fascinating laboratory – his 1920s light bulbs still burn brightly. The small museum on this side contains an education area with fact and activity sheets, including one explaining how to make a light bulb, and a Peanuts cartoon depicting the life, times and work of Edison and Henry Ford, founder of the Ford Motor Company.

Open *9am–5.30pm daily, last guided tours depart 4pm.* ***Admission***

Edison's Lab, Fort Myers

Laboratory and Museum tour US$11 (£5.50) adults, US$4.50 (£2.25) children aged 6–12, under 6s free, estate package US$20 (£10) adults, US$11 (£5.50) children. ***Credit*** *AmEx, MC, V.* ***Amenities*** *Café (10am–3pm). Shop. Baby-change facilities. Picnic area. Free buggy rental. Wheelchair rental US$1 (50p).*

The Ringling Estate ★★★

5401 Bay Shore Road, Sarasota, 941 359 5700 ***www.ringling.org***

This magnificent estate and legacy of circus showman John Ringling is the most outstanding attraction in the Sarasota area and it deserves a full day to appreciate. The rambling grounds are free to enter but there is a charge for admission to the four very different venues on this grandiose property. Housed in an enormous Italian palazzo-style building, the Museum of Art – Florida's official art museum – features a distinguished permanent collection of 17th century Baroque art as well as work from Europe, Asia and America.

A homage to Venetian gothic architecture, the 32-roomed Cà d'Zan stands on the edge of Sarasota Bay and was once Ringling's lavish winter home. The best place for children, and first of its kind, is the fabulous Circus Museum, which includes a fascinating collection of carved parade wagons, posters, props and an intricate miniature circus made up of eight tents, 1,300 performers and 300 animals. The final venue is the Asolo theatre, an 18th century Italian playhouse transported from Italy and painstakingly reassembled here.

FUN FACT King of Inventors

Edison was the king of inventors and held over 1,000 patents for everything from light bulbs to cement.

Two Sarasota Gardens

Overlooking Sarasota Bay, the beautiful and tranquil Marie Selby Botanical Gardens (811 S Palm Avenue, entrance off Hwy-41, Sarasota ☎ *941 366 5731* ***www.selby.org***. Open 10am–5pm daily. US$12/£6 adults, US$6/£3 children aged 6–11, under 6s free) feature a large collection of tropical plants, meandering pathways and koi ponds, making a pleasant break from the beach. Children particularly enjoy the rainforest area with its collection of dart bull frogs. Less tranquil is one of Sarasota's best-kept family secrets, the Children's Garden (1670 10th Way Sarasota ☎ *941 330 1711* ***www.sarasotachildrensgarden.com***. Open 10am–5pm Tues–Sun, US$10/£5 adults, US$5/£2.50 children aged 3–12, under 3s free). The mazes, sculptures and play areas in this creative garden make for a perfect pit-stop with under 5s. Turn east off Hwy-41 on to 10th Street, left on to Orange Avenue and right on to 10th Way for the garden.

Open *10am–5.30pm daily.* ***Admission*** *US$15 (£7.50) adults, US$5 (£2.50) children aged 5–12, under 5s free.* ***Credit*** *AmEx, MC, V.* ***Amenities*** *Café and restaurant. Shop. Some disabled access. Baby-change facilities.*

Salvador Dalí Museum ★★★

1000 3rd Street South, St Petersburg ☎ *727 823 3767* ***www.salvadordalimuseum.org***

St Petersburg is an unlikely place to find the world's most comprehensive collection of work by a

The Ringling Estate, Sarasota

FUN FACT **Destino**

In 1946, Dalí and Walt Disney worked together on a short animated film called *Destino*.

surrealist master, but a mile south of downtown you'll come upon the impressive home to 1,000 original works by this eccentric and renowned Spanish artist. It's worth bringing your children here just to see the giant *Discovery of America by Christopher Columbus* and *The Hallucinogenic Toreador*, but you can easily spend a couple of hours taking in the whole collection. Free hour-long narrated tours run regularly throughout the day.

Open *9.30am–5.30pm Mon–Wed and Sat, 9.30am–8pm Thurs, 9.30am–6.30pm Fri and noon–5.30pm Sun.* ***Admission*** *US$15 (£7.50) adults, US$4 (£2) children aged 5–9, under 5s free.* ***Credit*** *AmEx, MC, V.* ***Amenities*** *Disabled access. Shop.*

Child-friendly Tours

Babcock Wilderness Adventures Eco Tours ★★

GREEN

8000 State Road 31, Punta Gorda, ☎ *1 800 500 5583* ***www.babcockwilderness.com***

About an hour's drive from Fort Myers, Babcock Wilderness Adventures are perfect for a taste of the landscape and wildlife of the Everglades. Before you set off on a specially built swamp buggy into the heart of a 90,000-acre ranch, Babcocks' tour guides warn you to expect 'nature unscripted'. The ranch is farmed using traditional methods – its cowboys still ride horses – and is as eco friendly as possible. Tours take visitors through a range of natural environments including swamps, pinewoods and prairie flats, where you encounter cracker cattle, alligators, birdlife, cute wild pigs and wild, predatory cats. The wildlife experts leading the tours share their amazing knowledge of the ranch's history and animal life and you can expect a Florida critter to make a surprise appearance. Reservations and mosquito repellent both essential.

Open *9am–3pm daily Nov–May, mornings only June–Oct. Telephone for exact times and reservations.* ***Admission*** *US$18 (£9) adults, US$11 (£5.50) children aged 3–12, under 3s free.* ***Credit*** *AmEx, MC, V.* ***Amenities*** *Café (seasonal). Shop. Picnic area. Baby-change facilities. A wheelchair-accessible buggy is available, book a week in advance.*

Captiva Cruises

McCarthy's Marina, Andy Rosse Lane, Captiva Island, ☎ *239 472 5300* ***www.captivacruises.com***

Captiva Cruises' fleet of boats takes visitors on a range of tours around the tranquil waters surrounding Fort Myers Beach and Sanibel and Captiva islands. Recommended is their Dolphin and Wildlife tour, narrated by the

Pirate Ship Cruise, John's Pass

Sanibel Captiva Conservation Foundation, on which children can watch marine animals in their natural habitat. Families wanting to sunbathe, shell and picnic can pick either a full or half-day excursion to the glorious Cayo Costa State Park.

The trip to Cabbage Key allows visitors a couple of hours on this popular island, but there's little to keep children entertained. All trips are accompanied by a commentary on the history and geology of your destination and the islands you pass on the way. Reservations are required one week or less before a trip.

Open *Telephone for tour dates and times.* ***Admission*** *Prices range from US$20 (£10) adults, US$10 (£5) children aged 3–12, under 3s free to US$45 (£22.50) adults, US$25 (£12.50) children.* ***Credit*** *AmEx, MC, V.* ***Amenities*** *Parking US$5 (£2.50). Onboard bar and toilets.*

For Active Families

Captiva Kayaks & Wildside Adventures ★★★

McCarthy's Marina, Andy Rosse Lane, Captiva Island 📞 *239 395 2925*
www.captivakayaks.com

You don't have to be an experienced kayaker to get out and enjoy the placid coastal waters around Captiva with Captiva Kayaks, as this local company takes all ages and abilities on highly recommended tours. The shallow waters are perfect for children new to kayaking and little ones as young as two have been out with Greg and Barb, who run the tours. Experienced kayakers won't be disappointed either, as skimming around the island at water level is the perfect way to get up close to the environments and animals that live there. And, if you're lucky, the elusive manatee will get close to you.

Open 9am–5pm daily. ***Prices*** *The various guided tours range from US$35 (£17.50) adults, US$25 (£12.50) under 18s, to US$45 (£22.50) adults, US$35 (£17.50) under 18s. Kayak rental also available.* ***Credit*** *MC, V.*

J.N. 'Ding' Darling National Wildlife Refuge ★★★

Sanibel–Captiva Road, Sanibel Island ☎ *239 472 1100* ***www.fws.gov/ding darling***

Covering over half of Sanibel, this stunning reserve, famous for its multitude of birds and wildlife, contains numerous walking or cycling trails and a four-mile Wildlife Drive. The refuge's Education Center features interactive exhibits explaining the surrounding ecosystems and a hands-on area for children, and its gift shop stocks children's books. Bikes can be hired from Tarpon Bay Explorers ☎ *239 472 8900* ***www.tarponbayexplorers.com*** who run regular interpretive tram tours through the refuge (US$10/ £5 adults, US$7/£3.50 children under 12).

Open *7.30am to half an hour before sunset Sat–Thurs.* ***Admission*** *US$5 (£2.50) per car, US$1 (50p) per cyclist.* ***Amenities*** *Toilets. Picnic area.*

Pinellas Trail

Stretching from Tarpon Springs to St Petersburg, the Pinellas Trail is a 34-mile paved pathway through parks and along the coast with refreshment spots en route. Bikes can be hired at various points on the trail including Pinellas Trail Bike Shop (357 Scotland Street ☎ *727 734 5976*) and Energy Conservatory Bike Shop (745 Main Street ☎ *727 736 4432*) both in Dunedin (see p. 115).

Shopping

John's Pass Village and Boardwalk

www.johnspass.com

The meandering wooden waterfront boardwalks of John's Pass, an old fishing village at Madeira Beach (see p. 118) are crammed with quirky souvenir, clothes and crafts shops. This popular shopping hot spot is perfect for families, as there are a number of fun places to eat (see Sculley's, p. 135). It is right in the middle of St Pete's beaches (see p. 117), so you can hop back on to the sand the minute you've had enough of shopping.

St Armands Circle

Turn off Hwy-41 and drive over J Ringling Causeway, away from downtown Sarasota towards Lido Key and you'll hit the large landscaped roundabout of St Armands Circle. Filling the

FUN FACT **Haunted Bookshop** 

Haslam's on Central Avenue, St Petersburg ***www.haslams.com*** **opened** in 1933 and today is Florida's largest bookshop. It's a pleasure to browse through its endless shelves – but you might not want to do so alone, as the shop is reputed to be haunted.

pavements of this circle, and the four main roads that lead off it, is a collection of upmarket shops recommended for quality clothes and gift shopping. Keep children occupied in Kilwin's confectionery shop, with its fabulous ice cream and on-site fudge factory, or Scoop Daddy's retro memorabilia store serving delicious old-fashioned milkshakes.

INSIDER TIP

Parking on St Armands Circle can be difficult. Free parking is available on either north or south Adams Drive, which John Ring Boulevard crosses one block before the circle, and Fillmore Drive on the south side of St Armands.

FAMILY-FRIENDLY ACCOMMODATION

MODERATE/EXPENSIVE

Little Harbor ★★

611 Destiny Drive, Ruskin ☎ 813 645 3291 ***www.staylittleharbor.com***

Nestled on the edge of Tampa Bay and close to both Tampa and Sarasota, Little Harbor is a great base for families wanting to explore this area. The many facilities will keep all ages occupied and the resort's Tiki Bar is right by its private beach – so parents can relax and watch cruise ships drift in and out of Tampa Bay while children play on the sand. What I like about this resort is the range and quality of its accommodation, including hotel suites and town homes, all with waterfront views and most self catering. Many are owned by American families who rent them out for most of the year, which gives the resort a pleasant community feel. For those not wanting to self cater, the on-site eating options are better than average and this expanding complex plans new pools, spas and a children's programme.

Rooms *Varies.* ***Rates*** *Rooms from US$189 (£94.50), suites from US$209 (£104.50), town homes from US$279*

Little Harbor's private beach

Dunedin Heron

Tampa & Dunedin

Beyond Busch Gardens (see p. 72), the most tourist-focused area to stay in Tampa is Ybor City (see p. 113). Recommended is The Hampton Inn and Suites (1301 East 7th Avenue ☎ *813 247 6700* ***www.tampayborcitysuites.hamptoninn.com***. From US$120/£60). Right on the trolley line and within easy walking distance of Ybor's shops and restaurants, this comfortable chain hotel offers guests special deals to the local attractions. Park your car at the hotel (US$6/£3 a night) as car crime is high in this area.

Dunedin is a convenient base from which to visit Tampa – Busch Gardens is only 27 miles away – and nearby beaches, and has two family accommodation options. The Holiday Inn Express (972 Broadway ☎ *727 450 1200* ***www.hiexpress.com/dunedin***. From US$119/£59.50), a quiet, comfortable hotel on the corner of Alt-19 to Clearwater and SR-580 to Tampa, and Best Western Yacht Inn (150 Marina Plaza ☎ *727 733 4121* ***www.advantuscopr.com***. From US$110/£55) located in the marina and with excellent waterfront views. Both hotels have pools and are close to the downtown area.

Clearwater Beach & St Pete's Beaches

Clearwater Beach has a wide variety of accommodation, from new, multi-storey resorts to small, family-run motels. Stick to well-known chains or big resorts if you're booking unseen, as the quality of accommodation can be unreliable. At the time of writing, a considerable amount of long-term construction work is taking place, and this, combined with Clearwater's boisterous nightlife, makes Sand Key (see p. 116) a few miles south a better option for families with small children. If you do want to stay at Clearwater, choose a hotel north of SR-60, such as the Clearwater Beach Hilton (400 Manderlay Avenue *727 461 3222* ***www.clearwaterbeachresort.com***. From US$159/£79.50), which is set up for families, or south of the marina on Gulfview Boulevard, where you'll find a number of reputable chain hotels.

Long favoured by US families, St Pete's beaches have a comprehensive range of family-friendly accommodation. The beachside Sunset Vistas on Treasure Island Beach (12000 Gulf Boulevard *866 597 1600* ***www.sunsetvistas.com***. from US$190/£95) is within striking distance of St Petersburg and John's Pass, and contains two and three self-catering bedroom suites, a large pool area complete with fountains and beach access.

For further information on accommodation options in Clearwater Beach see ***www.clearwaterbeach.com*** and on St Pete's Beaches see ***www.saintpetebeach.com***.

(£139.50). ***Credit*** *AmEx, MC, V.* ***Amenities*** *Canoe and boat hire. Jet ski tours. Two pools. Whirlpool. Tennis and basketball courts. Fitness centre. Children's playground. Three restaurants. Bar.* ***In room*** *A/C. Cable TV (free premium movies). Internet access. Microwave. Mini-fridge. Full kitchen in suites and town homes. Cot US$5 (£2.50) per night.*

EXPENSIVE

Clearwater Marriot Suites on Sand Key ★

1201 Gulf Boulevard, Clearwater Beach (at Sand Key) 727 596 1100
www.marriott.com

It's hard to miss this massive white resort on the edge of Clearwater Bay, which is one of the best in the area for families. The large pool, featuring a 35 ft waterfall, is superb for children and Lisa's Klubhouse (named after the resort's resident macaw and costing US$5/£2.50 per child per day) provides daily supervised activities, including video games, film nights and arts and crafts. This resort also organises poolside dinner parties and trips to nearby islands. The energetic can enjoy morning fitness sessions, while those wanting more relaxing entertainment are catered for with trivia contests and poolside films. The roomy suites include a separate living area and balconies with memorable views.

Rooms *220.* ***Rates*** *from US$250 (£125). Check website for special deals.* ***Credit*** *AmEx, MC, V.* ***Amenities*** *Babysitting service. Salon. Spa. Pool. Children's pool. Whirlpool. Water sports centre and rentals. Shops. Fitness centre. Children's club. Three restaurants. Café and ice cream shop* ***In room*** *A/C. Cable TV. Video games (for a fee). Wi-Fi Internet access. Microwave. Cot (on request free).*

MODERATE/EXPENSIVE

Don CeSar Beach Resort ★★

3400 Gulf Boulevard, St Pete's Beach ☎ 727 360 1881 ***www.doncesar.com***

Built in 1928, this fabulous ornate pink hotel has hosted the famous and infamous, from F. Scott Fitzgerald to Al Capone, but today it distinguishes itself as a luxury resort with excellent facilities for families. Based on American summer camps, Camp CeSar is a special programme designed to provide 5–10-year-olds with daily supervised activities, including jewellery making, beach exploration, scavenger hunts – even etiquette lessons – and themed dinner parties. Parents (and older children) can enjoy water aerobics, beachside yoga, beach volleyball and much more. The resort's bedrooms have been recently renovated and are all spacious and comfortable – not that, with so much going on, your children will want to spend much time in them.

Rooms *277.* ***Rates*** *From US$179 (£89.50), plus US$10 (£5) per person resort fee. Check website for special packages.* ***Credit*** *AmEx, MC, V.* ***Amenities*** *Two outdoor pools. Children's camp. Spa. Five restaurants. Shops. Fitness centre. Babysitting.* ***In room*** *A/C. Cable TV. Safe. Mini bar. In room movies. Wi-Fi Internet access.*

MODERATE/EXPENSIVE

Captiva Island Inn ★

11508 Andy Rosse Lane, Captiva ☎ 239 395 0882 ***www.captivaislandinn.com***

This charming, eclectic inn is about as far away from generic resorts or bland hotels as you can

Fort Myers, Sanibel & Captiva Islands

Set up to fulfil any family's accommodation requirements and with an increasing number of British tourists arriving by package tour, this region can provide everything from a large lively resort on Fort Myers Beach, to quaint and quiet self-catering cottages on Sanibel. You can explore many of the options in this region at its visitor website ***www.fortmyers-sanibel.com***.

If you're looking for self-catering accommodation near Fort Myers, Sanibel and Captiva, there are a number of companies which rent holiday homes, including Sanibel and Captiva Central Reservations ***www.sanibel-captivarent.com*** and Resort Quest ***www.resortquestswfl.com***.

get. There are 13, all very different, cottages and suites to rent – my favourite is the Periwinkle Loft – some with two bedrooms, others with sofa beds and all with full kitchens. It's the location that appeals to me, as Captiva Island Inn is situated right in the heart of island life, has a great beach on its doorstep and McCarthy's marina, a number of shops and eating options are all within easy walking distance, making this the kind of place where you don't have to drive long distances in order to have a good time. Young children will love the laid-back feel and older teens can go off and explore alone without ever being too far away. Rates include full breakfast at the Keylime Bistro.

Rooms *13 cottages/apartments, a five-bedroomed house and three b&b rooms.* ***Rates*** *suites/cottages US$99–US$375 (£49.50–187.50).* ***Credit*** *AmEx, MC, V.* ***Amenities*** *Pool. Jacuzzi. Restaurant. Picnic area. BBQ grill. Water sport rentals.* ***In room*** *A/C. Cable TV. Fridge.* ***In cottages/suites*** *Full kitchen. Patio or balcony.*

Outrigger Beach Resort ★★

6200 Estero Boulevard, Fort Myers Beach ☎ 239 463 3131 ***www.outriggerfmb.com***

Overlooking a wide, pristine and quiet stretch of Fort Myers Beach, but still close enough to the lively Times Square, Outrigger is perfect for families and is my favourite place to stay along this stretch of coastline. The resort has a variety of rooms to suit all budgets, from beachfront suites with fantastic views, to smaller rooms facing the pool and, more private, garden rooms. Many of the resort's simple, yet comfortable rooms have kitchenettes and are set up for self catering, and there's a small restaurant on site or the larger Charley's Boathouse Grill across the road ☎ *239 765 4700* ***www.boathousegrill.net***. What I particularly like about this resort is that its popular Tiki Bar is full of life, and often live music, as the sun sets over the ocean in front of it, but with a closing time of 9pm, those wanting to party late into the night move on elsewhere. There's also a cinema and shops nearby.

Rooms *144.* ***Rates*** *Rooms US$100–US$200 (£50–100), beach-front suites US$160–US$270 (£80–135).* ***Credit*** *AmEx, MC, V.* ***Amenities*** *Watersport and bike rentals. Pool. Restaurant and bar. Shop. Putting green. Picnic area. Laundry facilities.* ***In room*** *Cable TV. Fridge. Safe. Wi-Fi Internet. Cots on request (free). Microwave on request (fee). Some rooms with kitchenettes.*

Sanibel Inn ★

937 E Gulf Drive, Sanibel ☎ 239 472 1400 ***www.sanibelcollection.com***

Situated a shell's throw away from the beach, Sanibel Inn has all you'd expect from a top hotel in a paradise island setting. Planted with native species to attract hummingbirds, butterflies and turtles, it's the hotel's grounds that I love, and children can enjoy numerous daily nature-based activities including shell safaris and dolphin watching. The large, airy rooms and suites reflect the hotel's natural surroundings and feature wicker furnishings and bamboo floors, and all have

Sarasota

Families wanting to stay in Sarasota should consider accommodation close to St Armands Circle because of its proximity to beaches, shops and restaurants. Lido Beach Holiday Inn (233 Ben Franklin Drive ☎ *941 388-5555* ***www.lidobeach.net***, from US$240/£120) and Lido Beach Resort (700 Ben Franklin Drive ☎ *941 388 2161* ***www.lidobeachresort.com***, from US$216/£108), are both close to a beautiful beach and just blocks away from St Armands Circle. Those looking for cheaper accommodation will find a number of decent chain motels on Hwy-41 north of John Ringling Causeway, including the convenient and attractive La Quinta (1803 N Tamiami Trail ☎ *941 366 5128* ***www.lq.com***. Rooms US$92/£46).

screened porches so you can enjoy the evening air without suffering the mosquitoes. The on-site Ellington Jazz Bar and Restaurant often features live jazz performances, while the cabana-style café next to the pool is set up for more casual dining.

Rooms *94.* ***Rates*** *Rooms from US$149 (£74.50), suites from US$225 (£112.50).* ***Credit*** *AmEx, MC, V.* ***Amenities*** *Beach access. Pool. Restaurant, Bar and café. Access to a golf course. Barbecue grills. Complimentary bicycles. Shop.* ***In room*** *A/C. Cable TV. DVD player. Fridge. Microwave. Safe. Wi-Fi Internet access.*

INSIDER TIP

Punta Gorda's Fisherman's Village (1200 W. Retta Esplanade, Punta Gorda ☎ *941 639 8721* ***www.fishville.com***. From US$140/£70 per night), a renovated fishing pier jutting into the Peace River, is an appealing place to break a journey between Sarasota and Fort Myers. Along with a peaceful waterfront park, shops and excellent villa-style accommodation, you'll find a number of restaurants – try Harpoon Harry's at the end of the pier.

MODERATE

Periwinkle Cottages

1431 Jamaica Drive, Sanibel ☎ *239 472 1800* ***www.periwinklecottages.com***

Built in 1959, these charming cottages have the distinct advantage of being located beside the J.N. 'Ding' Darling National Wildlife Refuge (see p. 127) and just 300 yards from a private beach, making them ideal for those seeking to stay off the beaten track and away from the region's more crowded beaches. Both peaceful and convenient, these four distinct cottages all have full kitchens and patios and are well set up for families. Three are one-bedroom cottages with a pull-out couch and rollaway bed, while the two-bedroom cottage sleeps four and is reserved for families with children over 8.

Cottages *Four.* ***Rates*** *From US$105 (£52.50) per night. US$700 (£350) per week.* ***Credit*** *MC, V.* ***Amenities*** *Book, puzzle, game and video library. Complimentary bicycles. Whirlpool. Laundry facilities.* ***In room*** *A/C. Cable TV. VCR/DVD. CD player. Beach chairs. Linen and towels. Charcoal grill. Wi-Fi Internet.*

FAMILY-FRIENDLY DINING

Tampa

INEXPENSIVE

Fresh Mouth Grill ★

Plaza Level at the Grand Staircase, Ybor City, Tampa ☎ 813 241 8845 ***www.freshmouthfl.com***

An authentic American dining experience in the heart of Ybor City, Fresh Mouth is a buzzing, laid-back restaurant packed with students, tourists and local business folk. Teenagers will love this hip eatery where you can squeeze into a booth, perch on a high stool at the bar or sit outside and enjoy the sights of Centro Ybor. Their burgers are excellent – the veggie burger is the best I've eaten in Florida – and I don't believe anyone's mouth is big enough to accommodate the enormous Lock Jaw burger.

Open *11am–11pm Sun–Thurs, 11am–2am Fri and Sat.* ***Main Courses*** *US$3–US$6 (£1.50–3).* ***Credit*** *MC, V.*

Dunedin

INEXPENSIVE/MODERATE

Casa Tina ★★

369 Main Street, Dunedin ☎ 727 734 9226 ***www.casatinas.com***

Extremely popular with locals and one of the friendliest restaurants in south west Florida, Casa Tina is lively and fun and welcoming to children. Whether you sit in a booth around the edge or at a table in the middle of the restaurant, you'll feel part of the amiable atmosphere maintained by subdued lighting, upbeat music and cheerful conversation. The authentic, gourmet Mexican cuisine is excellent and the menu features something to please all family members, even fussy vegetarian teens.

Open *11am–10pm Tues–Thurs and Sun, 11am–11pm Fri and Sat.* ***Main Courses*** *US$6–US$17 (£3–8.50).* ***Credit*** *AmEx, MC, V.* ***Amenities*** *Children's menu. Highchair.*

St Pete's beaches

MODERATE/EXPENSIVE

Guppy's ★

1701 Gulf Boulevard, Indian Rocks Beach, St Pete's Beaches ☎ 727 593 2032 ***www.3bestchefs.com/guppys***

Popular with both locals and visitors, the food at Guppy's is simply delicious and you'll be hard pushed to find a table at peak times without a reservation. I recommend this restaurant because it can be difficult to find anything other than fast food when driving along St Pete's beaches and if you're looking for something healthier, Guppy's is a fine option. The menu is refreshingly inventive and the adventurous can sample dishes including yellow fin tuna quesadilla or salmon with udon noodles. You can eat inside, but the shady outdoor seating is better for children.

Open *11.30am–10.30pm Mon–Thurs, 11am–11pm Sat and Sun.* ***Main Courses*** *US$13–US$24 (£6.50–12).* ***Credit*** *AmEx, MC, V.*

Columbia Restaurant

www.columbiarestaurant.com
Founded in 1905 by a Cuban immigrant, the Columbia restaurant is a Florida institution, with establishments in Sarasota (411 St Armands Circle *941 388 3987*), St Petersburg (800 2nd Avenue N.E. *727 822 8000*), Clearwater Beach (1241 Gulf Boulevard *727 596 8400*) and – best of all – Ybor City (2117 E. 7th Avenue *813 248 4961*), it is owned by the family who started it all off. The varied menu features variations on Spanish tapas and paella, but, as the children's menu is basic, get adventurous youngsters to try the tapas.

INEXPENSIVE/MODERATE

Sculley's

John's Pass, Madeira Beach 727 393 7749 ***www.sculleys.com***

John's Pass is awash with food outlets, but Sculley's stands out for me because of its waterfront location overlooking the marina and sea beyond. This open-air restaurant serves a variety of seafood, including tuna sushi, pasta dishes and a varied range of inexpensive sandwiches for lunch. Its rustic, relaxed atmosphere is welcoming to children and spiced up with live music most evenings.

Open *11am–10pm daily.* ***Main Courses*** *US$7–US$24 (£3.50–12).* ***Credit*** *AmEx, MC, V.* ***Amenities*** *Children's menu. Highchair.*

INSIDER TIP
Frozen custard is a delicious alternative to ice cream and you can try some at Sweet Berries Eatery in Bradenton (4500 Manatee Avenue W) or Sarasota (2881 Clark Road) ***www.sweetberries.com.***

Sarasota/St Armands Circle

MODERATE

Cha Cha Coconuts

417 St Armands Circle, Sarasota 941 388 3300

At first glance, many of the restaurants on St Armands Circle appear to focus on adult dining, however, if you're eating out in this area with children, especially in the evening, Cha Cha Coconuts is a family-friendly option. This bright, boisterous tropical-style restaurant has indoor seating, but I like the outside tables where you can feel a part of this lively area. The menu has a Caribbean twist and features seafood, jerk chicken sandwiches, burgers and steaks, and dishes on the children's menu (for the under 10s) come with island fries and a soft drink. In the evenings a steel drum player provides rhythmical entertainment.

Open *11am–11pm Mon–Thurs, 11am–midnight Sat and Sun.* ***Main Courses*** *US$7–US$14 (£3.50–7).* ***Credit*** *AmEx, MC, V.* ***Amenities*** *Children's menu. Gift shop.*

INSIDER TIP

If you're travelling through Venice, to the south of Sarasota, pop into the Soda Fountain (349 W. Venice Avenue *941 412 9860*. Open 11am–9pm Mon–Sat), a traditional diner where you sit in candy-coloured booths or on circular stools at the soda bar and enjoy creamy milkshakes or speciality cherry pop.

Fort Myers, Sanibel & Captiva

MODERATE/EXPENSIVE

The Bubble Room ★

15001 Captiva Drive, Captiva 239 472 5558 ***www.bubbleroom restaurant.com***

Packed with colourful memorabilia, this fascinating restaurant is entertaining for children because its décor is so much fun. All kinds of toys, old-fashioned paraphernalia and film memorabilia are crammed into every space possible and if you want to take a bit of the restaurant home, a separate emporium sells gifts and souvenirs. The restaurant consists of five wacky dining areas and a bubble train trucks through all of them at regular intervals.

Main courses are predominantly steak and seafood dishes and the enormous, fluffy home-made desserts are famous throughout the region.

Open *11.30am–3pm and 4.30pm–9.30pm daily.* ***Main Courses*** *lunch US$8–US$15 (£4–7.50), dinner US$19–US$29 (£9.50–14.50).* ***Credit*** *AmEx, MC, V.* ***Amenities*** *Children's menu. Highchair. Reservations recommended.*

The Bubble Room, Captiva

INEXPENSIVE/MODERATE

Lazy Flamingo

1036 Periwinkle Way 239 472 6939 and 6520-C Pine Avenue, (Blind Pass) Sanibel 239 472 5353 ***www.lazyflamingo.com***

Decorated with all things nautical, Sanibel's two Flamingo restaurants are renowned for fresh, reasonably priced seafood, although there are alternatives for non-seafood eaters on the menu and children will love the Dead Parrot Wings (don't anybody mention Monty Python). The restaurants, located at either end of the island, both overlook the gulf, making them ideal options for sunset dining, and I recommend the Blind Pass location for young children, as its ring-on-a string game will keep them entertained for hours.

Open *11.30am–1am daily.* ***Main Courses*** *US$8–US$16 (£4–8).* ***Credit*** *AmEx, MC, V.*

6 The North & Central East Coast

THE NORTH & CENTRAL EAST COAST

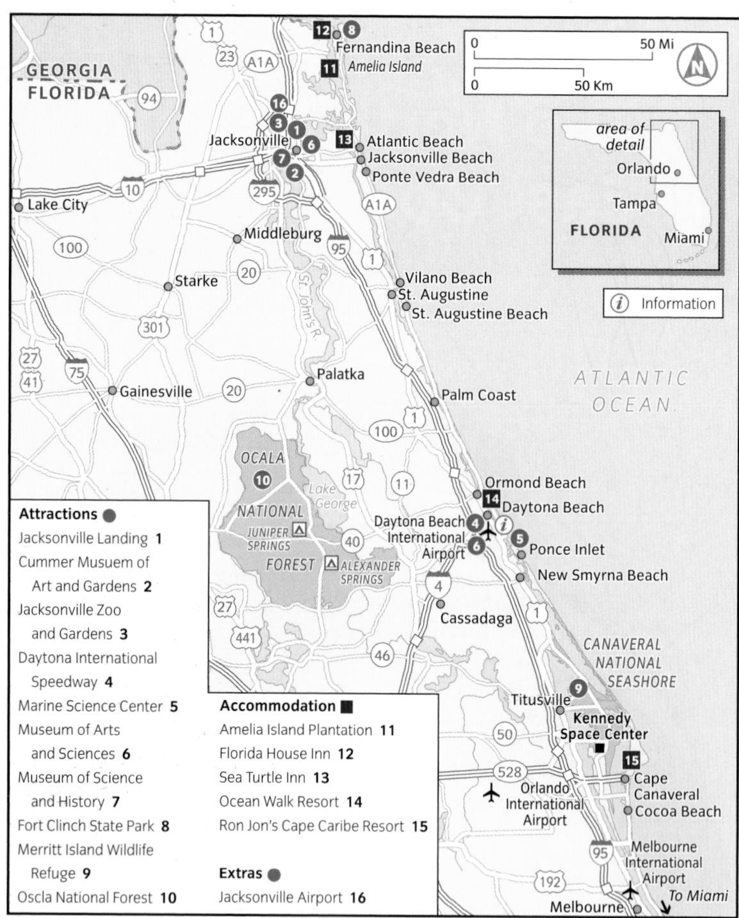

With its attractive mix of wide Atlantic-facing beaches, vibrant city life, untamed nature refuges and fascinating heritage, Florida's north and central east coast has something for all ages. From the windswept, sparsely populated Fernandina Beach in the far north, to the wildly popular surfer beach at Cocoa – the closest beach to both Disney and the Kennedy Space Center – this region's beaches are some of the wildest in Florida – although none come alive until April onwards due to cooler winters. History buffs will love the fascinating stretch of coastline from Amelia Island to St Augustine, known as the First Coast, in honour of the early European settlers who developed communities here. Families seeking culture and art should head inland to the thoroughly modern Jacksonville, home to some of the north east's finest museums and galleries. Further south, Daytona

Beach is famous for land speed records and its International Speedway, the best family-friendly attraction in the region, as well as many cultural attractions and even a turtle hospital. And nestled in between all of these are numerous places where visitors can simply get back to nature and enjoy the sun.

ESSENTIALS

Getting There

By Plane Jacksonville International Airport is located 12 miles north of the city's downtown. This airport *904 741 4902* ***www.jaa.aero*** is the north east's largest and receives regular flights from Miami, Tampa and Fort Lauderdale, operated by various American airlines.

By Car The quickest route to the central east coast from Orlando is via SR-528 (Bee Line Expressway) to I-95, the main interstate running the length of the east coast.

However, if you're headed for the north east take I-4, which joins I-95 at Daytona Beach after an hour's drive.

The most direct route from the Panhandle (see Chapter x) is via I-10, which joins I-95 at Jacksonville.

VISITOR INFORMATION

Jacksonville's most convenient visitor information centre is located in Jacksonville Landing on Independent Drive adjacent to the city's waterfront. It is open 10am–7pm Mon–Sat and noon–5.30pm Sun *904 791 4305* ***www.jaxcvb.com***. An information centre at the airport is open 9am–10pm daily. St Augustine's main visitor information centre is situated on Castillo Drive, opposite the Castillo de San Marcos

Visiting Daytona Beach

Daytona Beach is home to the Daytona International Speedway (see p. 150) and it's impossible to find accommodation in or around this town during Speed Weeks, which culminate in the Daytona 500 stock car race in February, Bike Week ***www.bikerbeach.com*** in March, Pepsi 400 weekend in early July and Biketoberfest ***www.biketoberfest.org*** in October. But Daytona Beach organises Spring Family Beach Break each year between mid-March and May to encourage holidaying families to the area – at this time you'll get discounts at hotels, sights, restaurants and shops. *1-866-845-1993* or visit ***www.familybeachbreak.com*** for more information.

St John's River Ferry

Anyone driving SR-A1A along the north east coast of Florida will take the car ferry over the river between St George's Island and Mayport, just north of Jacksonville Beach. Ferries operate every 15 minutes in alternate directions from 6.40am–10.15pm daily. US$3.25 (£1.63) fare in cash.

904 825 1000 ***www.visitoldcity.com***. It is open 8.30am–5.30pm daily. For information on Daytona Beach, visit the Convention and Visitor Bureau at 126 E Orange Avenue *386 255 0415* ***www.daytonabeach.com*** between 9am–5pm Mon– Fri.

Orientation

I-95 is the quickest route linking the towns and cities spread along Florida's central and north east coast. The slower Hwy-1 travels adjacent to I-95 before branching inland at Jacksonville. However, by far the most pleasant route is the SR-A1A, which winds along the coast.

Getting Around

With limited public transport options, the only feasible way to travel around the north and central east coast with children is by car. For details of car hire, see p. 29.

Child-friendly Festivals & Events

Ron Jon's Easter Surf Festival

Every Easter Ron Jon's Surf Shop (see p. 156) organises a vast surfing festival that takes Cocoa Beach by storm. This veteran event showcases world-championship surfers, aged 12–80, who compete in a variety of events over the weekend. A food court springs up on the edge of the beach and visitors watch surfing demonstrations and take part in an Easter Egg hunt. Check the website for exact dates.

Cocoa Beach 321 799 8888 ***www.eastersurffest.com***. *Free*

WHAT TO SEE & DO

Children's Top Five Attractions

1. **Getting** on to the track at Daytona International Speedway; p. 150.
2. **Exploring** St Augustine's historic streets; p. 143.
3. **Learning** about the care of sick sea turtles at the Marine Science Center; p. 152.
4. **Taking** a river taxi across St John's river in downtown Jacksonville; p. 142.
5. **Cycling** on wide, wild Fernandina Beach; p. 148.

Towns & Cities

Jacksonville ★★

South of the border with Georgia by 25 miles and spliced through the middle by the St John's river, Jacksonville is Florida's largest city by land mass. Its prosperity grew through proximity to both river and railway, and Jacksonville claims the largest deep-water port in the south. Gleaming skyscrapers housing banking and insurance giants characterise Jacksonville's cityscape and the main reason to bring your children into its glistening downtown is to relish its young, upbeat vibe and rich culture.

Divided by the St John's river, there are two sides to downtown Jacksonville – the north and south banks. Most visitors make Jacksonville Landing *904 353 1188* ***www.jacksonvillelanding.com***, their first stop. This is a snazzy two-storey waterfront semi-circle of shops, bars and restaurants on the north side of the river. Just north of Main Street Bridge, this complex is a convenient place to park and has a visitor information centre (see p. 139). It's also the best place to eat in the city, as there's an inexpensive food court containing Mexican, Thai and pizza outlets on the second floor and a range of moderately priced restaurants such as Benny's Steak and Seafood Restaurant *904 301 1014* at water level, all with stunning views of the St John's river and its many bridges.

Also on the north side of the river, just south of I-95, is the Cummer Museum of Art (see p. 152), the most impressive of the city's numerous art galleries. Jacksonville's downtown contains a cluster of galleries; to explore more pick up a map detailing the city's Art Walk from the visitor information centre (see p. 139). Many of the galleries are within walking distance of Jacksonville Landing – don't miss the Museum of Contemporary Art (333 North Laura Street

Jacksonville

Jacksonville – Movie Town

In the 1910s, Jacksonville was known as 'the winter film capital of the world' because so many New York-based filmmakers came to escape the cold and make movies. More than 30 studios were once based here and at the time of writing, the only one remaining – the Norman Studios, 6337 Arlington Road ***www.normanstudios.org*** – is being renovated and will open as a Silent Film Museum in 2008.

904 366 6911 ***www.mocajacksonville.org***. Open 10am–4pm Tues and Thurs–Sun, 10am–9pm Wed. US$6/£3 adults, US$4/£2 students, under 2s free. Sundays free for families), where the collections of work from the 1960s to the present day are accessible to children. The interactive Art Explorium on the fifth floor is great for budding young artists.

INSIDER TIP

Other than walking across Main Street Bridge, there are two ways to cross the St John's river in downtown Jacksonville. The Skyway monorail (6am–11pm Mon–Fri, 10am–11pm Sat *904 630 3191*. 35¢/17.5p) glides between Central Station on the north bank and San Marco Station close to the Museum of Science and History (see p. 153) on the south side and provides an elevated view of the city. Or cross at water level on a river taxi that operates between Jacksonville Landing and the south bank (*904 910 1227*. US$3/£1.50 adults, US$2/£1 children, under 3s free). The river taxis also run to Metropolitan Park (see p. 142). These fabulous taxis provide glorious views of Jacksonville's downtown and are a fun and inexpensive way to gad about the city.

The south bank of St John's river is home to the picturesque Riverwalk, a wooden boardwalk winding along the waterfront to the massive Friendship Fountain and Jacksonville's Museum of Science and History (see p. 153).

In contrast to its art- and culture-soaked downtown, Jacksonville has two attractions that appeal to families who enjoy the outdoors. Follow Bay Street east out of downtown, and directly across the street from Jacksonville's Municipal Stadium and you will arrive at the large, waterfront Metropolitan Park (1410 Gator Bowl Boulevard *904 630 0837*). Walk right to St John's river in this perfect picnic destination or head straight to Kids' Kampus, a large play area filled with climbing frames and slides, plus a splash water park – perfect for young children.

One of the main routes into downtown is the Arlington Expressway (Alt-90). Turn off the expressway on Arlington Road and right into Lone Star Road and you'll reach the Tree Hill Nature Center **GREEN** (7152 Lone Star Road, *904 724 4646* ***www.treehill.org***. Open 8am–4.30pm Mon–Sat. US$2/£1

FUN FACT **Saints Feast Day**

Pedro Menendez de Avilés named his settlement after St Augustine because he first sighted land on 28 August, the saint's feast day.

adults, US$1/50p children). With its hummingbird and butterfly gardens, this is a great place to visit with young children and a must if you are interested in alternative energy and living an eco-friendly life.

For information on Jacksonville Beach, see p. 150.

St Augustine ★★★

On 8th September 1565, 55 years before the pilgrims arrived at Plymouth Rock, Pedro Menendez de Avilés landed at the place he named St Augustine with a group of Spanish settlers. Unlike other early settlements, St Augustine survived to become the oldest continually occupied European settlement in North America.

Thirty-seven miles south of Jacksonville and a two-hour drive from Orlando, St Augustine is perfect for any British family that enjoys visiting historic sites at home. You can easily spend a couple of days delving into the heritage of Florida's most charming city – longer if you want to combine spending time on its beaches. There's so much history here that St Augustine feels like one big museum and wandering around the Mediterranean-style streets of its compact historic downtown is enjoyable for all ages.

INSIDER TIP

The best place to park in St Augustine is the car park behind the visitor information centre on Castillo Drive (US$3/£1.50 per day).

Pass through the old city gates at the south end of San Marco Avenue into pedestrianised St George Street, the spine of the historic district. A number of

Downtown, St Augustine

ST AUGUSTINE

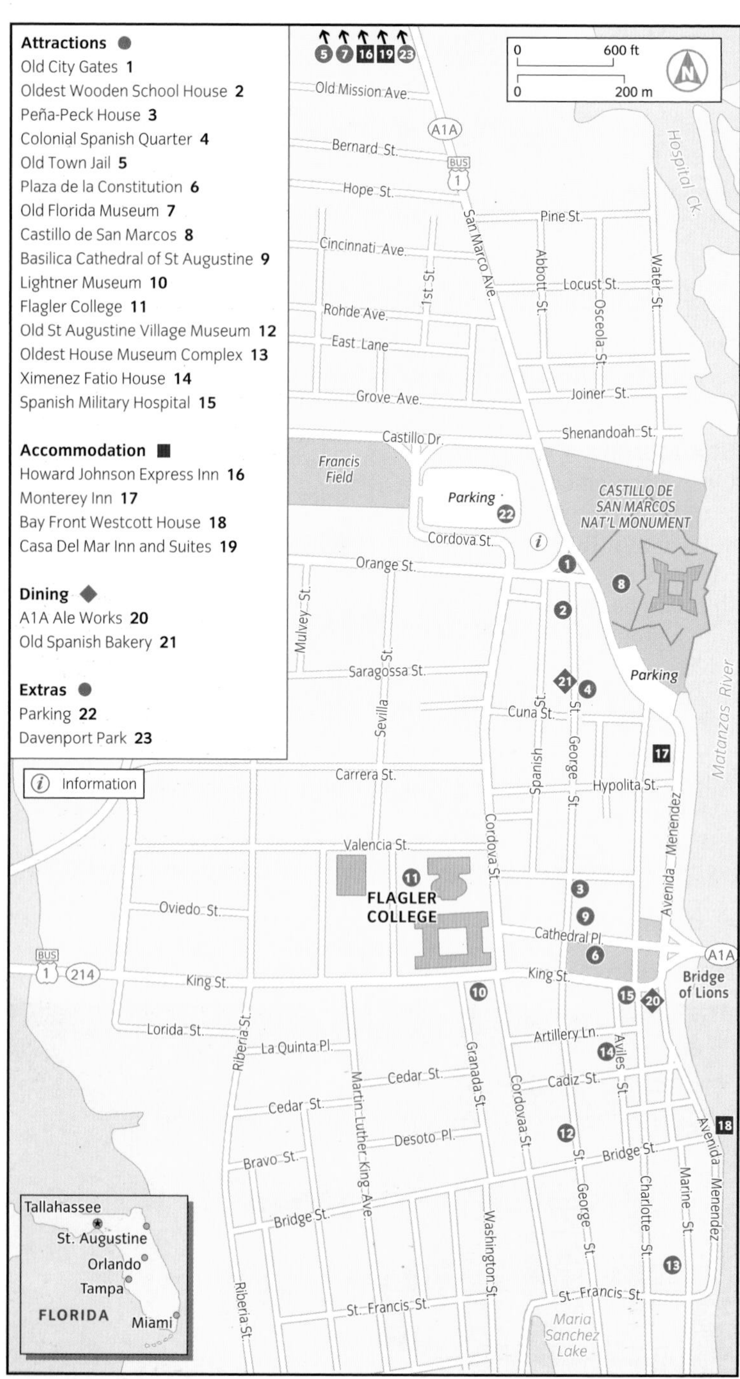

Tours of St Augustine

A great way for children to learn about St Augustine's history is on one of its colourful sightseeing trains. The Old Town Trolley Tours (*904 829 3800* ***www.trolleytours.com***. 8.30am–4pm. US$20/£10 adults, US$7/£3.50 children aged 6–12, under 12s free) depart from the Old Town Jail (see p. 147) on San Marcos Avenue and parking is provided. Tickets are valid for 3 days and the narrated journey makes about 20 stops around town. Hop on and off, or sit back and do the whole trip in one go.

Ghost Tours of St Augustine *904 461 1009* ***www.ghosttoursofst augustine.com*** offer evening walking tours (US$12/£6 per person), trolley tours (US$22/£11 per person) and sailing tours (US$35/£17.50 per person), which take visitors deep into the city's spookiest corners.

One of the most relaxing ways to tour is by horse-drawn carriage; these depart from the waterfront near the Castillo de San Marcos (*904 829 2391* ***www.staugustinetransfer.com***. From 10am. US$20/£10 adults, US$10/£5 children aged 5–11).

attractions lead off this street, including the quaint Oldest Wooden School House (14 St George Street *904 824 0192* ***www.oldestwoodenschoolhouse.com***. Open 9am–5pm daily. US$3/£1.50 adults, US$2/£1 children), which taught its last class in 1864; the Peña-Peck House (143 St George Street *904 829 5064*. Open noon–5pm Mon–Sat. Free), a restored 1740s house built for the Spanish Royal Treasurer, and, best for children, the Colonial Spanish Quarter (see p. 147). On this street the old Spanish Bakery is a good choice for lunch, as its cinnamon rolls and inexpensive Spanish dishes are good and tasty (42 St

Castillo de San Marcos

George Street ☎ *904 471 3046* ***www.thespanishbakery.com***. Open 9.30am–3pm).

At the point where St George Street meets King Street, St Augustine's architecture changes to a Spanish colonial style. Turn east and you'll enter the wide Plaza de la Constitution; pop into the Basilica Cathedral of St Augustine to view its beautiful stained glass. Heading west, away from the plaza, you'll encounter two of St Augustine's most impressive buildings, the Lightner Museum (see p. 153) and imposing Flagler College. Once an exclusive winter hotel, visitors can enter the college's main building, which boasts exquisite Tiffany stained glass and an intricate painted ceiling.

INSIDER TIP

If you are travelling with small children, pay a visit to Davenport Park at the corner of SR-A1A and San Marcos Avenue. This small park features an old-fashioned carousel (US$1/50p), children's playground and picnic tables.

Many visitors don't explore St George Street any further south than King Street – but persevere because the streets of this quiet end of town are one of the few places in Florida where it's safe to wander away from the main road and delight in discovering shady courtyards and tiny lanes dripping with Spanish moss.

Here you'll find the Old Augustine Village (see box p. 147) and the Oldest House Museum Complex (14 St Francis Street ☎ *904 824 2872* ***www.oldesthouse.org***. Open 9am–5pm daily. US$3/£1.50 adults, US$2/£1 children) which provides a feel for how people lived in 18th century St Augustine.

And on Aviles Street, Ximenez Fatio House (20 Aviles Street ☎ *904 829 3575* 11am–4pm Tues–Sat. Free) is an old Spanish merchant's house built in 1789, and the Spanish Military Hospital (3 Aviles Street ☎ *904 825 6830* ***www.spanishmilitaryhostital.com***. Open 9am–5pm Mon–Sat, noon–5pm Sun. US$3/£1.50 adults, US$2/£1 children) lets visitors view the grim health care of centuries past.

Best Beaches & Beach Communities

Cocoa Beach

www.visitcocoabeach.com

Orlando's closest beach and neighbour to the Kennedy Space Center (see p. 74), Cocoa Beach is the east coast's chilled-out surf capital, whose laid-back vibe has a genuinely family-friendly appeal. Cocoa's ramshackle old pier is a veritable institution and forms the beach's focal point. Its battered wooden boardwalk provides glorious views over the surfer-filled waves and is home to numerous shops, restaurants and bars serving a range of seafood and burgers, some with children's menus.

Cocoa is an active beach with plenty of beach volleyball courts and is well suited to families who like company or want to sit

St Augustine's Family-Friendly Historic Sights

There are many historic sites in St Augustine that will engage your children as well as Castillo de San Marcos (see p. 154).

The Colonial Spanish Quarter ★★ (33 St George Street ☎ *904 825 6830* ***www.historicstaugustine.com***. Open 9am–5.30pm daily. US$7/ £3.50 adults, US$5/£2.50 children) consists of a number of recreated old buildings. This working museum is brought alive by costumed actors demonstrating how people lived in early St Augustine.

Old St Augustine Village Museum ★ (246 St George Street ☎ *904 823 9722* ***www.old-staug-village.com***. Open 10am–4.30pm Mon–Sat, 11am–4.30pm Sun. US$7/£3.50 adults, US$5/£2.50 children) is another commendable reconstruction of life in olden times. Take a self-guided tour of the reconstructed properties or join one of the 30-minute guided tours.

At the Old Florida Museum ★ (254 San Marco Avenue ☎ *904 824 8874* ***www.oldfloridamuseum.com***. Open 10am–5pm daily. US$6/£3 adults, US$5/£2.50 children) children have fun with history and get stuck into the likes of pumping water, playing with hoops and grinding corn.

The Old Jail (167 San Marco Avenue ☎ *904 829 3800*. Open 8.30am–5pm daily. US$6/£3 adults, US$4/£2 children) highlights the grizzlier side of St Augustine's history. Visitors view maximum security and solitary confinement cells along with the old jailer's living quarters. Admission to the adjacent Florida Heritage Museum is free with tickets to the Old Jail.

back and watch surfers hone their skills. If watching isn't enough, Cocoa Beach Surf Company ***www.cocoabeachsurf.com*** adjacent to Fort Points by the Sheraton resort, rents boards from US$5 (£2.50) for 2 hours and organise surf lessons and camps for all ages.

Daytona Beach ★★

Daytona Beach is proud to be the world's most famous beach and the birthplace of speed. Before the opening of the International Speedway in 1959 (see p. 150), all kinds of 'horseless carriages' raced on its 23 miles of hard-packed sand and today cars are still allowed onto large areas of the beach.

Daytona is everything you'd expect from a developed beach, with clusters of arcades and rides around its pier. Daytona Lagoon ☎ *386 254 5020* ***www.daytonalagoon.com*** is an entertainment complex complete with go-karts,

FUN FACT **Surfing**

The ancient Polynesians invented surfing sometime between 500 and 1000 AD.

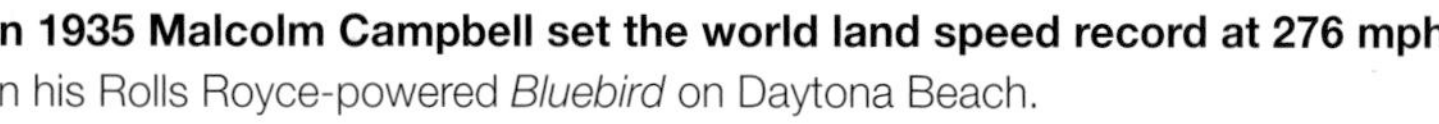

FUN FACT **Land Speed Record**

In 1935 Malcolm Campbell set the world land speed record at 276 mph in his Rolls Royce-powered *Bluebird* on Daytona Beach.

miniature golf and a small water park. While Ocean Walk is a brightly coloured complex of shops, restaurants and 10-screen cinema on Daytona's waterfront.

However, Daytona, which is far from the party beach it once was, has another side characterised by the likes of the old-fashioned Beach Avenue, where chocoholics will discover confectionery heaven at Angell and Phelps Chocolate Factory *386 257 2677* ***www.angellandphelps.com***. Here children are offered free tours to learn how chocolate is made.

INSIDER TIP

Daytona's Jackie Robinson Ballpark on E Orange Avenue is a great place for families to watch Minor League baseball games. Matches take place most evenings from April to September and tickets cost US$7 (£3.50) adults, US$6 (£3) children aged 13 and under. *386 257 3172* or visit ***www.daytonacubs.com*** for more information and to book tickets.

Away from its beach, Daytona is home to a collection of cultural attractions including the excellent Museum of Arts and Sciences (see p. 153) and the Museum of Photography *386 506 4475* ***www.smponline.org***. Housed in the Daytona Beach Community College on International Speedway Boulevard, this hosts world-class photography exhibitions and children can learn about the science of photography through optical illusions, kaleidoscopes and activity sheets.

Families with small children can seek out Ponce Inlet, just south of Daytona Beach, which has a quiet beach and play area and two good family-friendly eating options (see p. 162). Here you can also climb the tower of the Ponce de Leon Inlet Lighthouse *386 761 1821* ***www.ponceinlet.org***, Florida's tallest lighthouse, to enjoy views over the east coast and visit the Marine Science Center (see p. 152).

Fernandina Beach ★★★

Tucked away under the border with Georgia, Fernandina Beach on Amelia Island is rarely visited by European tourists. Proud to be undeveloped, this community is characterised by wooden sea-facing houses and manages to combine the ambience of New England with the laid-back charm of the Caribbean – this is a safe and welcoming place to bring children.

Washed by the Atlantic, Fernandina's wide, wild beach is never crowded and the park by its main entrance, with volleyball courts and picnic tables, is a favourite with local and visiting families.

FUN FACT Pirates

The deep waters off Fernandina Beach were a favourite haunt of pirates until the late 1800s.

Fernandina has plenty to keep children occupied, with attractions like Fort Clinch (see p. 154), the off-road cycling path along Egan's Creek Greenway and the beach itself (see p. 155). And no visit is complete without exploring the historic downtown, with its late-Victorian architecture.

Overlooking the Amelia river, a marina forms the hub of Fernandina's downtown, from which Amelia River Cruises (*904 261 9972* ***www.ameliarivercruises.com***. US$18–US$24/£9–12 adults, US$8–US$12/£4–6 children aged 12 and under) operate a variety of daily boat trips around the region's waterways. Polly the Trolley, a tourist sightseeing trolley, (*904 753 4486*. US$9/£4.50) departs on tours of downtown.

Situated close to the marina, Fernandina's visitor information centre is housed in an old station building (*904 277 0717* ***www.ameliaisland.org***. Open 9am–5pm Mon–Fri, 10am–2pm Sat) at the top of Center Street, downtown's main road, which is bursting with eclectic bookshops, boutiques, arts and crafts shops and great cafés. I recommend grabbing a Cuban snack at Angel's Porch Café (708 Center Street *904 321 2299*. Open 11am–4pm Mon–Tues and 11am–9pm Wed–Sat), which serves inexpensive food on a rustic porch crammed with plants.

INSIDER TIP

ZZ Toys and Kites (116 Center Street *888 499 8699*) sells a good range of kites and other beach toys.

Holiday Villa, Fernandina Beach

Jacksonville Beach

www.jaxcvb.com

Jacksonville Beach is the touristy area of a 15-mile strip of coastline east of Jacksonville. This stretch of sand has all the young vibe of the city's downtown and is populated with athletic locals who come to play volleyball, surf and jog. Families with teenagers who like to kick a ball around or play Frisbee will enjoy this lively, upbeat beach.

INSIDER TIP

Jacksonville Beach is popular with spring breakers, so is not suitable for families at this time.

Day-trippers park on the corner of 4th Avenue and 1st Street at the foot of a busy pier, which is the focal point of all activity. Here beachwear, souvenir and surf shops spill on to a walkway edging the beach – there are lots of bike rental outlets as well. A number of fast-food waterfront bars and restaurants jostle for attention around the pier; the most popular is Bukkets Ocean Front Grill (*904 246 7701*. Open from 11am daily), with a range of seafood, burgers and chicken dishes from US$9 (£4.50), and a children's menu for US$5 (£2.50).

Another draw to Jacksonville Beach for lively children is Adventure Landing (1944 Beach Boulevard (Hwy-90) *904 246 4386* ***www.adventurelanding.com***. Open 10am–10pm Sun–Thurs, 10am–1am Fri and Sat). Here you'll find pay-as-you-go activities including go-carts, miniature golf, laser tag and a water park, which is open in the summer. If you're looking for a quieter beach I recommend travelling a few miles north to Kathryn Abbey Hanna Park (500 Wonderwood Drive *904 249 4700*. Open daily 8am–8pm Apr–Oct and 8am–6pm Nov–March. US$3/£1.50 per car). Just south of Mayport and ideal for small children, this secluded park has an unspoilt beach, freshwater lake with a water play area, woodland trails and picnic tables.

Top Family Attractions

Daytona International Speedway ★★★

1801 International Speedway, Daytona Beach 386 947 6800
www.daytonausa.com

The Daytona 500 – 'the Great American Race' – and stock car racing in general is integral to the culture of the Southern US. A visit to the International Speedway is as much about learning about this race and the sport it represents as it is about

FUN FACT **Hurricane Damage**

Jacksonville Beach's original pier was destroyed by a hurricane in September 1999. The new pier opened in 2004.

Daytona Beach

getting up close to fast cars and the men who risk their lives driving them.

Allow at least half a day to experience everything here, especially if you have older children who'll want to try out Acceleration Alley, where they get to sit in a racing car and drive a video simulation of the Daytona 500. A visit also includes an IMAX 3D film covering the history of NASCAR from its beginnings as a race dominated by whiskey runners from the Appalachians during the prohibition era, to the multi-million dollar business it is today.

There's also a museum featuring winning stock cars and photographs of the original races on Daytona Beach, and the *Bluebird*, which set land speed records on these very sands.

Nothing beats getting out on to the track itself, and a speedway tour takes you behind the scenes of this, one of the world's biggest speedways. The tour includes privileged views of the track's famous steeply angled curves, around which drivers must maintain a speed of 95mph or lose the battle with gravity and get sucked to the bottom of the track. For an extra US$150 (£75) a professional driver will whizz you around the track in a stock car at 150mph.

Open *9am–7pm daily.* ***Admission*** *US$24 (£12) adults, US$19 (£9.50) children aged 6–12, under 6s free.* ***Credit*** *MC, V.* ***Amenities*** *Shop. Disabled access. Baby-change facilities.*

INSIDER TIP

To book tickets to a race at Daytona International Speedway, see ***www.racetickets.com***

Jacksonville Zoo and Gardens ★

370 Zoo Parkway, Jacksonville 📞 *904 757 4463* ***www.jaxzoo.org***

Situated halfway between Jacksonville's downtown and airport, the animals in this zoo are housed in a series of environmentally sensitive natural habitats. Each showcases species from a different part of the world; the African area is complete with elephant pool, cheetahs and giraffes, while the Inca-themed rainforest is home to South American animals from jaguar to anaconda. Small children enjoy the mazes and water pools at the play park, where they can watch playful otters swimming close by. The daily Keeper Talks, which are a fascinating way to learn more about the zoo's animals, are more frequent at weekends.

***Open** 9am–5pm daily. **Admission** US$11 (£5.50) adults, US$7.50 (£3.75) children aged 3–12, under 3s free. **Credit** MC, V. **Amenities** Restaurants and cafés. Picnic area. Shop. Disabled access. Baby-change facilities.*

Marine Science Center ★★

100 Lighthouse Drive, Ponce Inlet
*☎ 306 304 5545 **www.marinesciencecenter.com***

This brilliant organisation aims to increase understanding of Florida's diverse ecosystems and wildlife and the conservation and rehabilitation programmes in place to help protect them. Volunteer staff members encourage children to ask questions as they view turtles housed in rehabilitation pools, and there's information on hand detailing their chances of survival – have a few tissues handy! The centre features an artificial reef aquarium and an accessible nature trail leading to a bird-watching tower. A bird sanctuary is located across the car park – go to view injured pelicans, wood storks, owls and hawks as they recover.

***Open** 10am–4pm Tues–Sat, noon–4pm Sun. **Admission** US$3 (£1.50) adults, US$1 (50p) children aged 5–12, under 5s free. **Amenities** Shop. Disabled access. Baby-change facilities.*

Top Museums

Cummer Museum of Art and Gardens ★

829 Riverside Avenue, Jacksonville
*☎ 904 356 6857 **www.cummer.org***

The Cummer Museum of Art is home to an impressive collection of work covering 8,000 years of art history. Highlights of the permanent exhibitions include work by the American

Marine Science Center

Impressionists and a collection of Japanese wood block prints. The best section for youngsters is the Arts Connections building, which houses interactive exhibits designed to enhance an understanding of art. Here they can walk through a painting and listen to a sculpture. There are also two beautiful acres of English and Italian formal gardens to contemplate.

***Open** 10am–5pm Wed–Sat, 10am–9pm Tues, noon–5pm Sun. **Admission** US$8 (£4) adults, US$5 (£2.50) students, under 5s free. **Credit** MC, V. **Amenities** Disabled access. Shop.*

Lightner Museum ★★

*King Street, St Augustine ☎ 904 824 2874 **www.lightnermuseum.org***

Built in 1888 as a luxury hotel, the three floors of the impressive Lightner Museum are filled with collections of exquisite 19th century artefacts, including Tiffany glass, music boxes, costumes and mechanical musical instruments. This beautiful museum is more for older children, who'll probably get as much from walking around the stunning building as they will from the exhibits. Make time for a visit to the museum's café, housed in what was once the hotel's splendid swimming pool.

***Open** 9am–5pm daily. **Admission** US$8 (£4) adults, US$2 (£1) children aged 12–18, under 12s free. **Credit** MC, V. **Amenities** Disabled access. Café. Shop.*

Museum of Arts and Sciences ★★

*352 S Nova Road, Daytona Beach ☎ 386 255 0285 **www.moas.org***

Situated halfway between Daytona's beach and speedway, this Smithsonian-affiliated museum is one of the best for children in Florida. The museum stands inside a large nature reserve, which contains walking trails, an environmental education complex and sensory garden. Inside the most child-friendly exhibition is the Americana collection, full of Coca-Cola memorabilia, vintage cars and train carriages plus a display of 800 teddy bears. Other highlights include the largest collection of Cuban art outside of Havana, donated by former dictator Fulgencio Batista. Admission includes entry to a planetarium show and a special children's museum is scheduled to open in 2008.

***Open** 9am–4pm Tues–Fri, noon–5pm Sat and Sun. **Admission** US$11 (£5.50) adults, US$7 (£3.50) children aged 6–17, under 6s free. **Credit** AmEx, MC, V. **Amenities** Café. Shop. Disabled access. Baby-change facilities.*

Museum of Science and History ★

*1025 Museum Circle, Jacksonville ☎ 904 396 6674 **www.themosh.org***

Jacksonville's best attraction for families, the Museum of Science and History is an interactive children's museum with numerous displays and activities designed to encourage learning. There's plenty here to engage children who are into dinosaurs and other highlights include the Atlantic Tails exhibit, where you can learn all about whales, dolphins and manatees, and Kids Space is an imaginative play area for small children. Admission includes a planetarium show.

Open *10am–5pm Mon–Fri, 10am–6pm Sat, 1pm–6pm Sun.* ***Admission*** *US$9 (£4.50) adults, US$7 (£3.50) children aged 3–12, under 3s free.* ***Credit*** *AmEx, MC, V.* ***Amenities*** *Shop. Baby-change facilities. Disabled access.*

State Parks & Historic Sites

Castillo de San Marcos ★

1 Castillo Drive East, St Augustine ☎ *904 829 6506* ***www.nps.gov/casa***

One of Florida's most important national monuments, the impressive star-shaped Castillo de San Marcos fort was built by the Spanish in the late 17th century to protect St Augustine. The fort is made from coquina, a soft material made of seashells that can withstand cannonballs, and over the double drawbridge a self-guided tour leads through (haunted) prison cells, a chapel and guard rooms. Regular costumed events and demonstrations bring the fort's history to life, and children can pick up a free Junior Rangers Programme activity book at the ticket booth – it's crammed with ideas to keep youngsters occupied during a visit.

Open *8.45am–5.15pm daily, ticket booth closes at 4.45pm.* ***Admission*** *US$6 (£3), children under 15 free if accompanied by an adult.* ***Credit*** *AmEx, MC, V.* ***Amenities*** *Limited disabled access. Shop.*

INSIDER TIP

The grounds around Castillo de San Marco overlook St Augustine's waterfront and are a pleasant place for an evening's dolphin spotting and stroll.

Fort Clinch State Park

2601 Atlantic Avenue, Fernandina Beach ☎ *904 277 7274* ***www.floridastateparks.org/fortclinch***

Fort Clinch stands guard over Fernandina's natural deep-water port (see p. 148) at the northern end of Amelia Island and provides fabulous views out to sea

Fort Clinch

from its battlements. The fort's interior has been recreated to show how it looked when occupied by soldiers in 1864 and the sleeping quarters, storehouse and kitchens are interesting to poke around. A guide in Civil War dress is present to answer visitors' questions and historical re-enactments take place the first weekend of each month. If your visit coincides, join an evening candlelit tour held on the first Saturday of the month (US$3/ £1.50 per person. Reservations are essential via the number above). The surrounding grounds contain hiking and cycling trails and access to a quiet stretch of beach.

***Open** Park 9am–sunset, fort 9am–4.30pm daily. **Admission** park US$5 (£2.50) cars, US$1 (50p) cyclists and pedestrians; fort US$2 (£1) adults, children under 5 free. **Amenities** Toilets. Shop. Picnic area. Some disabled access.*

For Active Families

Egans Creek Greenway

Winding through the green space behind Fernandina's coast road (Fletcher Avenue), Egans Creek Greenway comprises a series of looping off-road cycling and hiking trails that are good to explore with small children, as they are flat. All kinds of bird and wildlife can be encountered on the Greenway – keep an eye open for alligators – and paths can be accessed from Jasmine Street or Atlantic Avenue, where you can also join the quiet road leading to Fort Clinch (see p. 154). Bikes can be rented from Beach Rentals & More (2856 Sadler Road at Fletcher Avenue *904 556 2395* ***www.beachrentalsandmore.com***), who rent trailers for children and offer discounts for families.

Merritt Island Wildlife Refuge ★★

Four miles east of Titusville on SR-402 321 861 0667 ***www.merrittislandwildlife.org***

Sharing a border with the Kennedy Space Center (see p. 74), the various ecosystems of this large, undeveloped wildlife refuge are teeming with around 500 species of wildlife, including dolphins, sea turtles, otters and bob cats. Children who love wildlife will enjoy the opportunities the refuge provides to witness many different animals. The visitor centre provides free maps and the refuge can be explored by foot on one of the walking trails – don't miss the Manatee Observation Deck – or via a 7-mile drive past salt and freshwater marshes. Like the Everglades (see p. 216), the beauty of this terrain is not immediately striking, but the minute you see a large flock of migratory birds take to the skies, you'll know what all the fuss is about. The refuge is closed on shuttle launch days.

***Open** 8am–4.30pm Mon–Fri, 9am–5pm Sat, 9am–5pm Sun, Nov-March.*

FUN FACT **Black Bear**

Ocala National Forest is one of the few remaining refuges for the endangered Florida black bear.

Ocala National Forest ★★

352 629 8051 ***www.stateparks.com/ocala***

Inland from Ormond Beach along SR-40 and north west of Orlando, Ocala National Forest is a vast untamed wildlife refuge, crossed by hiking trails and spring-fed rivers whose waters are delicious on a hot day. This is a great place for families to canoe together, as the waters are calm; outlets rent double canoes that accommodate an adult and child.

At Alexander Springs (8am–8pm. US$8/£4 per car) off SR-19, visitors can swim and snorkel in crystal-clear spring water, explore a mile-long interpretive trail through palm, cedar and cypress swamps and rent canoes. Further north, Juniper Springs (8am–8pm. US$8/£4 per car), off SR-40, west of SR-19, has a spring-fed swimming area where racoons keep an eye on visitors, and the canoe rental shop will drop canoeists 7 miles downriver to paddle back to the centre – last drop off is at noon.

INSIDER TIP

There are very few petrol stations in Ocala National Forest, so fill up before you enter.

Shopping

Ron Jon's Surf Shop ★

4151 North Atlantic Avenue 1 888 757 8737 ***www.ronjons.com***

Just like the beach, Cocoa's enormous store, dedicated to all things surf, never closes. Two million visitors pass through Ron Jon's doors every year to browse through its two floors of clothes, accessories, beach gear and, of course, surfboards. This shop is usually a big hit with teens and older children looking for a trendy beach outfit, and is a good place to shop for wacky souvenirs – flip-flop soap anyone?

Open *24 hours.* ***Credit*** *AmEx, MC, V.* ***Amenities*** *Parking.*

The Dinosaur Store ★★

299 W. Cocoa Beach Causeway (SR-520) 321 783 7300 ***www.dinosaustore.com***

Advertising itself as 'a Jurassic shopping experience', The Dinosaur Store is an Aladdin's cave for any child interested in these prehistoric giants. The shop's shelves and glass cabinets are cluttered with fossils, dinosaur teeth and claws, rocks, minerals and bones – a dinosaur skull will set you back US$40,000 (£20,000). There's also a good range of T-shirts, books and educational games.

Fernandina

Fernandina has numerous good accommodation options suitable for visiting families on varying budgets, and wherever you choose to stay you're never far from the beach. Several better than average chain motels can be found on Sadler Road, near the junction with Fletcher Avenue, including the Best Western Amelia Island 2702 Sadler Road *904 277 2300* ***www.bestwesternflorida.com***, which has a large pool and jacuzzi (rooms US$80/£40), and the ocean-facing Amelia Island Hotel and Suites, 1997 South Fletcher Avenue *904 261 5735* ***www.ameliahotelandsuites.com*** (rooms US$130–US$170/£65–85). If you want to stay downtown, the Hampton Inn and Suites 19 S 2nd Street *904 491 4911* ***www.hamptoninn.com*** is in keeping with Fernandina's historic ambience, despite being built in the last decade, and features wooden floors from a local church and sherbet décor (rooms US$170/£85).

Many of Fernandina's Victorian and Queen Anne-style houses and various quirky properties such as Katie's Light, an old wooden lighthouse on the beach, have been converted into holiday homes. For more information on self catering in Fernandina Beach, see Amelia Island Vacations *904 277 4851* ***www.ameliaislandvacation.com*** and Unique Amelia Island Vacations *800 940 3955* ***www.uniqueameliaisland.com***

Open *10.30am–5pm Mon–Fri, 10.30 am–7pm Sat.* ***Credit*** *AmEx, MC, V.* ***Amenities*** *Parking.*

One of the best places to find a designer bargain in the area is **The Avenue Mall** (*321 634 5390* ***www.theavenuealist.com*** open Mon–Sat 10am–9pm, Sun noon–6pm) situated off I-95 at exit 191 to the south of Cocoa. This large mall contains around 150 shops including Belk department store and smaller designer outlets.

FAMILY-FRIENDLY ACCOMMODATION

VERY EXPENSIVE/EXPENSIVE

Amelia Island Plantation ★

6800 First Coast Highway (SR-A1A), Fernandina Amelia Island, 6 miles south of Fernandina Beach 904 261 6161 ***www.aipfl.com***

Set amongst 1,350 acres of verdant beachfront complete with its own natural lagoon, this massive complex is an idyllic retreat for an active family. The resort's rooms are large and airy, and facilities include championship golf, tennis and cycling. Children love the large landscaped swimming pools and a wild, wonderful and quiet beach is right on the doorstep. Kids Camp Amelia

Amelia Island Plantation

offers 3–10-year-olds nature clinics, games and arts, or golf and tennis lessons. And older children are equally well catered for with a recreation programme designed for 11–19-year-olds. Amelia Island Plantation is a good base from which to explore Fernandina Beach, Jacksonville and even St Augustine.

Rooms *249.* ***Rates*** *Rooms US$166–US$366 (£83–183), villas US$206–US$967 (£103–484).* ***Credit*** *AmEx, MC, V.* ***Amenities*** *Two golf courses. 23 tennis courts. Children's clubs. Sports equipment rentals. Nature tours. Fishing. Two outdoor pools. Indoor pool. Fitness centre. Spa. Shops. Games room. Two restaurants. Two bars. Babysitting.* ***In room*** *Cable TV. Internet access. Safe.*

MODERATE/EXPENSIVE

Florida House Inn ★

20–22 South 3rd Street, Fernandina Beach ☎ 904 261 3300 ***www.floridahouseinn.com***

Built in 1857 and situated in the heart of Fernandina's historical district, this charming B&B is Florida's oldest operating hotel. I recommend it as I think children will love its unique qualities. The clapboard exterior is decorated with gingerbread-trimmed balconies and wraparound porches, while inside, each of the rooms is furnished with old-fashioned luxury, some containing four-poster beds, clawfoot bathtubs and working fireplaces. Family-sized accommodation consists of a choice of twin rooms or grander suites in the Carriage House that come with kitchens. Room rates include limited scooter rental, and local bluegrass musicians jam in the bar every Monday night.

Rooms *22.* ***Rates*** *Rooms US$129–US$259 (£64.50–129.50), Carriage House suites US$250–US$309 (£125–154.50).* ***Credit*** *AmEx, MC, V.* ***Amenities*** *Parlour. Restaurant. Bar.* ***In room*** *A/C. Cable TV.*

FUN FACT Cuban Uprising

It is said that José Marti stayed at the Florida House Inn while planning the Cuban uprising against its Spanish rulers in the 1890s.

MODERATE

Sea Turtle Inn

1 Ocean Boulevard, Atlantic Beach, north of Jacksonville Beach 📞 904 249 7402 ***www.seaturtle.com***

Atlantic Beach is a small friendly community north of Jacksonville Beach with wide, pristine sands and numerous lively restaurants. The Sea Turtle Inn is a good base for families who want to be within easy access of this laid-back town and have a quiet refuge away from it all. This recently renovated resort stands on the edge of the beach and children receive complimentary chocolate on arrival. The resort's pool overlooks sand and sea and provides safe swimming along with easy beach access for youngsters. An ocean-front lounge provides nightly live entertainment, while the on-site Plantains Restaurant serves unusual versions of local favourites.

Rooms *190.* ***Rates*** *Rooms from US$169 (£84.50), suites from US$200 (£100).* ***Credit*** *AmEx, MC, V.* ***Amenities*** *Restaurant. Lounge. Pool. Babysitting. Complimentary breakfast. Discounts to a nearby fitness centre and transport to Jacksonville and its airport.* ***In room*** *Cable TV. A/C. Wi-Fi Internet. Fridge.*

MODERATE

Casa Del Mar Inn and Suites ★

95 Vilano Road, St Augustine, at Vilano beach on SR-A1A 📞 904 827 9797 ***www.casadelmaroceanside.com***

Tucked away in a residential area, just a few minutes' drive from St

Jacksonville and Its Beaches

Most visitors to Jacksonville stay around the beach area, which is awash with accommodation options, particularly chain motels, including the Beach Front Best Western 305 North 1st Street 📞 *904 249 4949* ***www.bestwesternjacksonvillebeach.com***, which is right on the beach (rooms US$130–US$170/£65–85). If you prefer to stay on the outskirts of this at times busy area, a budget option on Neptune Beach to the north is the very pink Seahorse Oceanfront Inn 120 Atlantic Boulevard 📞 *904 246 2175* ***www.seahorseoceanfrontinn.com*** (rooms from US$100/£50). And for families wanting to stay in Jacksonville's downtown, a convenient option is the Hyatt Regency 225 East Coast Line Drive 📞 *904 588 1234* ***www.jacksonville.hyatt.com*** (rooms US$109–US$300/£54.50–150), which is adjacent to Jacksonville Landing and has Hertz car hire and two restaurants on site.

St Augustine

In contrast to most of Florida's coastal communities, many visitors to St Augustine prefer to stay in its historic downtown where numerous accommodation options can be found. A string of chain motels is located at the north end of downtown where SR-A1A becomes San Marco Avenue, including the Howard Johnson Express Inn, 137 San Marco Avenue ☎ *904 824 6181* ***www.hojo.com*** (rooms from US$50/£25), which is literally on the tourist trail as tram tours stop here to visit the Old Senator, a 600-year-old oak tree in the middle of the motel's car park.

A number of family-run accommodation options are to be found in the heart of the city's historic area, including the red-brick Monterey Inn, 16 Avenida Menendez ☎ *904 824 4482* ***www.themontereyinn.com*** (rooms from US$79/£39.50) with its sundeck facing Matanzas Bay, and the lovingly restored Bay Front Westcott House, 146 Avenida Medendez ☎ *940 824 4301* ***www.westcotthouse.com*** (family rooms US$150–US$230/ £75–115).

St Augustine has many fabulous Bed and Breakfasts set in old houses in the historic district. The St Augustine Historic Inns website ***www.staugustineinns.com*** details all of these properties and their rates.

Augustine's busy tourist centre and right on the beach, this friendly, old world style resort is an ideal base from which to explore St Augustine and the surrounding coast. I like this resort for families because it is located on the edge of a wild beach and close to the historic area. St Augustine sightseeing tours provide complimentary pick up from the hotel's lobby so you don't even have to drive into town, and after a hard day's taking in the sights, children can enjoy the sweet shop while parents relax in the heated whirlpool.

Rooms *94.* ***Rates*** *From US$140 (£70).* ***Credit*** *AmEx. MC. V.* ***Amenities*** *Pool. Whirlpool. Fitness centre. Complimentary breakfast. Laundry facilities. Shop.* ***In room*** *Cable TV with Play Station. Safe. Internet access. Fridge. Microwave. Cots available.*

MODERATE/EXPENSIVE

Ocean Walk Resort

300 N Atlantic Avenue, Daytona Beach ☎ *800 347 9851* ***www.oceanwalk.com***

Situated close to the Ocean Walk shopping and dining complex and Daytona's pier, this luxurious beach-front resort is perfect for families who want to be at the heart of a lively beach. The attraction of this section of Daytona's beach if you have small children is that it's car free, but you might never tear your children away from the enormous hotel pool with its giant waterslide, long lazy river and children's water play area. The accommodation consists of luxury suites set up for self catering and there are plenty of on-site activities laid on for families who like to play together.

Rooms *150.* ***Rates*** *US$120–US$270 (£60–135).* ***Credit*** *AmEx, MC, V.* ***Amenities*** *Two indoor pools. Three outdoor pools. Children's programme. Exercise equipment. Hot tub. Restaurant. Games room. Putting green. Waterslide. Bar. Spa.* ***In room*** *Full kitchen. Washer/dryer. Cable TV. A/C.*

MODERATE/EXPENSIVE

Ron Jon's Cape Caribe Resort ★★★

1000 Shorewood Drive, Cape Canaveral ☎ *866 854 4835* ***www.capecaribetour.com***

With the lobby of this fabulous new resort featuring both a large tropical fountain and framed astronaut suit, it's pretty clear that the two big attractions to this area are the nearby Kennedy Space Center and even closer chilled-out beach. The various sizes of self-catering suites have a home from home appeal and I really like the vast array of activities for children of all ages, including everything from football to coconut painting. The child-friendly pool area is enormous and the indoor jungle gym is good for youngsters on a rainy day; there's even a programme of family films shown throughout the day in an on-site cinema.

Rooms *Depends on availability.* ***Rates*** *US$175–US$425 (£87.50–213) depending on size and season.* ***Credit*** *AmEx, MC, V.* ***Amenities*** *Pool. Waterslide. Lazy river. Hot tub. Restaurant. Bar. Miniature golf. Exercise room. Children's play centre. Cinema. Shop.* ***In room*** *A/C. Full kitchen. Cable TV. Washer/dryer.*

Daytona Beach

Daytona Beach is crammed with accommodation options, from big brash ocean-facing resorts strung out along the beach to small charming B&Bs tucked away in quiet residential corners. Beach-front chain options include the Best Western Aku Tiki, 2225 S Atlantic Avenue ☎ *386 252 9631* ***www.bwakutiki.com*** (rooms from US$120/£60), with a huge, unmissable Tiki god carving right outside, this kitsch resort operates a family-friendly recreation programme for children and adults, and the equally distinctive Best Western Mayan Inn, 103 S Ocean Avenue ☎ *386 252 2378* ***www.bestwestern.com*** (rooms from US$100/£50) with its huge Mayan painting on the outside wall. The Days Inn Tropical Seas Oceanfront South, 3357 S Atlantic Avenue ☎ *386 767 8737* ***www.tropicalseasfla.com*** (rooms US$50–US$125/£25–63) is another basic chain option featuring some rooms with kitchenettes.

For details on the best times for families to visit Daytona Beach, see p. 139.

Cocoa Beach

Cocoa Beach's largest concentration of accommodation options is spread out along SR-A1A as it becomes Atlantic Avenue and on Ocean Beach Boulevard as it runs parallel to the beach behind SR-A1A. Recommended options are the Holiday Inn 1300 N Atlantic Avenue ☎ *321 783 2271* ***www.hi-cocoa.com*** (rooms US$90–US$150/£45–75), which has a large pool and water park complete with pirate ship, La Quinta 1275 N Atlantic Avenue ☎ *321 783 2252* ***www.lq.com*** (rooms US$100–US$110/£50–55) and the colourful Fawlty Towers Motel 100 E Cocoa Beach Causeway ☎ *321 784 3870* ***www.fawltytowersresort.com*** (rooms US$90–US$140/£45–70).

FAMILY-FRIENDLY DINING

MODERATE/EXPENSIVE

A1A Ale Works ★

1 King Street, St Augustine ☎ 904 829 2977 ***www.a1aaleworks.com***

Families love this friendly restaurant-cum-pub whose lively atmosphere is welcoming to children. Try to grab a table on the less crowded outside balcony facing the waterfront, an ideal spot from which to watch the decorated horse-drawn carriages plying their trade. The lunch and dinner menu is long and varied and, while seafood heavy, also features a decent range of sandwiches, pasta and lots of appetizers for smaller appetites. This has to be the only restaurant I've ever seen with smoked salmon, fish and chips and fried custard on the same menu.

Open *11am–10.30pm Sun–Thurs, until 11pm Fri and Sat.* ***Main Courses*** *US$10–US$28 (£5–14).* ***Credit*** *AmEx, MC, V.*

A1A Ale Works

Joe's 2nd Street Bistro ★★★

14 S 2nd Street, Fernandina Beach *904 321 2558* ***www.joesbistro.com***

Deep in the heart of Fernandina Beach's historic downtown, Joe's 2nd Street Bistro is the best place to dine with children away from the beach. You can choose to sit in a charming New Orleans-inspired courtyard decorated with an ornate fountain and tropical plants, or inside an old restored house but, if you can, get a table on the covered front porch, which has glorious views of Fernandina's waterways just as the sun is setting over them. What stands out for me is the fabulous food, influenced by flavours from all over the world. The pasta and mainly meat and seafood main courses are truly memorable, just make sure you leave room for dessert. Reservation recommended.

Open *6pm–9.30pm daily.* ***Main Courses*** *US$14–US$32 (£7–16).* ***Credit*** *AmEx, MC, V.* ***Amenities*** *Children's menu.*

MODERATE

Al's Pizza ★

303 Atlantic Boulevard, Atlantic Beach *904 249 0002* ***www.alspizza.com***

This jazzy diner-style pizza parlour is an inexpensive, friendly restaurant in the Jacksonville Beach area. It's located across the road from the Sea Turtle Inn (see Family-friendly Accommodation p. 157) and within walking distance of the glorious Atlantic Beach, and its create your own pizzas are famous for being some of the best in the whole north east. This place is well frequented by local families and the children's menu contains fresh pasta dishes with not a burger, chip or fried fish in sight. Adults will appreciate the extensive beer selection.

Open *11am–11pm Mon–Thurs, 11am–midnight Fri and Sat, noon–9pm Sun.* ***Main Courses*** *US$8–US$21 (£4–10.50).* ***Credit*** *MC, V.* ***Amenities*** *Children's menu.*

Lighthouse Landing Restaurant ★

4940 South Peninsular Drive, Ponce Inlet, Nr Daytona Beach *386 761 9271* ***www.lighthouselandingrestaurant.com***

The sign outside reads 'if you have a reservation you're in the wrong place', which sums up the deliberately downbeat ambience that the owners of this rustic waterfront restaurant are proud to uphold. Lighthouse Landing claims to be the last old Florida fish camp and its battered wooden porch overlooking Ponce Inlet has all the aura of Florida's adventurous, pre-theme park past. You'll find no frills here and children can relax and run around while parents enjoy the amazing views. None of the food is processed and dishes on the predominantly seafood menu vary depending on what's in season.

Open *11.30am–9pm Sun–Thurs, 11.30am–10pm Fri and Sat.* ***Main Courses*** *US$8–US$21 (£4–10.50).* ***Credit*** *MC, V.* ***Amenities*** *Children's menu.*

Sliders ★

1998 South Fletcher Avenue, Fernandina Beach ☎ 904 277 6652 ***www.slidersseasidegrill.com***

Themed with a Caribbean style, both in terms of décor and food, this casual beachfront restaurant is popular with locals and visitors alike. You can choose to eat inside, but the outside tables or covered porch area are preferable for children because they provide glorious views of the ocean and access to a beachside play area that's well set up for little ones. This is a good choice for lunch if you're having a day on the beach; however, better still is eating here in the evening when the cool sea breeze blows in and the moon rises above the Atlantic.

Open *Daily from 11.30am for lunch and dinner.* ***Main Courses*** *lunch US$7–US$13 (£3.50–6.50), dinner US$17–US$24 (£8.50–12).* ***Credit*** *AmEx, MC, V.* ***Amenities*** *Highchair. Children's menu. Children's play area.*

BUDGET/MODERATE

Bunkey's Raw Bar and Seafood Grill

315 West Cocoa Beach Causeway, Cocoa Beach ☎ 321 799 4677 ***www.bunkysrawbar.com***

With its rustic nautical décor, fish tanks and oyster-shaped bars, Bunky's is a quirky and fun place to eat and one of the better places to bring children in Cocoa Beach without having to resort to a big name chain. It's tucked away from the main drag and you can eat outside, but the inside booths are more set up for families. The food is mainly seafood, but there are some alternatives to standard dishes, including snow crab and clam linguini, and the children's menu features pasta and seafood options in addition to the usual burger and fries.

Open *4pm–10pm Mon, 11am–10pm Tues–Thurs, 11am–11pm Fri and Sat, 11am–9pm Sun.* ***Main Courses*** *US$7–US$21 (£3.50–10.50).* ***Credit*** *AmEx, MC, V.* ***Amenities*** *Children's menu.*

Ocean Deck

127 S Ocean Avenue, Daytona Beach ☎ 386 253 5224 ***www.oceandeck.com***

Although a popular party pub later in the evening, this rustic beachfront bar next door to the Mayan Inn (see p. 161) is a great place to eat with children for lunch and in the early evening and one of the best dining options on Daytona Beach. The main bar is downstairs and totally separate from the dining area, where you can enjoy inexpensive sandwiches and seafood accompanied by wide ocean views. The children's menu comes along with an activity sheet and includes Peanut Butter and Jellyfish with chips for US$4 (£2). But whatever they choose to eat, all children get to keep the Frisbee their meals are served on.

Open *11am–2am daily.* ***Main Courses*** *US$7–US$21 (£3.50–10.50).* ***Credit*** *AmEx, MC, V.* ***Amenities*** *Children's menu.*

7 Miami & the South East Coast

MIAMI & THE SOUTH EAST COAST

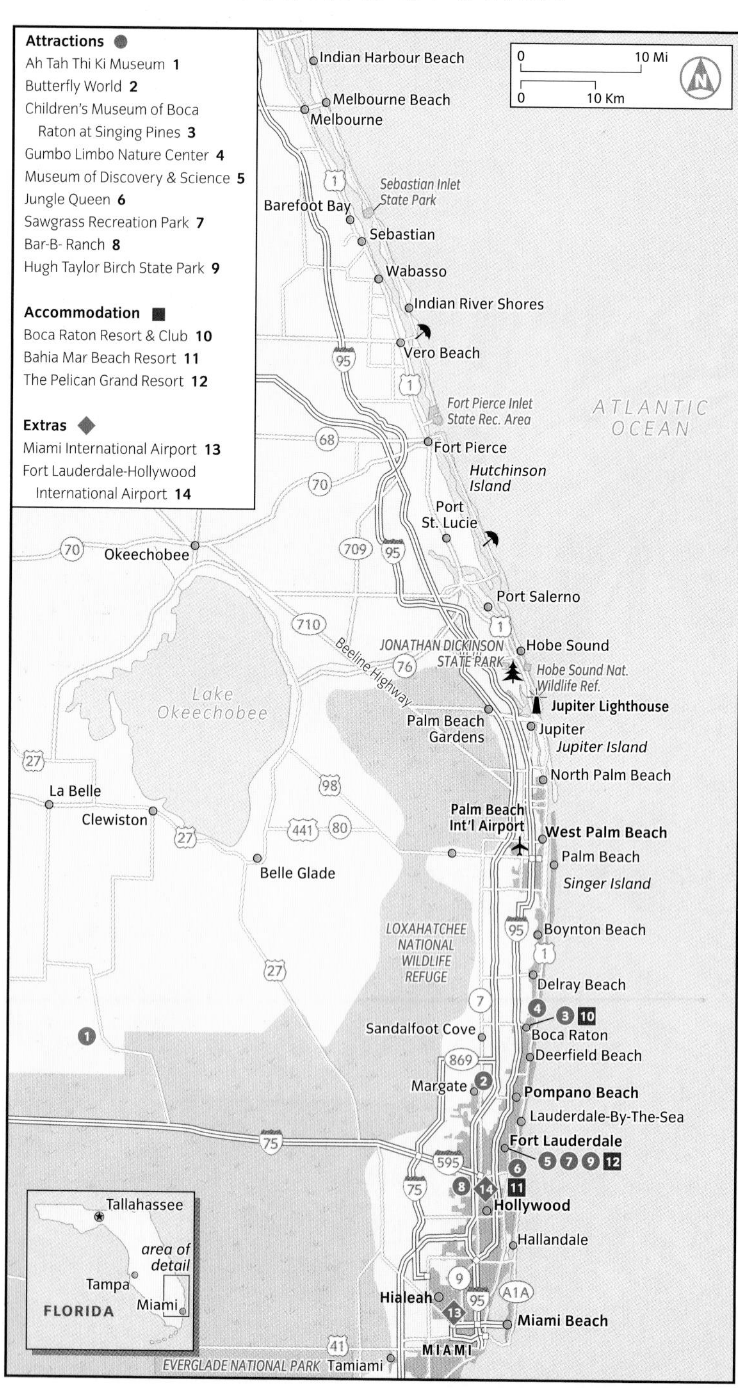

With glamorous Miami and its world famous Art Deco district as its central focus, Florida's south east coast is a region where celebrities and millionaires come to play and swathes of its glorious coastline are the exclusive territory of winter homes for the rich and famous. But swanky nightclubs, designer boutiques and plush mansions are just the brash side of the south east. Peel back the pages of celebrity magazines and property brochures and you'll find stunning undeveloped surfer beaches where sea turtles come to nest and families come to play. And away from its Atlantic-washed shores, expect to find some of the best museums, art galleries and family-friendly attractions in the whole state, many the result of the region's diverse cultural and historical influences and all accessible to visitors young and old. In contrast, large parts of the south east butt up against the undeveloped tropical wilderness of Big Cypress Swamp and the Everglades, where big city life soon dissolves into a timeless natural environment that's an easy day trip from the urban-soaked coast.

ESSENTIALS

Getting There

By Plane Miami International Airport ☎ *305 876 7000* ***www.miami-airport.com*** is situated six miles west of downtown and receives regular non-stop flights from London Heathrow operated by British Airways, Virgin Atlantic, Continental Airlines and American Airlines, and internal flights operated by various American airlines (see p. 33) from Fort Lauderdale, Tampa, Orlando, Jacksonville, Fort Myers, Key West, Pensacola and Tallahassee.

If you're driving from the airport, SR-112 is the Airport Expressway (toll) and leads through central Miami across the Julia Tuttle Causeway (I-195) to the beach.

Fort Lauderdale-Hollywood International Airport ☎ *866 4359 355* ***www.broward.org/airport*** is a 15-minute drive south from Fort Lauderdale and receives internal flights from Jacksonville, Key West, Tallahassee, Tampa, Orlando and Pensacola operated by various American airlines (see p. 33) but no non-stop flights from the UK.

For information on package tours, see p. 28.

By Car The most direct route from Orlando to the south east coast is Florida's Turnpike, which cuts across central Florida to run parallel with I-95, the most direct route from the north, at Fort Pierce onwards. Florida's Turnpike is a toll road, so have change handy.

If you're driving from south west Florida, the picturesque Hwy-41 (Tamiami Trail) cuts across the top of the Everglades from Naples and leads directly into the heart of downtown Miami. However, due to its relatively low speed limit, this road can be slow.

For a faster route take I-75, otherwise known as Alligator Alley (toll), which runs north of Hwy-41 from Naples.

At the point where I-75 turns south to lead into north Miami, the I-595 branches east to become the main route to Fort Lauderdale.

From the Florida Keys, Hwy-1 is an excruciatingly slow route directly into Miami. Faster options are to join the Florida Turnpike, which begins at Florida City, or take the Palmetto Expressway (SR-826), which heads north from Hwy-1 on the western edge of Miami.

By Ferry The Key West Express ferry travels between Miami and Key West. High-speed boats leave at 8.30am from the dock next to the Seaquarium on Rickenbacker Causeway and take approximately 4 hours to reach Key West. Boats depart for the return journey to Miami at 5.30pm. Single trips cost US$50 (£25)per person, round trips US$100 (£50) adults, US$68 (£34) children under 12. For further information ☎ *1 888 539 2628* ***www.seakeywestexpress.com***. This service also connects Key West with Fort Myers Beach (see p. 109).

VISITOR INFORMATION

Miami's main visitor information centre is the Greater Miami Convention and Visitor's Bureau, 701 Brickell Avenue ☎ *800 933 8448* ***www.miamiandbeaches.com*** open 8.30am–6pm Mon–Fri. However, the Miami Beach Visitor Center is more convenient at 1920 Meridian Avenue ☎ *305 672 1270* ***www.miamibeachchamber.com*** open 9am–6pm Mon–Fri, 10am–4pm Sat and Sun. Also try the Downtown Miami Welcome Center ***www.downtownmiami.com*** in the lobby of the Gusman Center for the Performing Arts at 174 E Flagler Street. If you're arriving by plane (see p. 167), the visitor information centre at Miami airport is open 24 hours.

INSIDER TIP

Booking accommodation in Miami online via ***www.reservation-services.com*** can be cheaper than booking direct.

For information on Fort Lauderdale, visit the Greater Fort Lauderdale Convention and Visitor Bureau, 100 E Broward Boulevard ☎ *954 765 4466* ***www.sunny.org*** open 8.30am–5pm Mon–Fri.

Orientation

Situated at the southern tip of the south east coast, Miami dominates the region. Heading north from Miami, I-95 is the fastest route up the east coast to the area's other major towns and cities. East of I-95, Hwy-1 leads directly through the region's coastal towns. For those not in a rush, the, coast-hugging SR-A1A is the most

Getting Around Miami

By Car Miami is straightforward to drive around, as major roads lead to all the tourist sights and the grid system is easy to follow. Avoid driving during weekday rush hours – 7am–9am and 4pm–6pm – when you won't go anywhere fast. Parking is plentiful except on South Beach, where your best bet is the two municipal car parks on Collins Avenue at 7th and 13th Streets.

By Bus Miami's Metrobus is a slow way to travel around, but its comprehensive service is easy to work out, covers most of Miami's attractions and is well used by the locals. Fares are US$1.50 (75p) per journey and 50¢ (25p) extra to transfer from one bus to another in a single journey (exact change required). To travel by bus around South Beach, the South Beach Local mini bus service runs every 10–15 minutes from 7.45am Mon–Sat and from 10am Sun until 1am daily, making numerous stops at South Beach's popular locations on the way. The fare is 25¢ (12.5p) per journey. All buses are wheelchair and bike accessible.

By Metromover A free monorail serves the downtown and business district. Its elevated tracks provide great views of the city.

By Metrorail A train service runs from south Miami into the city along a route close to Hwy-1. It travels through downtown and out to Medley, a region north of the airport. This is a commuter service and has few relevant stops for tourists.

The Metrobus, Metromover and Metrorail are all operated by Miami-Dade Transit and for more information ☎ *305 770 3131* or visit ***www.miamidade.gov/transit*** for routes and schedules. Timetables can be picked up from visitor information centres (see p. 168).

By Taxi Most people don't hail cabs in Miami. To book a cab call Metro Taxi ☎ *305 888 8888*, Yellow Cab ☎ *305 444 4444* or for Miami Beach, Central ☎ *305 532 5555*.

South Beach, Miami

scenic way to travel through the south east.

Getting Around

With limited public transport options, the only feasible way to travel around most of the south east coast with children is by car. For details of car hire, see p. 29. For information on getting around Miami, see box above.

Child-friendly Festivals & Events

Art Deco Weekend

The Miami Design Preservation League hosts a weekend of celebrations in South Beach's Art Deco region each January. The festival has a different theme each year and includes a parade, street entertainers, festival food and arts-and-crafts stalls. For exact dates and full details check *www.mdlp.org* or *305 672 2014*.

INSIDER TIP

If you plan to visit a lot of Miami's sights, a Go Miami Card *www.gomiamicard.com* could save you money. The card gives entry into over 40 attractions and is bought in days of usage from a single day to a week. The fees range from one-day US$59 (£29.50) adult, US$49 (£24.50) children 3–12 to 7 days US$209 (£104.50) adult, US$169 (£84.50) children 3–12. Cards can be purchased online or at the Miami Beach Visitor Center (see p. 168) and at Miami Duck Tours (see p. 180). But do the maths before you buy to check that this deal will work for you.

WHAT TO SEE & DO

Children's Top 10 Attractions

1. Discovering South Beach's amazing Art Deco; p. 175.
2. Taking a dip in Coral Gables' magical Venetian Pool; p. 179.
3. Learning about the care of injured sea turtles at the Gumbo Limbo Nature Center; p. 186.
4. Telling the time on Fort Lauderdale's Museum of Discovery and Science's giant gravity clock; p. 187.
5. Breakfast at Jerry's Famous Deli; p. 194.
6. Strolling around Fort Lauderdale's Riverwalk; p. 183.
7. Playing beach volleyball at Deerfield Beach; p. 184.
8. Shopping along South Beach's Lincoln Road; p. 182.
9. Speeding across Big Cypress Swamp on an airboat at Sawgrass Recreation Park; p. 188.
10. Getting up close to the animals at Miami's MetroZoo; p. 175.

MIAMI

Overlooking the Caribbean and with a distinctly Hispanic edge – Spanish is the predominant language in many areas – Miami, with its fashion-conscious beaches, sophistication and reputed high murder rate, might not be every parent's first choice as a holiday destination, but don't let 1980s cop shows or crime statistics put you off bringing children to this stylish city. For all its glamour and celebrities, Miami is surprisingly family friendly and its many world class museums, sumptuous art galleries and cool zoos are some of the best in Florida – there's plenty to keep all ages occupied for days.

MIAMI

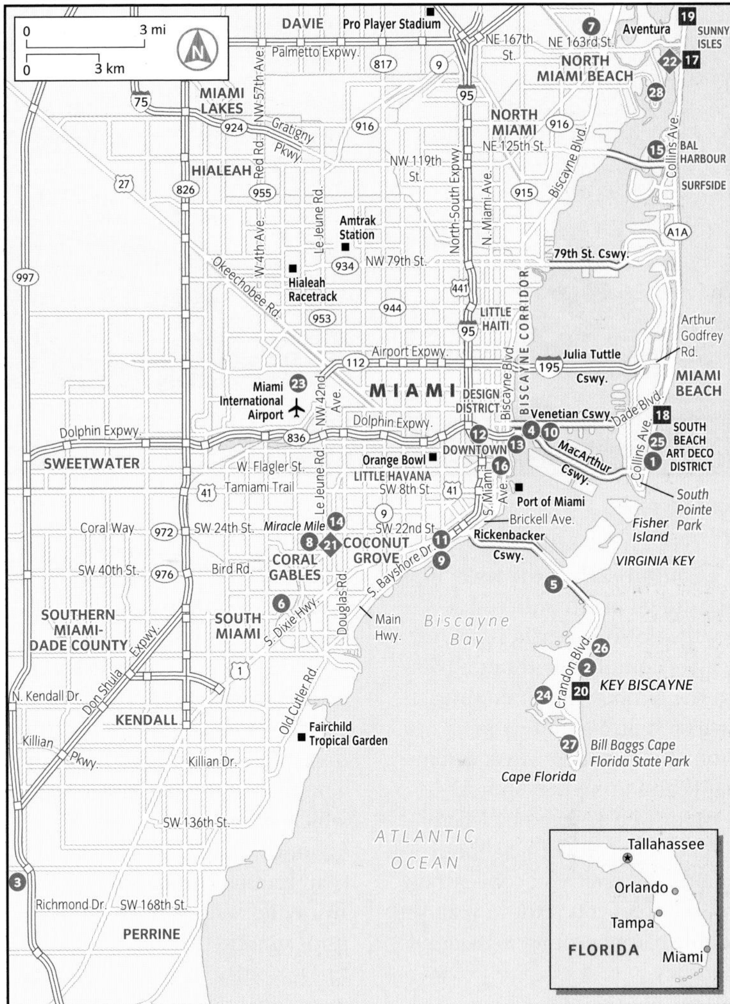

Attractions ●

Art Deco Welcome Center **1**
Marjory Stoneman Douglas Biscayne Nature Center **2**
Miami MetroZoo **3**
Parrot Jungle Island **4**
Miami Seaquarium **5**
Lowe Art Museum **6**
Spanish Monastery **7**
Venetian Pool **8**
Vizcaya Museum and Gardens **9**
Miami's Children's Museum **10**
Miami Science Museum **11**
Metro Dade Cultural Center **12**
Bayside Marketplace **13**
Miracle Mile **14**
Bal Harbour Shops **15**
Flagler Street **16**

Accommodation ■

Aqualina, A Rosewood Resort **17**
Loews Hotel **18**
Thunderbird Beach Resort **19**
Ritz Carlton Key Biscayne **20**

Dining ◆

Californian Pizza Kitchen **21**
Rascal House **22**

Extras ●

Miami Airport **23**
Key Biscayne **24**
South Beach **25**
Crandon Park Beach **26**
Bill Baggs Cape Florida State Park **27**
Oleta River State Park **28**

Art Deco District

South Beach is the jewel in the crown of Miami's consistently glorious beaches and no visit is complete without a trip to the famous Art Deco district, whose stylish architecture is home to countless swish restaurants and upmarket shops.

Don't be deterred by Miami's size, this is a city of neighbourhoods and once you concentrate on the areas you want to visit, the whole place becomes manageable.

Miami's Family-Friendly Beaches

Key Biscayne

Separated from the mainland by the Rickenbacker Causeway (US$1/50p toll), Key Biscayne is a family-orientated area of Miami whose leafy roads are pounded by joggers and cyclists and a relaxed atmosphere prevails. Two ideal beaches for children can be found on this island. The first, Crandon Park Beach, which sits on the east side of Crandon Boulevard (the main road leading through Key Biscayne) is open from 8am until sunset (US$5/£2.50 per car). Popular with local families, especially at weekends, this beach's 3 miles of golden sand is protected by a sand bar, making its waters safe for children to swim in.

FUN FACT **ATM for Rollerbladers**

Miami installed the world's first ATM just for its rollerbladers.

Miami Vice or Nice?

Once famous for car jacking, Miami has worked hard over the past two decades to clean up its act. Don't worry about visiting with children as long as you exercise all the usual cautions of being in a big city. Be careful from whom and where you ask directions, use ATMs in busy areas, leave valuables in your hotel and steer clear of quiet, unlit streets at night. And don't venture out of the tourist areas. If you're driving, stay on the main roads, keep your car doors locked and windows closed and never stop in unlit areas, even if someone flags you down. If you are bumped, drive to a busy street before getting out. Don't walk around downtown at night, be careful walking along Biscayne Boulevard and 2nd Avenue during the day and never be tempted to stay in any of the motels on Biscayne Boulevard.

INSIDER TIP

A large, landscaped park with a carousel and playground sits on the west side of Crandon Boulevard and is a shady, pleasant place to stop with pre-school toddlers.

The Marjory Stoneman Douglas Biscayne Nature Center ★ ☎ *305 361 6767* ***www.biscaynenaturecenter.org*** is situated at the north end of Crandon Beach and features exhibits explaining the region's marine environments as well as organising child-friendly, naturalist-led tours into nearby sea grass beds where you can scoop up nets full of small sealife for the guide to explain what you've found.

Hugging Key Biscayne's southern tip, Bill Baggs Cape Florida State Park (8am until sunset. US$5 per car) is a good choice for families who want more than just sea and sand. At weekends the Latin population is out in force and upbeat music livens up the whole beach. Standing at the end of the beach, the Cape Florida lighthouse is accessible via free ranger-led tours at 10am and 1pm Thurs–Mon. View the keeper's former living quarters and take in expansive views across the key. Bikes can be rented for US$8 (£4) per hour, or quadrocycles, which accommodate four people, for US$25 (£12.50) per hour, from a cycle outlet in the park's main car park.

The Boater's Grill ☎ *305 361 0080* at No Name Harbour is a small, mainly seafood, restaurant whose veranda overlooks a busy marina (mains approximately US$15/£7.50) or you can munch on takeaway pizza slices for US$3/£1.50 or take your own picnic.

Oleta River State Park ★★

3400 NE 163rd Street, North Miami
☎ *305 919 1846*

Half an hour's drive from downtown but convenient if you're staying at the north end of

Miami Beach, Oleta River is the largest urban park in Florida and the place to head for privacy and seclusion. The park features a small beach, mangrove-lined river and miles of biking trails. Visitors can rent kayaks, canoes and bikes, while a calm lagoon away from the beach area provides safe swimming for children. Keep a look out for cameras, as this park is a popular film and TV location.

Open *8am–sunset daily.* ***Admission*** *US$5 (£2.50) per car.*

South Beach ★★★

Running from South Pointe Park to 23rd Street, Miami's South Beach is one of the world's coolest beaches and is an entirely separate region from the rest of Miami Beach, which stretches up to Sunny Isles in the north. Despite its prestige, there's always room to be found on the beach itself, which is dotted with jaunty lifeguard huts and large blue and white boxes where attendants rent beach chairs. Unlike other sections of Miami Beach, this stretch isn't dominated by high-rise resorts and the landscaped Lummas Park separates the sand from the bustling Ocean Drive.

INSIDER TIP

If you want a night out in Miami without the children and your hotel does not have a babysitting service, contact Nanny Poppinz Child Care Services ☎ *954 752 6707* ***www.nannypoppinz.com*** and they will arrange childcare for you.

Away from the sand, South Beach is a place to be seen in for many, but for visiting families it's simply a place to see. Cafés and restaurants spill out onto the pavements along Ocean Drive and Lincoln Avenue, and the eclectic mix of boutiques and trendy chain stores will keep teenagers occupied for hours (see p. 182). South Beach's compact streets are easy to cover on foot and if you get tired of spotting Art Deco and shopping, the excellent art galleries (see p. 177) are a good diversion with older children.

At the north end of South Beach, near the Convention Center on Meridian Avenue, is the moving Holocaust Memorial (open 9am–9pm daily). Miami Beach is home to many Holocaust survivors and this emotive statue – a giant outstretched arm stamped with an inmate number from Auschwitz and surrounded by nearly a hundred life-sized grief-stricken bodies – is an unforgettable testimony to those who did not survive.

INSIDER TIP

Memorial Day weekend (the last weekend in May) is notorious on South Beach. Thousands of revellers descend to party the weekend away and a heavy police presence in recent years has resulted in scores of arrests. South Beach is no place to visit with children at this time.

Miami's Art Deco Historic District ★★★

South Beach is home to the world's largest collection of Art Deco buildings and the stunning assortment of pastel-hued, streamlined architecture that lines its streets is one of Florida's greatest attractions. The Art Deco District is a must see for every visitor and worth bringing your children to, as the memory of these unique buildings will stay with them forever.

Construction of this district began after WW1, with the earliest Art Deco dating back to the mid-1920s. This sleek style grew to become the height of modern fashion in the 20s and 30s. However, following WW2, Miami's fashionable residents moved further north and South Beach and its beautiful buildings went into a deep decline, with some even calling for its total demolition. The campaign to preserve this district began in the late 1970s with the establishment of the Miami Design Preservation League. Their battles with developers and careful restoration work are responsible for saving this historic area and making it Miami's most fashionable neighbourhood once more.

Today the Art Deco Historic District is bordered by the Atlantic to the east, Alton Road to the west, 6th Street to the south and 23rd Street to the north and contains around 800 listed Art Deco buildings – even Burger King is Art Deco. The biggest concentration can be found along sea-facing Ocean Drive, Collins Avenue, Washington Avenue and Lincoln Road. Take a stroll along Ocean Drive as dusk settles and the neon lights start to flicker on and watch these glorious old buildings come to life.

The Art Deco Welcome Center on Ocean Drive 📞 *305 531 3484* ***www.mdpl.org*** is open 9.30am–7pm daily and contains a small shop selling souvenirs. Take a self-guided walking tour of the area (self-guided audio tours are available to hire from 10am–4pm), or join one of the Welcome Center's guided tours on Wednesdays, Fridays, Saturdays and Sundays at 10.30am, or Thursdays at 6.30pm (US$20/£10 adults, US$15/£7.50 children). For details of a cycling tour around the Art Deco Historic District, see p. 181.

Miami's Top Animal Attractions

Miami MetroZoo ★★

12400 SW 152nd Street 📞 305 251 0400 ***www.miamimetrozoo.com***

Situated south of Miami, towards Homestead and about 45 minutes from downtown, this huge zoo is one of the most impressive in Florida. Hundreds of animals roam through spacious habitats representing locations such as an African plain and Asian jungle. Animal highlights include majestic Bengal tigers and too cute to be true koalas and the daily wildlife show aims to educate through entertainment. Children wanting to learn more can ask questions at the Keeper's Talks, and while the

MetroZoo tiger

petting zoo provides the opportunity for all ages to get up close to some species, older children tend to gravitate towards the Wild Earth Simulator (US$5/£2.50 per person) to take a virtual African safari. The MetroZoo takes some walking around, but you can catch a tram tour or monorail. Better still, the funky safari cycles (US$16/£8 to hire), big enough to accommodate the whole family, are the most entertaining way to travel.

Open *9.30am–5pm daily. Ticket booth closes at 4.30pm.* ***Admission*** *US$11.50 (£5.75) adults, US$7 (£3.50) children.* ***Credit*** *AmEx, MC, V.* ***Amenities*** *Café. Shop. Play area. Buggy rental single US$7 (£3.50), double US$9 (£4.50). Disabled access. Baby-change facilities. No food or drink can be brought into the zoo, but there are picnic tables near the front entrance.*

INSIDER TIP

Arrive early at Miami MetroZoo; it gets very hot in the midday sun and most of the animals take a snooze.

Miami Seaquarium

4400 Rickenbacker Causeway ☏ 305 361 5705 ***www.miamiseaaquarium.com***

Worth a visit if you haven't been to SeaWorld (see p. 68), the Miami Seaquarium is a much smaller and older version. The park features sharks, manatees

Seaquarium dolphins

Miami's Art Scene

With many cultural and historical influences pouring into its creative melting pot, Miami's art scene contains galleries large and small to inspire the artistic imagination of any child. In addition to the **Miami Art Museum** (see p. 181), these are some of the galleries on offer.

Situated inside the University of Miami's Coral Gables Campus, the **Lowe Art Museum** *305 284 3535* ***www.lowemuseum.org*** (open 10–5pm Tues, Wed, Fri and Sat, noon–7pm Thurs and noon–5pm Sun. US$7/£3.50 adults, children under 12 free) exhibits old masters and contemporary artists.

In the heart of the Art Deco district, the **Bass Museum of Art** ★ at 2121 Park Avenue *305 673 7530* ***www.bassmuseum.org*** (open 10am–5pm Tues–Sat, 11am–5pm Sun. US$8/£4 adults, under 6s free) displays an overview of major European work and contemporary art from around the world.

Also on South Beach, the **Wolfsonian-FIU** ★★ *305 531 1001* ***www.wolfsonian.org*** (open noon–6pm Mon, Tues, Sat and Sun, noon–9pm Thurs and Fri. US$7/£3.50 adults, US$5 children 6–12) exhibits mainly North American and European art from 1885–1945. Collections include work from Art Nouveau artist and architect Charles Rennie Mackintosh and Arts and Crafts practitioner William Morris, plus collections of historical political propaganda and American industrial design.

Within walking distance of the Wolfsonian, **ArtCenter/South Florida** on Lincoln Road *305 674 8278* ***www.artcentersf.org*** (open 11am–10pm daily. Free) is a collection of eclectic artists' studios and exhibition space whose fun, sometimes challenging, work appeals to teenagers.

and turtles as well as numerous species of seabird. The main attractions are Seaquarium's animal shows, of which Lolita the killer whale is the star, Salty the sea lion the cheesiest and Flipper the dolphin the most famous – the original **Flipper** TV show was filmed here. The Dolphin Harbor area runs a programme of dolphin interaction sessions, all of which need to be booked in advance and come with an extra fee attached.

Open *9.30am–6pm daily.* ***Admission*** *US$32 (£16) adult, US$25 (£12.50) children aged 3–9, under 3s free.* ***Credit*** *AmEx, MC, V.* ***Amenities*** *Parking $7 (£3.50). Disabled access. Cafés. Shop. Baby-change facilities.*

Parrot Jungle Island ★

1111 Parrot Jungle Trail 305 400 7000 ***www.parrotjungle.com***

One of Miami's more expensive family attractions, Parrot Jungle Island takes half a day to explore and is recommended for children who love birds and primates. The

FUN FACT Left-handed Parrots

Most parrots are left-handed.

hundreds of macaws, cockatoos, parrots and other exotic birds are as loud as they are colourful – get up close to them in Manu Encounter, a large walk-through aviary, or in the nursery where newly fledged birds are raised. Other animals include a host of entertaining primates – look out for twin orang-utans Peanut Butter and Pumpkin Pie – and ligers, hybrids of lions and tigers with distinctive striped and spotted fur. 'Winged Wonder' features birds performing amazing tricks and is one of three animal shows to watch. In the Everglades Habitat, visitors travel via wooden boardwalks through a recreation of south Florida's famous landscape to encounter a striking albino alligator. Bring swimming costumes so you can splurge down a massive waterslide on the beach, and if the squawking birds get too much, the calm flamingo lake will soothe all fraught nerves.

Parrot Jungle Island

Open *10am–6pm daily.* ***Admission*** *US$28 (£14) adults, US$23 (£11.50) children aged 3–10 under 3s free.* ***Credit*** *AmEx, MC, V.* ***Amenities*** *Parking US$7 (£3.50). Disabled access. Café. Shop. Baby-change facilities.*

Miami's Top Historic Attractions

Spanish Monastery

16711 W. Dixie Hwy, North Miami Beach ☏ *305 945 1461* ***www.spanishmonastery.com***

Controversial newspaper tycoon William Randolph Hearst bought this medieval Spanish monastery in Segovia in 1925 and had it dismantled and shipped to North America. Despite his intention to rebuild the monastery in his Californian home, financial troubles forced Hearst to sell it before it was unpacked and the new owners brought the pieces to Miami to be reconstructed. Today this charming monastery is a working Episcopal church. Older children might not be interested in a visit, but the tranquil grounds and peaceful cloisters are pleasant to amble around with little ones.

Open *10am–4pm Mon–Sat, noon–4pm Sun.* ***Admission*** *US$5 (£2.50) adults, US$2 (£1) children under 12.*

Venetian Pool

Venetian Pool ★★★

2701 DeSoto Boulevard, Coral Gables ☎ 305 460 5356 ***www.venetianpool.com***

Tucked away in a shady corner of Coral Gables in south Miami, the Venetian Pool was an unsightly limestone quarry until it was transformed in the 1920s into one of the most enchanting places in the world to swim. The pool is fed by sparkling spring water and surrounded by pink stucco towers, palm trees, waterfalls and caves, while Venetian bridges lead over its stunning blue waters. Despite its beauty and upmarket location, the Venetian Pool is a municipal swimming pool and popular with locals. The warm waters and magical surroundings make for a pleasant break from salty seawater and chlorine-soaked hotel pools.

Open *11am–5.30pm Tues–Fri, 10am–4.30pm Sat and Sun.* ***Admission*** *US$10 (£5) adults, US$5.50 (£2.75) children aged 3–12, no under 3s (proof of age may be required).* ***Amenities*** *Café.*

INSIDER TIP

When visiting the Venetian Pool, take a quick peek at the nearby world-famous Biltmore Hotel ***www.biltmorehotel.com*** on Anastasia Avenue.

Vizcaya Museum and Gardens ★★★

3521 S Miami Avenue ☎ 305 250 9133 ***www.vizcayamuseum.org***

This sumptuous neo-Renaissance villa was built on the banks of Biscayne Bay in the early 20th century as a winter residence for Chicago industrialist James Deering. It's a must for families who enjoy exploring stately homes. Miami's most breathtaking attraction is entered via a fountain-strewn walkway into a museum crammed with fabulous furnishings from all over Europe. Each room is decorated in a different style and in amongst all the gorgeous antiques you'll discover an old telephone switchboard and an outdoor swimming pool reached from a grotto beneath the house.

The highlight for children of the large, formal French and Italian gardens is an orange jasmine maze, and the Venetian water landing commands expansive waterfront views towards Key Biscayne.

Open *9.30am–4.30pm.* ***Admission*** *US$12 (£6) adults, US$5 (£2.50) children aged 6–12, under 6s free.* ***Credit*** *AmEx, MC, V.* ***Amenities*** *Café. Shop. Disabled access. Baby-change facilities.*

Miami's Child-Friendly Museums

Miami Children's Museum ★★

980 MacArthur Causeway ☎ 305 373 5437 ***www.miamichildrensmuseum.org***

The two floors of this imaginative museum are filled with interactive exhibits designed for pre-school age children. Through the arts, culture and lifestyle-orientated exhibits, children are encouraged to learn through play skills, including how to look after pets, how banks work and what goes on inside the human body. They can also explore Miami's neighbourhoods, record music in a sound studio and peek behind the scenes of a TV studio.

After all that learning they can bounce around slides and tunnels in the Castle of Dreams.

Open *10am–6pm daily.* ***Admission*** *US$10 (£5) adults, children under 12 months free.* ***Credit*** *MC, V.* ***Amenities*** *Parking US$1 (50p) per hour. Shop. Café. Baby-change facilities*

Miami Science Museum ★

3280 South Miami Avenue ☎ 305 646 4200 ***www.miamisci.org***

Aiming to make science easy to understand, this museum is entertaining and informative and contains around 140 hands-on exhibits revealing secrets of the universe to young minds. At the adjoining Wildlife Center, visitors view reptiles and rehabilitating birds and the arachnophobics in your family can face their fears by petting a tame tarantula. A visit includes an astronomy show ★★ at the adjacent Space Transit Planetarium as well as numerous demonstrations requiring audience participation.

Open *10am–6pm daily.* ***Admission*** *US$20 (£10) adults, US$13 (£6.50) children aged 3–12, under 3s free.* ***Credit*** *MC, V.* ***Amenities*** *Shop. Disabled access. Baby-change facilities.*

Miami's Child-Friendly Tours

Duck Tours ★

1665 Washington Avenue, South Beach ☎ 786 276 8300 ***www.ducktoursmiami.com***

Take your children on the 'quackiest' way to see Miami. Otherwise you'll be too embarrassed travelling around style-conscious Miami in a giant duck-shaped vehicle. That said, these 90-minute tours on land and water are an entertaining way to discover Miami, especially if you have limited time. Tours leave from Watson Island near Parrot Jungle (see p. 177) and depart every hour between

The Metro Dade Cultural Center

Situated in the heart of Miami's downtown, the Mediterranean-style Metro Dade Cultural Center contains two first-class and inexpensive draws. **The Historical Museum of Southern Florida** ★ *305 375 1492* ***www.hmsf.org*** (open 10am–5pm Mon–Sat, noon–5pm Sun. US$5/£2.50 adults, US$2/£1 children aged 6–12, under 6s free) promotes an understanding of the history of south Florida and the Caribbean through stories. The recreations of old Miami are good for children to engage with, and the old photographs of the city are worth the entrance fee alone for adults.

On the other side of the courtyard, the **Miami Art Museum** ★★ *305 375 3000* ***www.miamiartmuseum.org*** (open 10am–5pm Tues–Fri, noon–5pm Sat and Sun. US$5/£2.50 adults, under 12s free) exhibits art from the 20th century to the present day. Every second Saturday of the month is family day, when admission after 1pm is free for parents and children, and live music, storytelling and games liven up the exhibitions for young ones.

9am and 6pm daily. Tickets cost US$32 (£16) for adults, US$18 (£9) for children, under 3s free.

South Beach Bike Tours

305 673 2002 ***www.southbeachbiketours.com***

Two-and-a-half-hour cycling tours around the famous and infamous nooks and crannies of the Art Deco Historic District are both informative and fun. Experienced guides lead cyclists through the history of the area and take in film locations, celebrity homes and cool hotels. Tours depart daily at 10am from the junction with 5th Street and Washington Avenue and reservations must be made in advance by phone or at the Art Deco Welcome Center on Ocean Drive (see p. 175).

Tickets *US$50 (£25) per person including refreshments.* ***Credit*** *MC, V.*

INSIDER TIP

The tranquil Deering Estate at Cutler ***www.deeringestate.org*** on the edge of Biscayne Bay to the south of Miami organises half-day naturalist-led canoe tours through the mangroves that hug the bay's coastline. Children over 9 can join a tour and tickets cost US$25 (£12.50) for adults, US$15 (£7.50) for children aged 9–14. For more information and to make reservations call *305 235 1668.*

Miami's Shopping Hot Spots

In a city that personifies style, it comes as no surprise that Miami's streets contain sophisticated shopping to indulge all budgets and age groups.

Bal Harbour Shops

Collins Avenue, just north of the SR-22 ***www.balharhourshops.com***

FUN FACT Miracle Mile

Miracle Mile is only half a mile long.

Anyone seeking designer brands at bargain prices gravitates to Bal Harbour Shops on Miami's North Beach, with its exclusive but generic stores and valet parking.

Bayside Marketplace, Downtown *www.baysidemarketplace.com*
More orientated towards tourists, this downtown waterfront marketplace on Biscayne Boulevard is suited to shopping with young children and contains a fairground carousel, comic stores, funky T-shirt shops and souvenir stalls plus reasonably priced family dining options.

Flagler Street, Downtown
Flagler Street offers affordable Miami fashion and big chain stores such as Macy's, but has none of the glamour of other shopping areas.

Lincoln Road, South Beach
www.lincolnroadmiamibeach.com
Designed in 1957 and saved through millions of dollars worth of restoration, the pedestrianised section of Lincoln Road, with its palm trees and Art Deco fountains, is shopping heaven for the fashion-conscious teen, who'll be hard pushed to decide between surf wear and cute boutiques.

Miracle Mile, Coral Gables
A family highlight of Coral Gables's Miracle Mile is Boy Meets Girl ☎ *305 445 9668,* a designer clothes shop for newborns to pre-teens and one of the distinctly upmarket clothes and gift shops on this famous road – look out for the Jedi master post boxes.

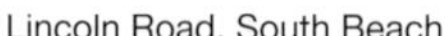

Lincoln Road, South Beach

THE SOUTH EAST COAST

Fort Lauderdale

Three hours' drive from Orlando and less than an hour from Miami, Fort Lauderdale is an inviting mix of relaxed beach and smart downtown, whose cultural and historic attractions, and great shopping, will appeal to all ages. Fort Lauderdale is known as the Venice of America thanks to hundreds of miles of inland waterways, many lined with exclusive houses, others with sleek shops and restaurants.

Getting out on to the water is an essential part of any visit (see "Child-friendly Tours," p. 187). An entertaining and inexpensive way to travel on Fort Lauderdale's waterways is by water bus ☎ *954 467 6677* **www.watertaxi.com**. The service runs between Oakland Park Boulevard and South East 17th Street and its stops are convenient for many of the city's attractions. Day passes cost US$10 (£5) and a map and timetable are available online or from the visitor information centre (see p. 168).

Once famous for its regular deluge of spring breakers, Fort Lauderdale has cleaned up its image and today you're more likely to find locals reading or jogging on its fine beach. However, the real appeal of these palm-lined sands is that they are not dominated by high-rise resorts and are accessible from an oceanfront promenade that's enjoyable to stroll along. The teen-focused Beach Place, with its shops, restaurants and bars, forms the focal point, but you don't have to walk far to find a peaceful spot to play if you've small children. Watch out for the turtle nests dotted in the soft sand in season (May to early autumn) and marked with yellow tape.

North of Beach Place, Bonnet House ☎ *954 563 5393* **www.bonnethouse.org** was once the home of American artist Frederic Clay Bartlett and today visitors can explore his beautiful old house and studios – children enjoy the gardens and ponds where you'll spot monkeys, swans and even the odd manatee.

The swish Las Olas Boulevard (see p. 189) leads inland from the beach to Fort Lauderdale's downtown – a charismatic blend of gleaming new buildings and charming historic district. The main tourist draws here are the waterfront Stranahan House ☎ *954 524 4736* **www.stranahanhouse.org**, an old trading post restored to provide an intimate glimpse into the life of an early settler, and the Museum of Discovery and Science (see p. 187).

The most relaxing and enjoyable thing for families to do together is simply meander along Fort Lauderdale's tropical Riverwalk, a shady, brick walkway where you can take in the sights – old and new – shop and enjoy lunch at one of the inviting restaurants (see p. 195).

Fort Lauderdale

Best Beaches & Beach Communities

Deerfield ★★ FIND

www.deerfield-beach.com

With its rustic pier reaching out into the Atlantic and busy, friendly waterfront, Deerfield Beach is one of the south east coast's best-kept secrets and a great place for families to chill out away from the commercialisation of the region's more famous beaches. This is a young, vibrant beach where picnic tables nestle beneath shady palm trees and volleyball courts are strewn along its golden sands. A paved walkway stretching along the edge of the beach contains accommodation options and a range of places to eat – try Kelly's Ocean Grill ☎ *954 421 4550* next to the pier for inexpensive burgers and sandwiches, or JB's on the Beach ☎ *954 571 5220* ***www.jbsonthebeach.com*** for pasta, seafood and paninis. Parking is metered with a 4-hour limit (US$1.50/75p per hour) and is hard to find when the beach is very busy. Alternative parking is available at North Ocean Drive, one block east of SR-A1A.

INSIDER TIP

Just north of Pompano Beach on SR-A1A, Hillsboro Inlet Park is a perfect place to picnic with small children. This picturesque spot overlooks an old lighthouse and has a children's play area, picnic tables, toilets and a large ship's bell commemorating the keepers of the lighthouse.

Top Family Attractions

Ah-Tah-Thi-Ki Museum

Big Cypress Seminole Reservation 17 miles north of I-75 at exit 49 ☎ *863 902 1113* ***www.ahtahthiki.com***

Located on the large Big Cypress Reservation inland of Fort Lauderdale, the Ah-Tah-Thi-Ki Museum is the place to bring children who want to learn about the traditions and culture

Three Beach Parks

Florida's south east coast is home to several parks containing family-friendly beaches and other outdoor activities. South of Fort Lauderdale, the broad beach at **John U Lloyd State Park** is a favourite with nesting sea turtles and if you're in the area in June or July, book a place on their turtle awareness programme *954 923 2833* – you can visit the beach at night to view females coming ashore to nest. **Red Reef Park** near Boca Raton spreads over both sides of SR-A1A and contains the **Gumbo Limbo Nature Center** (see p. 186) and a boardwalk leading to a quiet beach popular with small children and snorkellers. Also in Boca Raton, **Spanish River Park** on SR-A1A contains a large children's play area, nature trail, viewing tower and lagoon as well as a glorious beach. All of these parks charge a small fee for cars.

of Florida's Seminoles – the only Native American Indian tribe who did not sign a peace treaty with the US government. The museum consists of a living village where Seminoles work with traditional crafts, exhibitions of rare clothing and artefacts and a mile-long boardwalk leading into Cypress Swamp containing interpretive boards explaining the function of different plants.

Deerfield Beach

A visit includes an impressive five-screen film detailing historical and cultural information about the tribe. Billie Swamp Safari Wildlife Tours are connected to the museum and run airboat and swamp buggy tours into Big Cypress Reservation, ***www.seminoletribe.com/safari***.

Open *9am–5pm daily.* ***Admission*** *US$6 (£3) adults, US$4 (£2) children aged 4–12, under 4s free.* ***Credit*** *AmEx, MC, V.* ***Amenities*** *Shop. Disabled access.*

Butterfly World

Tradewinds Park, 3600 W Sample Road, Coconut Creek 954 977 4400 ***www.butterflyworld.com***

Butterfly World contains around 5,000 multicoloured butterflies in lush tropical surroundings and a collection of exotic hummingbirds and macaws that eat out of your hand. The recreated rainforest environment, complete with mist-filled cave and waterfall, is an evocative habitat to explore, and the Bug Zoo

FUN FACT **Butterflies Life**

Butterflies live for around seven days in the wild.

contains millions of amazing insects – children love it. No food is allowed in the park but there is a picnic area near the entrance.

Open *9am–5pm Mon–Sat, 11am–5pm Sun, last admission 4pm.* ***Admission*** *US$22 (£11) adults, US$16 (£8) children aged 3–11, under 3s free.* ***Credit*** *AmEx, MC, V.* ***Amenities*** *Shop. Cafe. Disabled access. Baby-change facilities.*

Children's Museum of Boca Raton at Singing Pines

498 Crawford Boulevard, Boca Raton 📞 *561 368 6875* ***www.cmboca.org***

Located in one of the oldest houses in Boca Raton (circa 1912), 17 miles north of Fort Lauderdale, this tiny museum is for children aged between 3 and 12. All the exhibits are designed to stimulate their imagination and contain activity centres where they can play at shopping, creating works of art and making postcards to send to friends.

Open *Noon–4pm Tues–Sat.* ***Admission*** *US$3 (£1.50) per person, infants free.* ***Amenities*** *Baby-change facilities.*

Gumbo Limbo Nature Center

★★★

1801 North Ocean Boulevard, Boca Raton 📞 *561 338 1473* ***www.gumbolimbo.org***

The Gumbo Limbo tree is known as the 'tourist tree' because of its red, peeling bark and the nature centre named after it is a fabulous facility where children can learn about the plants and animals found in the area. Located inside Red Reef Park (see p. 185), the nature centre contains large sea-water tanks filled with all kinds of marine life, some of which are being nursed back to health – try to coincide your visit with

Museum of Boca Raton

feeding times (2.30pm daily or 11am on Saturdays) as children love to watch the sharks' frenzy. A boardwalk leading through the surrounding hardwood hammock ends at a 40-ft observation tower from which you can gaze down at the surrounding tree canopy or out to the Atlantic, where on a clear day you can spy the Gulf Stream. Many families combine a visit to this centre with time on the surrounding beautiful beach, where sea turtles come to lay their eggs in season.

Open *9am–4pm Mon–Sat, noon–4pm Sun.* ***Admission*** *Free.* ***Amenities*** *Shop. Disabled access. Baby-change facilities.*

INSIDER TIP

Although most of the collections in Boca Raton's Sport Immortals Museum *561 997 2575* ***www.sportsimmortals.com*** feature North American sports, its amazing memorabilia includes a pair of Muhammad Ali's boxing gloves and a football signed by Pele.

Museum of Discovery and Science ★★

401 SW 2nd Street, Fort Lauderdale 954 467 6637 ***www.mods.org***

An enormous and wacky gravity clock (tell the time by counting balls) marks the entrance and sets the scene for this inventive museum designed for children. The interactive exhibits are equally entertaining for adults and it's easy to while away a couple of hours exploring the likes of Gizmo City, which explains how science infiltrates all aspects of our lives. Aimed at under-7s, the Discovery Center is an educational play area designed to stimulate young minds and the IMAX cinema screens a changing programme of documentaries throughout the day.

Open *10am–5pm Mon–Sat, noon–6pm Sun, extended IMAX hours most evenings.* ***Admission*** *US$10 (£5) adults, US$8 (£4) children aged 2–12, under 2s free exhibits only; US$9 (£4.50) adults, US$7 (£3.50) children IMAX only; combination tickets available.* ***Credit*** *AmEx, MC, V.* ***Amenities*** *Café. Shop. Picnic area. Baby-change facilities. Disabled access.*

Child-Friendly Tours

Jungle Queen

801 Seabreeze Boulevard (SR-A1A), Bahia Mar Beach Resort 954 462 5596 ***www.junglequeen.com***

The **Jungle Queen** is a majestic old riverboat whose entertaining sightseeing trips explore Fort Lauderdale's maze of inland waterways, taking in exclusive neighbourhoods and historic districts along the way. Narrated tours depart at 9.30am and 1.30pm daily and travel all the way to the edge of the Everglades. Trips include a stop at a recreated Native American village where visitors are treated to a round of alligator wrestling.

Rates *US$16 (£8) adults, US$11 (£5.50) children under 12.* ***Credit*** *MC, V.*

INSIDER TIP

The three-hour *Jungle Queen* Cruise is long for small children. Take a water bus instead (see p. 183); you'll still a get a taste of Fort Lauderdale's waterways but youngsters won't get bored.

The *Jungle Queen*

Sawgrass Recreation Park ★

1005 N. Hwy-27, Fort Lauderdale 📞 *954 389 0202* ***www.evergladestours.com***

A short drive from Fort Lauderdale brings you to the edge of Big Cypress Swamp, a vast flat expanse of land dotted with small cypress trees and shallow marshes. Sawgrass Recreation Park, on the edge of the swamp, runs daily airboat tours that whizz visitors out into this extraordinary subtropical environment, riddled with native wild and bird life. Tours last 30 minutes, throughout which the captain shares stories of the Seminole tribe and region's wildlife.

First tours leave at 9am, after which they depart every half an hour until 5pm. Reservations are not required. ***Admission*** *US$20 (£10) adults, US$10 (£5) children aged 4–12, under 4s free.* ***Credit*** *MC, V.* ***Amenities*** *Shop.*

For more information on airboat tours, see p. 185.

For Active Families

Bar-B-Ranch

3500 Peaceful Ridge, Davie 📞 *954 424 1060* ***www.bar-b-ranch.com***

Located west of Fort Lauderdale in the small community of Davie, Bar-B-Ranch is the place to saddle up and try your hand at horse riding on one of the ranch's scenic guided trails. Rides last 90 minutes. The ranch caters to first-time and experienced riders, but children must be seven or over to join in. Rates start at US$45 (£22.50) per person and advance reservations are required.

Hugh Taylor Birch State Park

3109 East Sunrise Boulevard 📞 *954 564 4521* ***www.floridastateparks.org/hughtaylorbirch***

Just north of Fort Lauderdale's beach, the Hugh Taylor Birch State Park stands on the edge of a calm intercoastal waterway where visitors can rent canoes and paddle a long freshwater lagoon. Walking trails lead through tropical hammocks and its shady picnic tables are a pleasant alternative to the beach.

***Open** 8am until sunset. **Admission** US$5 (£2.50) per car.*

Shopping

Las Olas Boulevard, Fort Lauderdale

www.lasolasboulevard.com

This isn't the area to come with the children to souvenir shop, visit Beach Place for that (see p. 183), but older children will enjoy browsing through the clothes, gifts and accessories shops or sipping coffee in one of the cafés along this exclusive street.

Mizner Park

433 Plaza Real, Boca Raton www.miznerpark.com

Minutes from Boca Raton's beach, Mizner Park mall contains a range of shops and family-friendly places to eat. It is right next door to the town's impressive Museum of Art *www.bocamuseum.org*

Saw Grass Mills

12801 West Sunrise Boulevard, Sunrise www.sawgrassmills.com

At the other end of the shopping spectrum from Las Olas, Saw Grass Mills is a bargain-hunter's heaven, containing a branch of Ron Jon's surf shop and lots of factory outlets. If the children get bored with shopping, take them to Wannado City *www.wannadocity.com*, a role-playing theme park where they get to act out different career choices.

FAMILY-FRIENDLY ACCOMMODATION

VERY EXPENSIVE

Aqualina, A Rosewood Resort

17875 Collins Avenue, Sunny Isles Beach ☎ 305 918 6777 www.aqaualinaresort.com

Styled around a Mediterranean hotel, this ultra luxurious resort with its marble floors, large chandeliers and multiple beachfront pools is the place to stay if you want to pamper your children as much as yourselves. A large proportion of this exclusive resort's visitors is families and it's easy to see why, as rooms include children's bathrobes and rubber ducks for the bath. The AquaMarine Kids Program organises a multitude of different activities for young guests each day, from cookery classes to underwater photography, and evening 'popcorn, dinner and a movie' sessions leave parents free to enjoy Miami's nightlife.

***Rooms** 97. **Rates** Winter US$675–US$950 (£338–475) double, US$1,075–US$5,000 (£538–2,500) suite; off season US$425–US$675 (£213–338) double, US$775–US$5,000 (£388–2,500) suite. **Credit** AmEx, MC, V. **Amenities** Three restaurants. Three pools. Bar. Luxury spa. Watersports equipment rental. Valet parking US$25 (£12.50). **In room** A/C. TV. Wi-Fi Internet. Safe. CD player.*

Miami Beach

The majority of Miami's accommodation is located on the beach, as this is where most visitors stay. Many of South Beach's hotels don't accept children, rooms are on the small side in the old Art Deco buildings and this is an adult area at night. Exceptions include the Comfort Inn and Suites 1238 Collins Avenue 📞 *305 531 3406* ***www.choicehotels.com*** whose basic accommodation includes rooms and suites (rooms US$109–US$149/£54.50–74.50, suites US$129–US$149/£64.50–74.50), Best Western South Beach 1050 Washington Avenue 📞 *305 674 1930* ***www.bestwestern.com*** (rooms US$105–US$139/£52.50–69.50) and Days Inn South Beach at 21st Street and Collins Avenue 📞 *305 538 6631* ***www.daysinn.com*** (rooms US$80–US$140/£40–70). With some of South Beach's hotels you have to pay to park in a municipal car park overnight as the old buildings have limited on-site facilities.

As South Beach gives way to Miami's central and north beach areas, sprawling high-rise resorts characterise the ocean front and families won't have any problems finding accommodation. Budget options here include Howard Johnson Plaza Hotel 8701 Collins Avenue 📞 *305 865 6661* ***www.hojo.com*** (rooms US$99–US$140/£49.50–70), Days Inn 4299 Collins Avenue 📞 *305 673 1513* ***www.daysinn.com*** (rooms US$80–US$190/£40–95) and two Best Westerns – Atlantic Beach Resort 4101 Collins Avenue 📞 *305 673 3337* (rooms US$120–US$170/£60–85) and Ocean Front Resort 9365 Collins Avenue at Bal Harbour 📞 *305 864 2232* (rooms US$150–US$200/£75–100) ***www.bestwesternflorida.com.***

Miami's high season is January to March, when visitors arrive to escape winter elsewhere. Low season runs from June to August, when temperatures, humidity and rainfall can be high, but accommodation rates drop by as much as half. In between these two periods, the weather is still hot and bargains can still be found.

EXPENSIVE

Loews Hotel ★

1601 Collins Avenue, South Beach
📞 *305 604 1601* ***www.loewshotels.com***

Situated smack in the middle of the Art Deco district, you can stay in style on South Beach with children in this luxury, child-friendly resort. Butting up against the waterfront, guests can either sunbathe on the sand or laze around a large, landscaped pool. The Loews Loves Kids programme provides children with a special welcome gift and programme of activities throughout the day, while teenagers are treated as VITs (Very Important Teens) and given a welcome backpack on arrival. The hotel's babysitting service leaves parents free to enjoy South Beach's nightlife or one of the resort's own luxury restaurants.

Rooms *790 rooms, 52 suites.* ***Rates*** *Winter from US$400 (£200), low season from US$250 (£125). Valet parking US$19 (£9.50).* ***Credit*** *AmEx, MC, V.* ***Amenities*** *Pool. Jacuzzi. Three restaurants. Three bars. Watersports equipment rental. Café. Spa. Fitness centre.* ***In room*** *A/C. Cable TV. Internet access.*

MODERATE

Thunderbird Beach Resort

18401 Collins Avenue, Sunny Isles Beach ☎ 305 931 1700 ***www.thunderbirdresortmiami.com***

Located in north Miami's Sunny Isles Beach, and once a hang out for Hollywood's legendary Rat Pack, the Thunderbird Beach Resort is a good value for money, family-friendly hotel that's popular with European package tourists. The beach is quieter in this area and the resort's pool is large enough to accommodate all those who prefer its heated, calm waters. A large supermarket, delis and restaurants are all within walking distance and the resort operates free shuttle buses to the Adventura shopping mall and South Beach.

Rooms *180.* ***Rates*** *US$80–US$140 (£40–70).* ***Credit*** *AmEx, MC, V.* ***Amenities*** *Pool. Bar. Café. Jacuzzi. Children's pool. Hairdressers/beauty salon. Shop. Free parking.* ***In room*** *A/C. Cable TV. Safe. Fridge. Kitchenettes in some rooms.*

Elsewhere in Miami

Key Biscayne's laid-back atmosphere makes it a popular choice for visiting families and one that is still close to excellent beaches and all the major attractions. One of the nicest and cheapest accommodation options in this area is the Silver Sands Beach Resort ☎ *305 361 5441* ***www.key-biscayne.com/accom/silversands/*** (rooms US$129–US$169/£64.50–84.50, cottages US$279–US$329/£139.50–164.50, weekly rates available). A decent chain option in Coral Gables is the Extended Stay America 3640 SW 22nd Street ☎ *305 443 7444* ***www.extendedstayhotels.com*** (rooms US$100–US$110/£50–55). And for those needing to stay near Miami's airport there are a host of chain motels to choose from, including the Airways Inn and Suites 5001 NW 36th Street ☎ *305 883 4700* ***www.miamiairwaysinnandsuites.com*** (rooms US$80/£40) which provides a 24-hour airport shuttle service.

If you're also planning to split your visit with the Florida Keys and Everglades you can stay in the cheaper chain motels in Florida City, from which it will take about an hour to drive into Miami. See the Family-Friendly Accommodation section of The Florida Keys and Everglades chapter, p. 221.

Biscayne Bay

EXPENSIVE/VERY EXPENSIVE

Ritz Carlton Key Biscayne

455 Grand Bay Drive, Key Biscayne
305 365 4500 ***www.ritzcarlton.com***

Ritz Carlton has created an exclusive tropical island sanctuary in this large oceanfront resort. The beach area is very family friendly and the resort's swimming pools are nestled amongst acres of tropically landscaped gardens. The Ritz Kids children's programme caters for the 5 to 12-year-old age range and features tonnes of activities that will make them not want to leave the resort. And after a hard day taking in Miami's attractions, the casual oceanfront restaurants are a perfect place to end the day.

Rooms *402.* ***Rates*** *Winter US$450–US$590 (£225–295) double-suite, low season US$260–US$490 (£130–245) double-suite.* ***Credit*** *AmEx, MC, V.* ***Amenities*** *Restaurant. Café. Three bars. Two pools. Whirlpool. Fitness centre. Spa. Watersports equipment rental.* ***In room*** *A/C. Cable TV. Internet access. Safe.*

EXPENSIVE

Boca Raton Resort and Club

501 E Camino Real, Boca Raton
561 395 3000 ***www.bocaresort.com***

This distinctive 1920s luxury resort is set in large landscaped grounds that contain a number of leisure facilities and its own half-a-mile-long private beach. I like this resort because the sheer amount of activities guests can enjoy ensures that children won't have time to get bored, and if parents want time off alone, Camp Boca is an excellent children's programme for ages 3–11. In addition to the numerous restaurants, a number of family-orientated films are screened in the evening to keep guests occupied well into the night.

Rooms *963.* ***Rates*** *Winter US$290–US$760 (£145–380) double, low season US$190–US$495 (£95–247.50)* *double.* ***Credit*** *AmEx, MC, V.* ***Amenities*** *Water park. Fitness centre. Beach activities and cruises. 12 restaurants. Six bars. Six pools. Spa.* ***In room*** *A/C. Cable TV. Safe.*

MODERATE

Bahia Mar Beach Resort

801 Seabreeze Boulevard, Fort Lauderdale 1 888 802 2442 ***www.bahiamarhotel.com***

At the south end of Fort Lauderdale's Beach, Bahia Mar stands on the edge of a large marina where boat trips depart and water buses stop. This resort is also a short walk from the lively Beach Place and close to the city's downtown and Riverwalk areas, making it a good base for families who don't want to do a lot of driving in order to see Fort Lauderdale's sights. There are plenty of activities to keep older children occupied and a quiet stretch of beach nearby where all ages are safe to play. Children under 12 eat free with a paying adult at the resort's restaurants.

Rooms *300.* ***Rates*** *US$80–US$200 (£40–100).* ***Credit*** *AmEx, MC, V.* ***Amenities*** *Swimming pool. Fitness centre. Restaurant. Bar. Shop.* ***In room*** *A/C. Cable TV. Safe.*

The Pelican Grand Resort ★★

2000 North Ocean Boulevard, Fort Lauderdale 954 568 9431 ***www.pelicanbeach.com***

Just north of Fort Lauderdale's beach, this popular resort is ideal for families. The rooms have a separate living room area so parents can relax and watch TV while children sleep, and all have private balconies overlooking a glorious beach. A fabulous wraparound oceanfront veranda is a perfect place to relax while the children mess around in the heated pool, and the on-site shops sell ice cream and children's confectionery. But it's the small touches, such as board games that can be borrowed in the lobby, that make this exceptionally friendly, laid-back resort one of the best places to stay in the south east.

Rooms *159.* ***Rates*** *US$90–US$120 (£45–60). Valet parking US$15 (£7.50).* ***Credit*** *AmEx, MC, V.* ***Amenities*** *Restaurant. Bar. Swimming pool. Water ride. Shop/ice cream parlour.* ***In room*** *A/C. Cable TV. Fridge. Wi-Fi Internet.*

The Rest of the South East Coast

Deerfield Beach has two beachside options: the Comfort Inn Oceanside 50 S Ocean Drive *954 428 0650* ***www.comfortinnoceanside.com*** (rooms US$120–US$200/£60–100), which has a large pool with a waterslide and mini golf on site, and the Howard Johnson Plaza Resort 2096 NE 2nd Street *954 428 2850* ***www.thehojo.com/deerfieldbeach00450*** (rooms US$150–US$270/£75–135). At Boca Raton, the Best Western University Inn 2700 N Federal Hwy *561 395 5225* ***www.bestwestern.com*** (rooms US$70–US$90/£35–45) is a good budget chain option.

FAMILY-FRIENDLY DINING

Miami

MODERATE

Big Pink ★

157 Collins Avenue, South Beach ✆ *305 532 4700* ***www.bigpinkrestaurant.com***

One of the most family-friendly options on South Beach, Big Pink actively encourages children to eat here and not worry about making a noise to distract other diners. Which is just as well, because this restaurant is famous for its long tables and bar stools, so there's little privacy but lots of fun to be had. The American-style food of pizzas, burgers, sandwiches and salads is prepared under the motto of 'Real Food for Real People' and the enormous portions are surprisingly good. I particularly recommend their all-day breakfasts.

Open *8am–midnight Mon–Wed, 8am–2am Thurs, 8am–5.30am Fri–Sun.* ***Main Courses*** *US$7–US$20 (£3.50–10).* ***Credit*** *AmEx, MC, V.* ***Amenities*** *Children's menu.*

Californian Pizza Kitchen

300 Miracle Mile, Coral Gables ✆ *305 774 9940* ***www.cpk.com***

The Coral Gables branch of this small county-wide chain is one of the better family-friendly restaurants on the upmarket Miracle Mile. This is a laid-back, but still stylish, eatery whose menu includes a varied range of pizzas, pasta, sandwiches and salads. The children's menu for the under-10s has an unusually high number of options and choice of pizza, pasta and salads, including healthy options and free drink refills.

Open *11.30am–10pm Sun–Thurs, 11.30am–11pm Fri and Sat.* ***Main Courses*** *US$5–US$18 (£2.50–9).* ***Credit*** *MC, V.* ***Amenities*** *Children's menu. Highchair.*

Jerry's Famous Deli ★★★

1450 Collins Avenue, South Beach ✆ *305 5328 030* ***www.jerrysfamousdeli.com***

Jerry's Famous Deli is a Miami institution and well frequented by locals and visitors alike. This large, white Art Deco building stands on the corner of Collins Avenue and Espanola Way and its décor, complete with large ceiling fans, old framed photographs and 50s ambience, will hold even the most active child's attention. However, it's the enormous menu I love, including sandwiches, steaks, burgers, pizzas, pasta and fabulous breakfast dishes, but leave plenty of time to make up your mind, as the options are endless. You can sit outside and watch South Beach life pass by or inside in a large booth and be entertained by TV shows.

Open *24 hours.* ***Main Courses*** *US$11–US$20 (£5.50–10).* ***Credit*** *AmEx, MC, V.* ***Amenities*** *Children's menu.*

Rascal House ★

17190 Collins Avenue, Sunny Isle ✆ *305 947 4581*

Sister restaurant to Jerry's Famous Deli (see above), this no frills,

Jerry's Famous Deli, South Beach

vintage family-friendly American diner in Miami's North Beach opened in 1954 and claims to have served an estimated 60,000,000 meals since. The reasonably priced menu features fountains and floats, soups, salads, sandwiches and baked potatoes. Breakfasts are my favourite, with an amazing range of baked treats available from the on-site bakery. However, portions are enormous and you're almost expected to take away what you can't manage. There's no children's menu but half sandwiches are available and there's plenty for every taste.

Open *7am–10pm Sun–Thurs and until 11pm Fri and Sat.* ***Main Courses*** *US$10–US$20 (£5–10).* ***Credit*** *AmEx, MC, V.*

INEXPENSIVE

Pasha's ★

900 Lincoln Road, South Beach
☎ 305 673 3919 ***www.pashas.com***

This small Miami chain has a number of branches dotted around the city, including a funky branch in the South Beach. Situated in the middle of the bustling Lincoln Road, older children and teens will love the comfy couches and small stalls, but all ages are welcome in this friendly restaurant. The healthy Mediterranean-style menu includes inexpensive wraps, kebab platters and numerous vegetarian options.

Open *8am–midnight Sun–Thurs, 8am–1am Fri and Sat.* ***Main Courses*** *US$4–US$12 (£2–6).* ***Credit*** *MC, V.*

The Rest of the South East Coast

INEXPENSIVE/MODERATE

Briny Riverfront Irish Bar and Restaurant

305 S Andrews Avenue, Fort Lauderdale ☎ 954 376 4742

Decorated with a distinctly nautical theme, the Briny is the place to head for if you're missing a family-friendly pub atmosphere and craving a pint of beer. Children will love its crazy décor and scenic views of a small drawbridge over the river, where you can watch boats as they drift through. The menu is famous for its homemade burgers, large sandwiches and wraps, all served with fries, as well as good old pub grub including shepherd's pie and bangers and mash, making this a good choice if your children are missing familiar food.

***Open** for lunch and dinner. **Main Courses** US$8–US$15 (£4–7.50). **Credit** MC, V.*

Oasis Café

600 Seabreeze Boulevard, Fort Lauderdale ☎ 954 463 3130

Situated across the road from Fort Lauderdale's beach and close to numerous hotels, the Oasis Café is perfect for lunch or dinner if you're having a day on the sand, as its outdoor seating is sheltered from the sun and cooled by a sea breeze. You can rock back and forth in swinging outdoor booths – you have to see them to understand what I mean, but children love them. The relatively small menu features a range of sandwiches, wraps, salads and pizzas and while there's no children's menu, the starters are good for small appetites.

***Open** for lunch and dinner. **Main Courses** US$8–US$18 (£4–9). **Credit** MC, V.*

INEXPENSIVE

Ugly Tuna

300 SW 1st Avenue, Fort Lauderdale ☎ 954 467 8862 ***www.uglytunasaloona.com***

There are two sides to this informal and laid-back restaurant on Fort Lauderdale's popular Riverwalk. One side features an outdoor and at times noisy bar, but the other, better for families, side includes a quieter seating area with pleasant views overlooking the river itself. The menu is mainly seafood and includes traditional English fish and chips for US$10 (£5), there is also a range of sandwiches, salads and pastas, but few options for vegetarians. The small children's menu includes fish and chicken dishes and comes along with fish-themed cartoons to colour in.

***Open** for lunch and dinner. **Main Courses** US$5–US$10 (£2.50–5). **Credit** MC, V. **Amenities** Children's menu. Highchair.*

8 The Florida Keys & Everglades

THE EVERGLADES

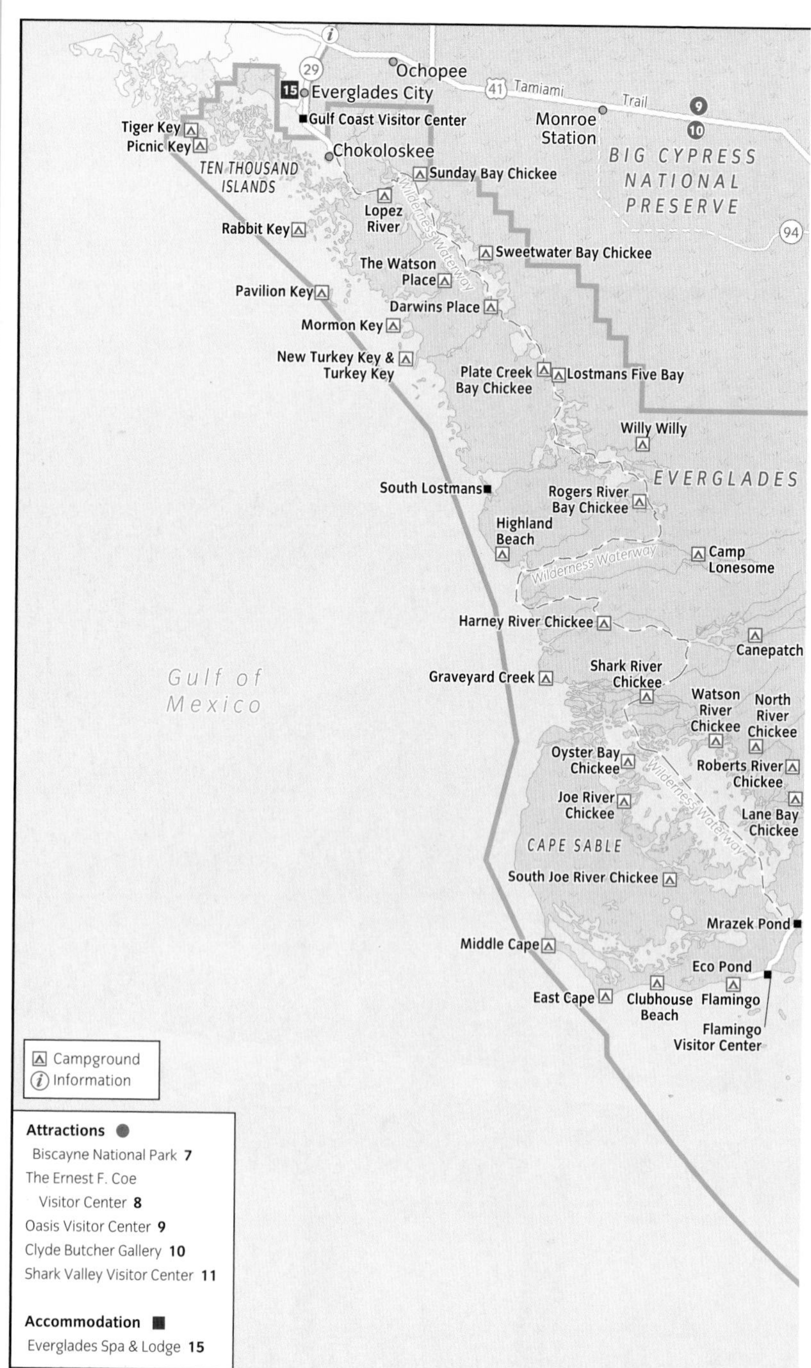

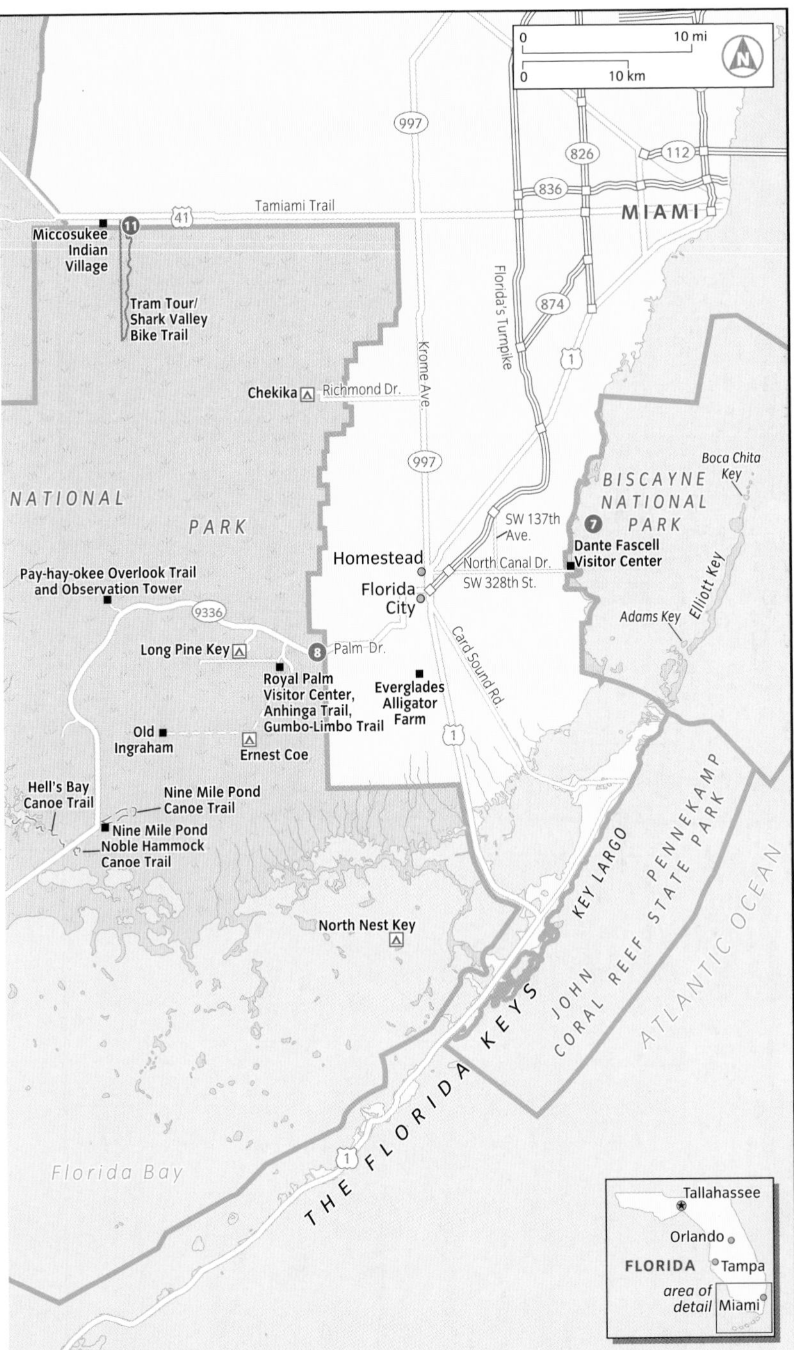

0
10 mi
0
10 km
N
997
826
112
836
MIAMI
Tamiami Trail
41
Miccosukee Indian Village
11
Tram Tour/ Shark Valley Bike Trail
Florida's Turnpike
874
Krome Ave.
1
Chekika
Richmond Dr.
997
NATIONAL
PARK
BISCAYNE NATIONAL PARK
Boca Chita Key
SW 137th Ave.
7
Dante Fascell Visitor Center
Homestead
North Canal Dr.
SW 328th St.
Florida City
Elliott Key
Adams Key
Pay-hay-okee Overlook Trail and Observation Tower
9336
Card Sound Rd.
Long Pine Key
8
Palm Dr.
Royal Palm Visitor Center, Anhinga Trail, Gumbo-Limbo Trail
Everglades Alligator Farm
Old Ingraham
Ernest Coe
1
Hell's Bay Canoe Trail
Nine Mile Pond Canoe Trail
Nine Mile Pond
Noble Hammock Canoe Trail
KEY LARGO
JOHN PENNEKAMP CORAL REEF STATE PARK
ATLANTIC OCEAN
North Nest Key
THE FLORIDA KEYS
Florida Bay
1
Tallahassee
Orlando
FLORIDA
Tampa
area of detail
Miami

FLORIDA KEYS

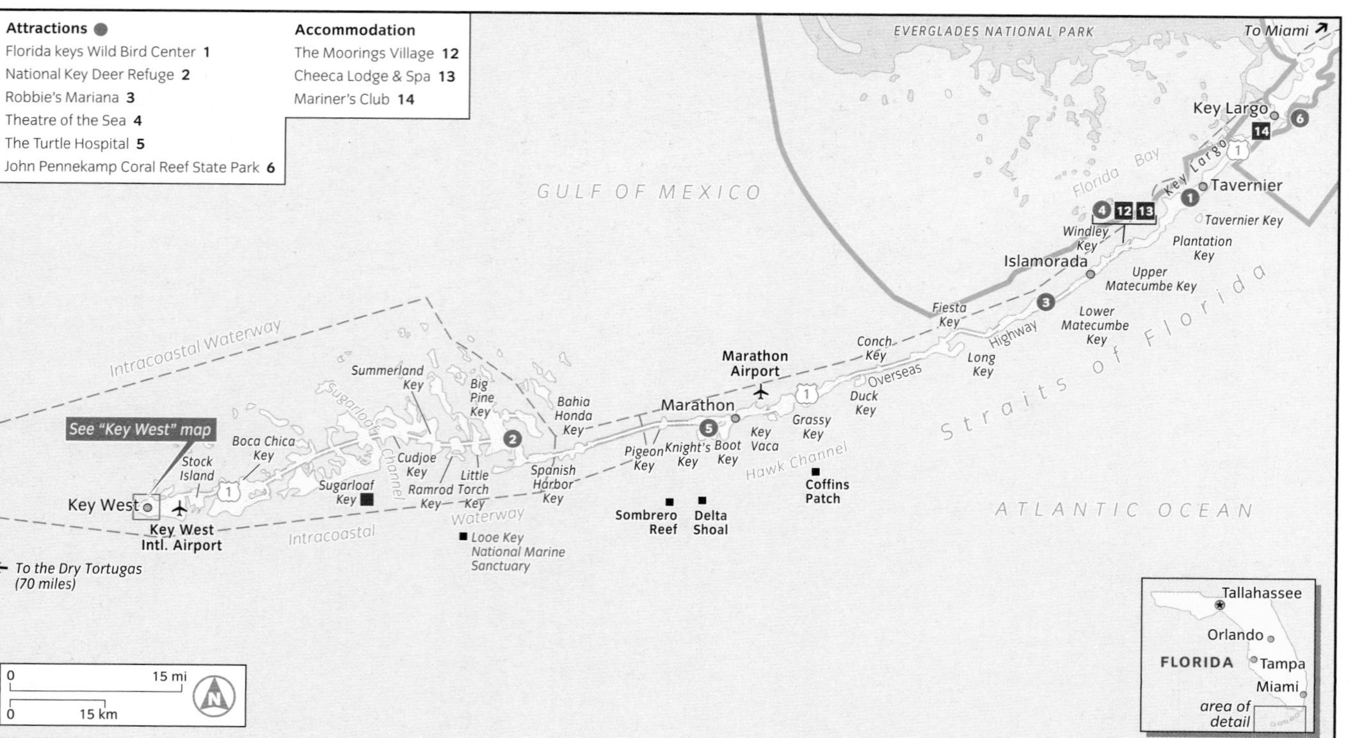

The two regions that make up Florida's southern tip couldn't be more different in personality. The vast, endangered, Everglades tumble off dry land as Florida falls into the Gulf of Mexico and provide many ways for outdoor-loving families to delve deep into intricate ecosystems and encounter endless birdlife, fragile flora and the ubiquitous alligator. Dangling off the edge of Florida, the chain of islands leading east to west known as the Florida Keys is the place to kick back and relax. The main draw for children in the Upper and Middle Keys is their many animal-focused attractions, where they can learn about rescue and rehabilitation programmes and get up close and personal to all kinds of marine species and birdlife. Key West, at the end of Hwy-1, is bursting with character and characters, and its vibrant, if eccentric, atmosphere and rich history of pirates, sunken treasure and wreckers has a natural appeal to young visitors. However, both these unique regions constantly negotiate a precarious existence in a region dominated by water. Any visit to either the Everglades or the Florida Keys is enriched by getting off dry land to experience reef-protected translucent seas, home to a myriad of exotic fish and colourful corals, or the tangled maze of mangrove-lined waterways that blend into these two incredible landscapes.

ESSENTIALS

Getting There

By Plane The main airport in the Florida Keys is the Key West International Airport, situated in the north east corner of the island on 3491 South Roosevelt Boulevard ☎ *305 296 7223* ***www.keywestinternationalairport.com***, which receives flights from Miami, Fort Lauderdale, Fort Myers, Orlando, Tampa and Naples operated by various American airlines (see p. 33). Most visitors to the Keys who arrive by air fly into Miami International Airport (see p. 167) and hire a car (see p. 29). Miami is also convenient for the eastern side of the Everglades. For visitors to the west side of the Everglades, the closest airport is Naples Municipal Airport ☎ *239 643 0733* ***www.flynaples.com***, which runs regular scheduled flights between Naples and Key West operated by Yellow Air Taxis ☎ *1 888 935 5694* ***www.flyyellowairtaxi.com.***

By Car From central Florida or the east coast including Miami, take the Florida Turnpike to Florida City and join Hwy-1, the main road to the Florida Keys. From the west, join SR-997 at either the junction with Hwy-27 or Hwy-41 to join Hwy-1 at Florida City. Key Largo is about half an hour from Florida City, Key West is approximately a further 2 hours' drive.

Goodland Island

If you're driving to the Everglades from the west, Goodland is a little-known place to break a journey with children. This ramshackle old fishing village is situated south east of Marco Island off SR-92, which branches south from Hwy-41. You'll find a cluster of friendly waterfront seafood restaurants including Little Bar *239 394 5663*, Old Marco Lodge Crab House *239 642 7227* and Stan's Idle Hour *239 394 3041*, and Island Woman *239 642 6166,* a quirky gift, clothes and jewellery shop. As you drive out of Goodland back to Hwy-41, the bridge off the island provides a stunning view over the Ten Thousand Islands, a large cluster of tiny deserted mangrove islands strewn around the Everglades' north west coastline.

INSIDER TIP

Hwy-1 is extremely busy with traffic into the Keys on a Friday afternoon, especially in winter, and out of the Keys on a Sunday afternoon. Avoid travelling at these times, as you will end up sitting in your car for hours.

The only way to reach the Everglades is by car. From the west, join Hwy-41, the main road into the Everglades, at Naples. From the east, follow directions to Florida City (see p. 201), the gateway into the Everglades.

By Ferry Key West is served by the Key West Express *1866 593 3779* ***www.seakeywestexpress.com*** ferry service from Fort Myers (see p. 109) and Miami (see p. 168).

VISITOR INFORMATION

The Florida Keys Visitor Centre on Hwy-1 at MM106 (Bayside) is located in Key Largo as you arrive at the Keys. *305 451 1414* ***www.keylargochamber.org*** (open daily 9am–6pm).

In Key West, visitor information can be obtained at the Greater Key West Chamber of Commerce 402 Wall Street, Key West *305 294 2587* ***www.keyschamber.org*** (open 8.30am–6.30pm Mon–Fri, 8.30am–6pm Sat and Sun).

Tourist information centres are also located in Islamorada *305 664 4503* ***www.islamoradachamber.com***, Marathon *305 743 5417* ***www.floridakeysmarathon.com*** (open 9am–5pm daily) and the Lower Keys *305 872 2411* ***www.lowerkeyschamber.com.***

The UK website for visitor information to the Florida Keys is ***www.fla-keys.co.uk*** and for more information *01564 79499*.

INSIDER TIP

In late October the week-long Fantasy Fest (***www.fantasyfest.net***), Key West's annual colourful

Bacchanal, takes place. If you're planning a visit at this time, book accommodation well in advance.

The Everglades Chamber of Commerce 239 695 31 72 *www.evergladeschamber.org* is housed in a large wooden triangular building at the junction of Hwy-41 and SR-29 north of Everglades City and is good for information on the National Park and various tour operators in the region (open 9am–4.30pm daily). On the east side of the Everglades, the visitor centre 305 245 9180 *www.tropicaleverglades.com* is located on the same grounds as the Fairway Inn on Hwy-1 in Florida City and contains information on the Everglades, Florida Keys and Miami (opening times vary). Also check *www.evergladesonline.com* for more information on this area.

Orientation

There is only one road through the Florida Keys: Hwy-1, also known as the Overseas Highway because its 42 bridges connect over 100 islands along the 126-mile route. Every address along Hwy-1 is identified by its Mile Markers (MM), indicated by small signs dotted the length of the road, starting at MM0 in Key West at the junction of Fleming and Whitehead Streets and ending at MM127 just south of Homestead. Each address is also identified as either Bayside or Oceanside, indicating which side of the highway it is on, with everything on the north being Bayside and everything on the south Oceanside.

In the Everglades, SR-29 branches south from Hwy-41 in the west to lead into Everglades City and Chokoloskee on the coast. In the west, SR-9336 travels from Florida City to Flamingo and is the only road into the Everglades National Park.

Getting Around

The only way to get around the Florida Keys and Everglades is by car. For details of car hire, see p. 29.

Child-friendly Festivals & Events

Earth Day Celebration
Every April, Cheeca Lodge in Islamorada (see p. 222) 305 267 1845 *www.cheeca.com* organises an event in celebration of Earth Day. Activities include live music, sand sculpting, a beach barbeque and environmental education booths. Whether you're staying at the resort or

Highway of Bridges

Over 18 miles of the Overseas Highway consist of bridges, with the longest spanning nearly 7 miles.

not, this is an entertaining day out for the whole family.

Independence Day Celebrations, Islamorada
Every 4th July, Islamorada, the Village of Islands, celebrates with a family day of activities at the beach and at Founders Park, MM87. The festivities include a bouncy castle, clowns and family playground.

Pirates In Paradise
Over a long weekend in late November or early December, Key West and Fort Taylor are transformed into a pirates' stronghold and all visitors are encouraged to shiver their timbers and join in the celebrations. Pirate entertainers and arts-and-craft stalls are enjoyed on land while out to sea, tall ships and pirate sails take to the waters in this celebration of Key West's maritime history.

305 296 9694 ***www.piratesinparadise.com***

WHAT TO SEE & DO

Children's Top Five Attractions

1. Snorkelling at John Pennekamp Coral Reef State Park; p. 215.

2. Feeding tarpon at Robbie's Marina; p. 212.

3. Learning about the environment at the Florida Keys Eco-Discovery Center; p. 207.

4. Shopping along Key West's eclectic Duval Street; p. 211.

5. Taking a tram or bicycle ride through Shark Valley; p. 220.

INSIDER TIP
Whatever the time of year, bring plenty of mosquito repellent when visiting the Florida Keys and Everglades.

Key West

Key West stands at the southernmost point of continental USA and its distinct devil-may-care identity is more influenced by its Caribbean neighbours than any legislation from Washington – hardly surprising considering it's only 90 miles from Havana but 150 miles from the nearest Wal Mart. Proud of its lawless past, rich with pirates and wreckers, Key West and its party atmosphere has a noticeable ambivalence towards the present, and its sun-drenched streets will impress on children a very different experience of the Sunshine State from Miami or Orlando.

Southernmost Point, Key West

KEY WEST

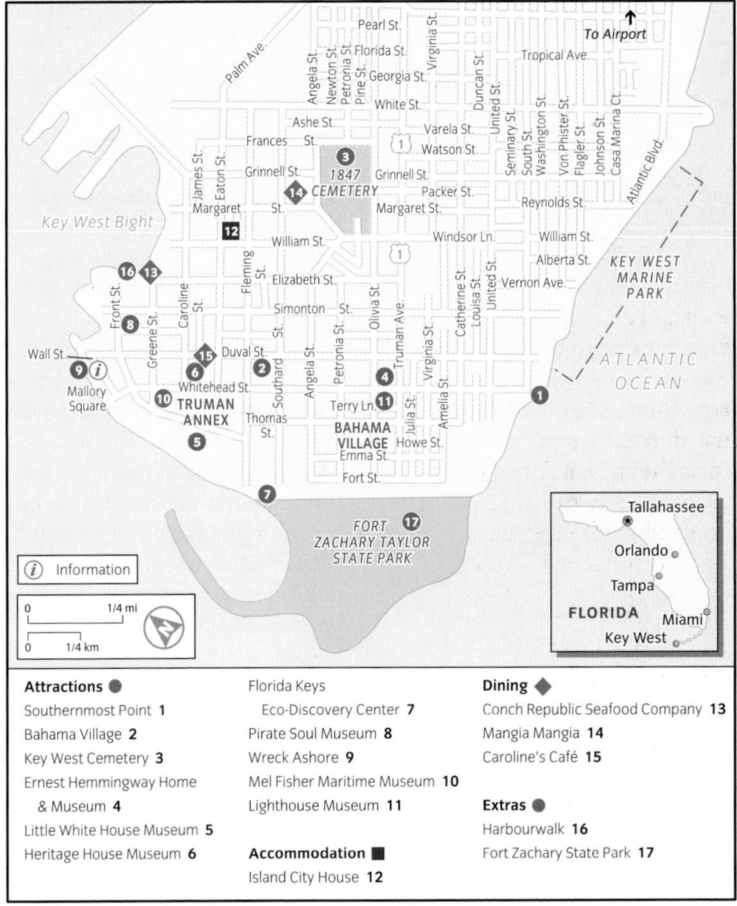

The best way to start a visit is to walk around the bustling streets of the attractive Old Town, Key West's historic heart, but if the heat's too much, or your children are too small to walk, take a trolley tour instead (see p. 210), which will provide some insight into the city's attractions. Most of Key West's attractions are on or around Duval Street, the famous shop- and restaurant-filled road, which leads from the waterfront near Mallory Square to the southernmost point. One block to the west, a large red, yellow and black buoy marks the southern tip of continental USA.

At the other end of Duval Street, near the waterfront, life picks up apace. The nearby tourist-focused Mallory Square, with its free-roaming chickens and multitude of market stalls bursting with all kinds of tourist

FUN FACT Conch Republic

In Key West, the term 'conch' (pronounced conk) is used to describe someone born there. The whole city is known as the Conch Republic after it unofficially declared a one-minute war and secession from the United States in protest at road blocks set up to search for Cuban refugees in the 1980s.

fare from hula girl garlands to hand-woven hats, is brilliant to explore with children of all ages. Tourists, locals and street performers gather in Mallory Square each evening to celebrate the setting sun ***www.sunsetcelebration.org*** – ironic considering this is one of the worst places on the island to see the sun set – but an essential part of any visit nonetheless.

INSIDER TIP
Watch your wallet in Mallory Square; it's a favourite haunt for pickpockets.

West of Duval Street, off Petronia Street, is an area known as Bahama Village, whose streets lined with old wooden houses, the former homes of Cuban cigar rollers, are an oasis of calm away from Key West's more touristy districts. Shop for souvenirs at Bahama Village Market.

East of Duval Street, with an entrance at the corner of Angela and Frances Streets, the Key West Cemetery might seem a morbid place to bring children, but with gravestones featuring such epitaphs as 'I told you I was sick', 'devoted fan of singer Julio Iglesias' and 'a good citizen for 65 of his 108 years', a visit can be more fun than you think.

INSIDER TIP
Key West is a cycle-friendly town, and visitors and locals use bikes to get around. Bikes with children's

Tourist Train passes Sloppy Joe's

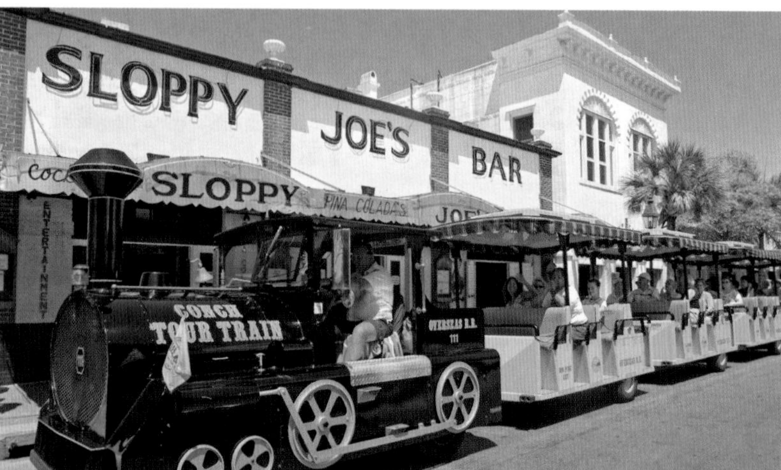

Famous Key West Residents

It's impossible to separate Key West's history from that of its most famous residents. Undoubtedly the most well known is author Ernest Hemingway, whose beautiful old Spanish colonial-style home on Whitehead Street, where he wrote *A Farewell to Arms*, is one of Key West's most visited historic sights ☎ *305 294 1136* ***www.hemingwayhome.com***. Hemingway was a regular at Sloppy Joe's, although it's debatable whether the bar of the same name on the corner of Greene and Duval Streets was really the author's favourite watering hole; Captain Tony's Saloon on Greene Street, once also called Sloppy Joe's, claims this honour.

While never a resident, President Harry S. Truman was a frequent visitor to Key West and the Little White House on Front Street ☎ *305 294 9911* ***www.trumanlittlewhitehouse.com*** was his favourite retreat – it functioned as the White House for 175 days of his presidency. Tours of this simple house provide a glimpse into a small piece of American history.

Tucked away on Caroline Street, the appealing Heritage House Museum ☎ *305 296 3573* ***www.heritagehousemusuem.org*** contains a charming garden cottage where poet Robert Frost came to write in the winter. Tour guides dish up gossip on some of the famous visitors, including Tennessee Williams and Gloria Swanson.

With the exception of the hoards of six-toed cats that live in the grounds around the Ernest Hemmingway House and Museum, none of these places is engaging for small children.

attachments can be rented from Sunshine Rentals ☎ *305 294 9990* ***www.sunshinekeywest.com*** with outlets on Truman Avenue, Duval, Eaton and Greene Streets.

Key West's Family-Friendly Attractions

Florida Keys Eco-Discovery Center ★★★

35 East Quay Road (opposite Fort Zachary Taylor State Historic Site) ☎ *305 809 4750* ***www.floridakeys.noaa.gov/eco-discovery***

Owned and created by the Florida Keys National Marine Sanctuary, the Eco-Discovery Center opened in January 2007 and is one of the few child-focused exhibits in Key West. The centre contains interactive recreations of the landscapes found in the Keys, such as a Living Reef – peering through the plate glass at the myriad of sealife and living coral is as good as snorkelling but doesn't involve getting wet.

One exhibit allows you to 'Be The Manager' and decide, after listening to all the arguments, what you would do if you were in charge of the Florida Keys' different natural environments.

Eco-Discovery Center

And have the outcomes of your decisions revealed.

See the mock-up of Aquarius, the world's only underwater ocean laboratory, where marine scientists live and work; NASA astronauts are sent here to get used to isolation. Other activities include a virtual 1,600ft dive, the opportunity to check local weather and reef conditions and an impressive film about the Keys made by the cinematographer from *Free Willy*.

***Open** 9am–4pm Tues–Sat. **Admission** Free. **Amenities** Shop. Disabled access. Baby-change facilities.*

INSIDER TIP

An old WW2 Mohawk combat ship docked at the waterfront adjacent to the Florida Keys Eco-Discovery Center has been converted into a museum *305 799 1143* ***www.ussmohawk.org.***

Pirate Soul Museum ★

524 Front and Simonton Streets 305 292 1113 ***www.piratesoul.com***

There's nothing subtle about this proud-to-be-a-pirate family attraction, which urges all visitors to swash their buckle and get in touch with their inner Captain Kidd. Any child remotely interested in pirates will love this place, as its themed exhibitions contain fascinating artefacts including a genuine pirates' treasure chest and original Jolly Roger flag. Recreations of Jamaica's Port Royal and the demise of Blackbeard bring the so-called Golden Age of Piracy to life and the creators of this imaginative museum claim that if visitors look closely enough they'll spy a pirate's soul.

***Open** 9am–7pm. **Admission** US$14 (£7) adults, US$8 (£4) children*

A Wrecking Good Time

In the mid 19th century, Key West was the richest city in the southern US thanks to wrecking – the 'salvaging' of goods and wares from ships stricken on the region's perilous reefs. To find out more about Key West's wrecking history, pay a visit to Wreck Ashore! ☎ *305 292 8990* ***www.shipwreckhistoreum.com***, a wooden shipwreck historeum in Mallory Square where actors and exhibits recreate the shady world of Key West's wreckers in 1856. Try the Mel Fisher Maritime Museum on Greene Street ☎ *305 294 2633* ***www.melfisher.org*** where discoveries from wrecks stretching back to the late 15th century have been spruced back to their former glory. For a panoramic view of Key West's treacherous waters and to learn more about its lighthouse, visit the Lighthouse Museum on Whitehead Street ☎ *305 294 0012* ***www.kwahs.com/lighthouse.***

aged 10 and under. ***Credit*** *MC, V.* ***Amenities*** *Shop. Disabled access. Baby-change facilities.*

Key West's Child-Friendly Tours

Ghost Tours of Key West ★★

These creepy tours are a fun way of discovering Key West's ghostly goings on for any child not afraid of things that go bump in the night. The lantern-lit tours, led through the shadowy corners of the city's darkest streets, last around 90 minutes and cover a mile and a half of Key West's 'most haunted' streets. Buy a ticket if you dare from the Ghost Tour shop at the corner of Duval and Fleming Streets, open 11am–11pm ☎ *305 294 9255* ***www.hauntedtours.com***.

Tours depart at 8pm and 9pm daily. ***Tickets*** *US$15 (£7.50) adult, US$10 (£5) children aged 4–12, under 4s free.* ***Credit*** *MC, V.*

Liberty Tall Ships ★★

Pier B, Westin Marina, Key West ☎ *305 292 0332* ***www.libertyfleet.com***

One of the most memorable ways to experience the seas around Key West for all ages is to take a cruise on one of the Liberty Fleet's traditional tall ships. These graceful old ladies of the sea provide visitors with a real feel for the region's sea-faring past and

Wreck Ashore!

Fort Jefferson & the Dry Tortugas

The Florida Keys don't end at Key West, but 70 miles further west at the Dry Tortugas **www.nps.gov/drto** – a designated National Park consisting of seven islands, the largest featuring the huge Fort Jefferson. These remote grassy islands are home to an amazing array of bird and marine life and a perfect day out for families who love to snorkel, bird watch or hike. Children can pick up a free Junior Ranger handbook from the visitor centre to learn about the park's history and wildlife. Two ferries serve the park from Key West: the *Yankee Freedom* ☎ *305 294 7009* ***www.yankeefreedom.com*** departs at 8am from the seaport on Margaret Street and returns at 5.30pm (tickets US$129/£64.50 adults, US$89/£44.50 children under 16, food and snorkelling equipment included). The faster and cheaper Sunny Days Catamaran ☎ *305 292 6100* ***www.drytortugas.com*** departs Key West at 8am and returns by 5pm (tickets US$120/£60 adults, US$85/£42.50 children under 16. Food, snorkelling equipment and a tour of the fort included). If you prefer to arrive in style on a trip your children will never forget, hop aboard a seaplane ☎ *305 294 0709* ***www.seaplanesofkeywest.com***, which will fly you there in next to no time and provide breathtaking views of the Keys along the way (tickets US$199/£99.50 adults, US$149/£74.50 children aged 6–12, US$119/£49.50 children aged 2–6, under 2s free).

close-up views of its glorious sunsets. Tours include food, drink and commentary from the captain and are the right length to hold children's attention, although for adults it's impossible not to feel disappointed when you arrive back on dry land.

Tours depart in the morning, afternoons and at sunset. ***Tickets*** *US$35–US$57 (£17.50–28.50) adults, US$25–US$35 (£12.50–17.50) children 12 and under.* ***Credit*** *MC, V.*

Trolley Tours ★★

Get to know Key West and its history via its informative and fun trolley tours. Two companies run regular tours: the Conch Tour Train's ☎ *305 294 5161* ***www.conchtourtrain.com*** 90-minute tours depart at regular intervals from Mallory Square from 9am–4.30pm, or you can hop on and off the Old Town Trolley at any of its stops around the

Key West Clipper

Lime Pie Shoppe

city 📞 *305 296 6688* **www.historic tours.com**. Tickets to both cost US$27 (£13.50) adults and US$13 (£6.50) children aged 4–12, under 4s free. Call ahead for wheelchair-accessible vehicles.

Key West's Shopping Hot Spots

Duval Street, with its eccentric mix of clothes and gift shops, and arts, crafts and cigar stalls, is a shopper's paradise – allow plenty of time to browse. Tucked away towards the marina, Harborwalk offers brightly painted arts and craft shops and stalls but no visit to Key West is ever complete without a trip to Kermit's Key West Key Lime Pie Shoppe on the corner of Elizabeth and Greene Streets 📞 *800 376 0806* **www.key limeshop.com**, where you'll be amazed at just how many things you can do with a Key Lime – I've even seen the eccentric owner pretending to fling pips at the tram tours as they pass by his shop. If your children are bored with writing postcards, head to the Key West Kite Store on Greene Street 📞 *305 296 2535* **www.keywestkites. com** where for US$20 (£10) you can send a message on a coconut instead.

The Florida Keys' Top Animal Attractions

Florida Keys Wild Bird Center ★

Hwy-1 at MM93.6 (Bayside), Tavernier
📞 *305 852 4486* **www.fkwbc.org**

Dedicated to nursing and rehabilitating sick and injured birds, the Florida Keys Wild Bird Center consists of several large, ramshackle cages housing rescue birds, most of which are released back into the wild as soon as possible. However, it's the more permanent residents that provide the entertainment. Pickle the cockatiel will do anything to grab children's attention and imitates a telephone answering machine and the 'beeps' of a reversing truck to keep them entertained. All kinds of animals have made their home around the centre and you'll spy lazing cats and feeding squirrels as you wander around. At 3.30pm the wild birds are fed by the ocean – if you hear footsteps behind you, it's likely to be a cheeky pelican seeing if you've left the odd snack in your pocket.

***Open** 8.30am–6pm daily. **Admission** Free, donations requested.*

National Key Deer Refuge ★

Hwy-1 at MM33 (Bayside), Big Pine Key ☎ 305 872 0774 ***www.fws.gov/nationalkeydeer***

Key deer, with their enormous brown eyes, large ears and white-tipped tails, are as cute as they are endangered, and most of the remaining population lives on Big Pine Key. Although they are free to wander wherever they like, the refuge is the best place to catch a glimpse of the deer, with good times for viewing being early in the morning or at dusk when the temperatures are cooler. If you're here in the spring, visiting the refuge is a must, as this is the season when hinds give birth to tiny fawns. Never feed the deer, it's illegal and reduces their chances of survival.

***Open** Sunrise–sunset daily. The visitor centre inside the Big Pine Shopping Center is open 8am–5pm Mon–Fri. **Admission** Free.*

INSIDER TIP

The speed limit of a section of Hwy-1 drops to 45mph in the day and 35mph at night as it passes through Big Pine Key in an attempt to reduce the number of deer deaths through collisions with cars.

Tarpon Feeding at Robbie's Marina ★★

Hwy-1 at MM84.5 (Bayside), Islamorada ☎ 305 664 9814 ***www.robbies.com/tarpon***

The owners of Robbie's Marina first fed an injured tarpon 31 years ago. Today, masses of these giant fish swish around in the water waiting to be fed. Spending US$3 (£1.50) on a bucket of fish to feed the tarpon guarantees slapstick fun, as they jump high out of the water to snatch food from your hands before splashing back into the sea. A webcam is poised over the feeding spot, so your children can text their mates to get them to watch the action online at home. And once your fish run out, Robbie's Hungry Tarpon café and the jewellery stalls make this a friendly place to hang out. Alternatively, join one of the regular snorkelling trips or eco tours.

***Open** 8am–5pm. **Admission** US$1 (50p) to enter the marina.*

Theatre of the Sea ★

Hwy-1 at MM84.5 (Oceanside), Islamorada ☎ 305 664 2431 ***www.theatreofthesea.com***

Theatre by the Sea opened in 1946 and is the oldest marine land in the world. Despite its age, the park has risen to the challenge of keeping up with the modern world and its enormous lagoon and holding tanks are

FUN FACT **Tarpon**

Tarpon can grow up to 8 ft long.

Swimming with Dolphins in the Keys

A number of attractions along Hwy-1 offer visitors the opportunity to interact or swim with dolphins. For more information about how to choose which organisation to visit, see p. 34 of Chapter 2.

filled with rescue animals that can't be released back into the wild. You'll see turtles, countless tropical birds, iguanas, a rather shy owl and an ever-increasing number of cats, which live around the gift shop.

It's easy to spend a day here, as there are lots of animal shows to watch, with performing sea lions, dolphins and parrots plus a glass-bottom boat ride to take. A small beach area, where visitors can snorkel with parrot and angel fish, is open from 11am–4pm and is a good opportunity for children who don't want to snorkel in the sea to see some marine life. A number of animal encounters are in place for an extra fee (book in advance) for those who want to interact with sea lions, sting rays or dolphins, but Theatre by the Sea endeavours to keep the amount of time its animals interact with humans to a minimum. There are also snorkel cruises into the Atlantic and Florida Bay for US$69 (£34.50) adults and US$45 (£22.50) children (children must be over three to participate).

Mimi at Theatre of the Sea

Open *9.30am–5pm daily, ticket office closes at 4pm.* ***Admission*** *US$24 (£12) adults, US$16 (£8) children aged 3–12, under 3s free.* ***Credit*** *AmEx, MC, V.* ***Amenities*** *Disabled access. Baby-change facilities. Café. Shop. Snorkel equipment hire US$3 (£1.50).*

The Turtle Hospital ★★

Hwy-1 at MM48.5 (Bayside), Marathon
305 743 2552 ***www.turtlehospital.org***

The Turtle Hospital started life as a motel with a saltwater pool; however, when a storm surge from hurricane William damaged the building, the hotel was ditched and the owners concentrated their efforts on saving sea turtles instead. Today, visitors are given a fascinating glimpse into the efforts to care for the injured sea turtles brought to the hospital. Most are rehabilitated into the wild but others, like April

Bahia Honda

who is almost blind and has to be hand fed, have become permanent residents. Tours around the hospital last around 90 minutes.

Tours depart at 10am, 1pm and 4pm daily, reservations are required. **Admission** *US$15 (£7.50) adults, US$7.50 (£3.75) children aged 4–12.* **Credit** *MC, V.*

Getting Out Onto the Water

Biscayne National Park ★★

9700 SW 328th Street, Homestead *305 230 1100* ***www.nps.gov/bisc***

You'll wonder where on earth you're going when driving down 328th Street (North Canal Drive) surrounded by farmland and incongruous views of the Homestead Miami Speedway, but when the road runs out nine miles after the turning off Hwy-1, you'll arrive at Convoy Point and Biscayne National Park. North of the actual Keys, 95 per cent of this park is underwater, and the visitor centre, with its touch table for children and family-fun activities such as jetty bingo, is well set up to engage children with the surrounding environment.

However, you need to get out on the water to make a visit worthwhile. Glass-bottom boat tours depart at 10am and 1pm (US$25/£12.50 adults, US$17/£8.50 children under 12) and allow visitors to view some of the most astonishing coral reefs in the US. Snorkelling trips leave once a day at 1.30pm (US$35/£17.50 adults, US$30/£15 children under 12) and park

FUN FACT **Perky's Bat Tower**

Perky's Bat Tower – turn north after MM17 to reach it – was built in 1929 by businessman Ricter C Perky. He hoped his tower would host a thriving bat population, which would eat all the area's mosquitoes, so he could build a resort. Perky's tower was an outstanding failure; the bats never came and the resort was never built.

The Best Beaches in the Florida Keys

The Florida Keys are surrounded by the third-largest coral reef in the world, which protects the islands from storms and hurricanes, but prevents the waves that make sand from reaching the shore. As such, there are few natural beaches in the Keys and these three are the best options for children.

Fort Zachary Taylor State Historic Site ★★ Southard Street on Truman Annex is home to Key West's finest beach, whose glorious but rocky sands are well used by local families. You can also explore an old fort or rent kayaks and snorkelling equipment.

Bahia Honda State Park ★★★ off Hwy-1 at MM37 contains some of Florida's most beautiful beaches, with the palm-lined, white coral sands of Calusa beach at the western tip providing the best swimming. This popular state park also runs snorkelling tours and contains various amenities including a gift shop and snack bar.

Sombrero Beach off Hwy-1 at MM50 is a small beach, which gently slopes into impossible blue waters halfway along the Florida Keys. It contains a children's playground, picnic tables and plenty of shade.

rangers share their knowledge of the reefs before letting visitors loose to experience their beauty first hand. Canoes and kayaks can be rented to explore alone (US$12–US$16/£6–8 per hour).

Call in advance to book places on a tour and check that the marine conditions are suitable for boats to go out.

Open *9am–5pm.* ***Admission*** *Free.* ***Amenities*** *Shop. Picnic tables. Baby-change facilities.*

John Pennekamp Coral Reef State Park ★★★

Hwy-1 at MM102.5, Key Largo (Oceanside) ☎ *305 451 1202* ***www.pennekamppark.com***

John Pennekamp Coral Reef is an undersea state park reaching three miles into the Atlantic from dry land and stretching for around 25 miles along the coast. The park's visitor centre features displays, films and aquariums explaining the underwater environment, but the real reason to come here is to get out into the water for yourself. There are various ways to do this, catering for all age groups and abilities, including glass-bottom boat tours which depart at 9.15am, 12.15pm and 3pm (US$22/£11 adults, US$15/£7.50 children under 12) and each providing a window into the amazing aquatic world below. For a closer look, book a snorkelling tour; these depart at 9am, noon and 3pm (US$29/£14.50 adults, US$24/£12 children under 18) and accept any age as long as the child can swim. Kayak and boat rentals, sailing tours and diving instruction are available; book in advance during peak periods. For

FUN FACT African Queen

The African Queen boat that starred in the 1951 movie is moored in a marina next door to the Holiday Inn at MM100 near John Pennekamp Coral Reef State Park.

glass-bottom boat and snorkelling tours *305 451 6300*, for diving tours *305 451 6322* and for boat rentals *305 451 6325*.

Many organisations in the Keys operate snorkelling and diving tours, some with stronger environmental credentials than others. This state park is committed to protecting the fragile underwater world it allows visitors to experience and is recommended for all those concerned about the protection of the Keys' delicate reefs.

Open *Park 8am until sunset, visitor centre 8am–5pm.* ***Admission*** *US$3.50 (£1.75) one person, US$6 (£3) two people then an extra 50¢ (25p) for every additional member of your party.* ***Amenities*** *Shop. Takeaway. Picnic tables. Baby-change facilities. Changing rooms and showers. Glass-bottom boat tours and snorkelling vessels are wheelchair accessible, consult the park for details of participation in snorkelling and scuba diving.*

The Everglades National Park ★★★

305 242 7700 **www.nps.gov/ever**

A designated World Heritage Site, the Everglades National Park is a vast subtropical wilderness and most visitors will achieve little more than dipping their toes into these timeless, yet acutely fragile and endangered, 'rivers of grass'. Before visiting the Everglades, assure your children that the closer they look, the more the beauty of this intricate protected landscape, teeming with wildlife large and small, will reveal itself.

Kayaking in John Pennekamp State Park

INSIDER TIP

There are few places to buy petrol in the Everglades. Petrol stations are found in Everglades City and at the junction of Hwy-41/SR-29 on the west side, and Homestead and Florida City in the east.

INSIDER TIP

The only place to buy food and drink on the east side of the National Park is at Flamingo. Options here are limited and many visitors bring their own supplies.

The Everglades are so big that it takes first-time visitors some planning to tackle them and a lot depends on which side of the National Park you are. From the east, the park is entered via SR-9336 near Homestead; in the west it is entered in or around Everglades City. There are various places to stop along Hwy-41 (the Tamiami Trail, see p. 220), with Shark Valley being the most popular.

Via SR-9336

Most visitors enter the vast, eternally flat, subtropical wilderness of the Everglades from the east via SR-9336, which leads south west from Homestead and where everything is set up for day visitors.

The Ernest F. Coe Visitor Center

305 242 7700 (open 8am–5pm daily) is 12 miles from Homestead on SR-9336 and an essential stop before heading into the National Park. The imaginative displays help children understand the environment they are about to encounter, and its threats, through reconstructions of its habitats, such as the ominous gator holes and a 15-minute film. Make sure youngsters pick up a Junior Rangers booklet (see p. 210) to make a visit more entertaining for them. At the same time, pick up a timetable of ranger talks, walks and boat tours in the park and plan your visit accordingly.

When to Visit the Everglades

When planning a visit, be aware that the Everglades has two distinct seasons – wet and dry. Lasting from mid-December to April, the dry season is when the majority of visitors arrive – there are fewer insects and lower temperatures. The wet season, which runs from May until November, is very hot and humid and a significant rise in water levels causes the population of pesky biting insects to increase. This isn't a good time to bring children into the Everglades, the temperatures and insects will drive them mad and, with afternoon thunderstorms common, the number of ranger-led tours drops. For more information check the Everglades National Park's website ***www.nps.gov/ever***.

Robert is Here

SW 344th Street, Homestead ☎ *305 246 1592* ***www.robertishere.com***
It's impossible to miss Robert is Here, a massive fruit store on the side of the road leading to the Ernest F. Coe Visitor Center (see p. 217). Specialising in the rare and exotic, the store's shelves are crammed with sugar apples, key limes, passion fruit and papaya and many visitors call in on their way to the National Park to stock up on fruit and fluids to combat the heat and humidity of the glades. Established in 1959, the store is named after the founder's son who, at the age of 6, was sent to stand on the edge of the road to sell his father's cucumbers. After failing to sell any on the first day, Robert's father made a large sign proclaiming 'Robert Is Here'. The next day all the cucumbers were sold and a fruit store was born.

Open 8am–7pm daily. Closed Sept–Oct.

The official entrance to the National Park is south of the visitor centre (US$10/£5 per car) and from here, SR-9336 leads south west for 38 miles to Flamingo, passing several places where you can park and walk into the glades via a series of boardwalks and trails. Each leads deep into a different ecological zone and all have interpretive boards explaining the surrounding environments. Most of these trails are about half a mile long and easy for children to tackle. The minute you step away from the road, your senses are engulfed by the nature that surrounds you and the infinite beauty of this most subtle of natural wonders reveals itself.

INSIDER TIP

Never feed any wildlife you might encounter while in the Everglades.

At the time of writing, Flamingo, at the end of SR-9336, is still recovering after the 2005 hurricane season when it took severe batterings from Katrina, Rita and Wilma. There's currently little to see at the visitor centre, and the main reason to drive this far is to join one of the organised boat tours, which depart from the marina at 10am, 1pm and 3.30pm every day except Tuesdays and Wednesdays (US$18/£9 adults, US$10/£5 children aged 6–12, under 6s free). Leading deep into the waters that separate the Everglades from the Florida Keys, these tours are led by rangers who share their in-depth knowledge along the way.

Everglades City

On the west side of the Everglades, visitors head to Everglades City – a 45-minute drive from Naples and three miles south of Hwy-41 along

SR-29 – for a base from which to explore this side of the park. The glades have a different personality here, as the coastline fragments into the lush Ten Thousand Islands and this once-prosperous town, which had the life ripped out of its infrastructure by hurricane Donna in the 1960s, is now the haunt of fishermen and hunters.

If you're tackling the Everglades from the west, there's no formal entrance into the park and it can be confusing to know where to begin. Many visitors start at the Gulf Coast Visitor Center ☎ *239 695 2591* half a mile south of Everglades City on SR-29 (open 8.30am–5pm daily) and hop aboard one of their National Park Boat Tours, which depart every half hour from mid-December to mid-April (US$27/£13.50 adults, US$14/£7 children aged 5–12). These tours venture deep into the startling array of offshore waterways and a maze of mangrove islands, where you're likely to spy manatees, herons, alligators and even the odd dolphin.

INSIDER TIP

Hamilton Observation Tower stands behind the Everglades City Chamber of Commerce on SR-29 south of Everglades City and provides glorious views of the National Park and nearby Ten Thousand Islands (open office hours. US$2/£1 per person).

The Havana Café (open 7am–3pm Tues–Sat) is an excellent place to stop for breakfast before heading into the glades – it also serves fabulous Cuban sandwiches for lunch. The café is situated in the Chokoloskee Mall on SR-29 south of Everglades City. Consisting of only a post office and the café, this has to be the world's smallest shopping mall.

If you prefer to picnic, head to the Small Wood Store, an old Indian Trading Post built in 1906 ☎ *941 695 2989* on the waterfront

The Ernest F. Coe Visitor Center

Airboat Rides

As Hwy-41 approaches Miami, airboat tour operators compete furiously for tourists' attention and cash, and although these distinctive boats are synonymous with the Everglades, there are a number of factors to consider before taking one. Firstly they are very noisy, which could scare some young children. Some operators are more environmentally concerned than others and those that are not can cause damage through pollution, scarring the landscape and feeding the animals. If you are concerned about which operator to use, seek advice from one of the visitor centres.

in Chokoloskee (open 10am–5pm daily 1st Dec–1st May and 11am–4pm 2nd May–30th Nov) where you'll find picnic tables and magnificent views of the Ten Thousand Islands.

Driving Hwy-41 – the Tamiami Trail Hwy-41

Also known as the Tamiami Trail, runs from Naples in the west through Big Cypress Preserve and across the top of the Everglades National Park to Miami in the east. There are several places to stop and experience the Everglades along this road and it's important if you're travelling with children that you do stop, otherwise life will be very boring for them.

Situated 50 miles east of Miami, the Oasis Visitor Center *239 695 1201* (open 8.30am–4.30pm daily) has a good bookshop and a small boardwalk where you're guaranteed to encounter plenty of gators. Half a mile east, the gallery of award-winning landscape photographer Clyde Butcher *239 695 2428* ***www.clydebutcher.com*** features his breathtaking black and white images of the Everglades and Big Cypress Preserve and is an essential stop.

The closer to Miami Hwy-41 gets, the more tacky tourist attractions start to line the route. Head for the Shark Valley Visitor Center *305 221 8776* (open 9.15am–5.15pm. US$10/£5 per car) to get into the park. At this point a 15-mile trail with an observation tower at the end loops into the park and back again, which visitors can either walk, cycle (bike hire US$7/£3.50 per hour) or join a two-hour tram tour to explore. The narrated tram tours depart every hour on the hour from 9am–5pm (US$15/£7.50) and reservations are recommended between December and March.

For Active Families

Everglades Hostel

20 SW 2nd Avenue, Florida City
305 248 1122 ***www.evergladeshostel.com***

On the east side of the National Park in Florida City, the Everglades Hostel rents bicycles for US$15 (£7.50) per day along with bike racks for cars (US$6/ £3 per day) and will drop off and pick up cyclists from the park's entrance if required. This organisation runs a series of full and half-day canoeing tours from November to March, which include transportation, park entrance fee and food.

***Rates** US$95 (£47.50) per person or US$65 (£32.50) for visitors staying at the hostel. **Credit** MC, V.*

Canoes can also be rented at the marina in Flamingo from US$22 (£11) per day.

Everglades Rentals and Eco Adventures

*Ivey House Bed and Breakfast, Camellia Street, Everglades City ☎ 941 695 4666 **www.evergladesadventures.com***

Based on the west side of the Everglades, Everglades Rentals and Eco Adventures organise naturalist-led kayak tours into the Everglades backcountry from 1st November to mid-April. They also rent canoes and kayaks to those who prefer to explore alone. Children have to be 10 or older to join in and 10–12-year-olds must share a parent's boat.

***Rates** US$99–US$119 (£49.50–59.50), visitors staying at Ivey House receive a 20% discount. **Credit** MC, V.*

FAMILY-FRIENDLY ACCOMMODATION

INSIDER TIP

Book accommodation ahead of time before travelling to either the Keys or the Everglades in high season – January to April – when there is a high demand and limited options.

MODERATE/EXPENSIVE

Island City House Hotel ★★★

*411 William Street, Key West ☎ 305 294 5702 **www.islandcityhouse.com***

Island City House is one of the few hotels in converted historic properties in Key West that accepts children, and is one of my favourite places to stay in the whole of Florida. This beautiful hotel consists of three rambling wooden houses, which share tropically landscaped grounds and a shady swimming pool. Well suited for families because of its proximity to the hustle and bustle of Duval Street and many of Key West's attractions, Island City House is also an oasis of calm that feels as though it's a million miles away from the intensity of downtown. Seven friendly cats laze around the hotel's gardens, where breakfast is served each morning, and staff can organise trips and activities for guests or bike rentals for US$12 (£6) per day.

***Rooms** 24. **Rates** US$150–US$399 (£75–199.50). **Credit** AmEx, MC, V. **Amenities** Free street parking. Pool. Complimentary breakfast. Wi-Fi Internet. **In room** A/C. Cable TV. Kitchens or kitchenettes.*

VERY EXPENSIVE

The Moorings Village ★★★

*123 Beach Road, near MM81.5 (Oceanside), Islamorada ☎ 305 664 4708 **www.mooringsvilllage.com***

Key West

A cluster of chain motels and resorts is located on the outskirts of Key West as Hwy-1 reaches the island, including a Holiday Inn 3850 N Roosevelt Boulevard ☎ ***1 305 294 6681 www.holidayinnkeys.com*** (rooms US$140–US$180/£70–90), Travelodge 3444 N Roosevelt Boulevard ☎ ***305 296 7593 www.travelodgekeywest.com*** (rooms from US$110/£55) or Radisson 3820 N Roosevelt Boulevard ☎ ***305 294 5511 www.radisson.com/keywestfl*** (rooms from US$200/£100).

A large number of the small accommodation options in Key West's old town do not take children, but one small family-run option that does is the Wicker Guesthouse 913 Duval Street ☎ ***305 296 4275 www.wickerguesthouse.com*** (rooms US$179–US$455/£89.50–227.50) or for a more luxury hotel try the Crown Plaza Hotel 430 Duval Street ☎ ***305 296 2991 www.holidayinnkeys.com*** which overlooks Key West's waterfront (rooms US$207–US$342/£103.50–171). For self catering, check Travelers Palm ☎ ***305 294 9560 www.travelerspalm.com***, who rent a small number of cottages and apartments in Key West (US$188–US$328/£94–164 per night).

Moorings Village is a small collection of luxurious, yet rustic, cottages of varying sizes set in 35 acres of tropically landscaped grounds and the kind of place where families from Key West come to get away from it all. Although close to a number of attractions and right across the road from its restaurants Pierre's and Morada Bay (see p. 226), Moorings might as well be on its own island, making it perfect for families who want space to relax together yet also be within driving distance of all the Keys' attractions. A bonus for children is the resort's large beach, one of the few on the Keys, and off the sand, older children can enjoy tennis, kayaking and windsurfing.

Rooms *18 cottages.* ***Rates*** *Weekly rentals for a small cottage US$3,850–US$5,075 (£1,925–2,538), large cottage US$6,650–US$7,700 (£3,325–3,850). Some small cottages available for a minimum of two nights' stay from US$395–US$425 (£198–213) per night.* ***Credit*** *MC, V.* ***Amenities*** *Pool. Tennis. Watersports equipment rental.* ***In room*** *Cable TV. Full kitchen. Washer/dryer in most cottages. DVD. CD players.*

EXPENSIVE/VERY EXPENSIVE

Cheeca Lodge & Spa ★★

Hwy-1 MM82 (Oceanside), Islamorada ☎ ***305 664 4651 www.cheeca.com***

Cheeca Lodge & Spa is one of the Keys' veteran luxury resorts, where the likes of George Bush have been known to spend the odd night. Despite its rates, this is a chilled-out, friendly place, which welcomes all age groups and one of the most popular resorts in the Keys for families because of its excellent children's club, Camp Cheeca. This club, aimed at 5–12-year-olds, organises activities such as fishing, swimming, games and crafts, and children's nights out. The on-site dining options have special children's menus or there's a babysitting service for parents wanting a romantic night out alone at its beautiful Atlantic Edge restaurant.

Rooms *199.* ***Rates*** *US$249–US$878 (£125–439).* ***Credit*** *AmEx, MC, V.* ***Amenities*** *Two restaurants. Two bars. Two pools. Nine-hole golf course. Jacuzzi. Hot tubs. Watersports equipment and bike rental. Spa.* ***In room*** *A/C. Cable TV. DVD. CD player. Wi-Fi Internet. Fridge. Kitchenette (in suites).*

Mariner's Club ★★

Hwy-1 at MM97.5 (Oceanside), Key Largo ☎ *305 853 1111* ***www.marinersclub.com***

Just like its sister resort Little Harbor in Tampa Bay (see p. 128), the Mariner's Club with its collection of town homes and villas is a great base from which to explore the Keys and ideal for families who want to self cater and feel like they're part of a wider community where American families come to stay. The luxurious accommodation has a comfortable, family home feel and there's plenty to keep children occupied if you want a day off from driving, including tennis, basketball, kayaking and two pools, one of which is simply enormous and the other features its own private grotto. The resort also owns the adjacent waterfront Mandalay restaurant ***www.themandalay.com***, and the largest supermarket in the Keys is just a few miles away.

Rooms *Varies depending on availability.* ***Rates*** *Nightly rates become less the more nights are booked, a two-bedroomed town house starts at US$500 (£250) per night for a single night and drops to US$250 (£125) per night for seven nights.* ***Credit*** *AmEx, MC, V.* ***Amenities*** *Two pools. Jacuzzi. Fitness centre. Restaurant and bar. Kayak and canoe rental.* ***In room****. A/C. Cable TV. DVD. Full kitchen.*

The Rest of the Keys

On arrival at Key Largo, visitors are greeted with numerous accommodation options including a Holiday Inn at MM100 ☎ *305 451 5592* ***www.holidayinnkeylargo.com***, a resort-style hotel (rooms US$135–US$200/£67.50–100), the Marriott Key Largo at MM104 ☎ *305 453 0000* ***www.marriottkeylargo.com*** (rooms US$160–US$300/£80–150) and The Pelican at MM99.4 ☎ *305 451 3576* ***www.thepelicankeylargo.com*** a small collection of self-catering cottages and rooms tucked away by a private waterfront (US$85–US$185/£42.50–92.50).

Further down the Keys near Islamorada at MM80 is a Hampton Inn and Suites ☎ *305 664 0073* ***www.keys-resort.com*** (rooms US$190–US$250/£95–125) and further south still at Marathon is a Holiday Inn at MM54 ☎ *305 289 0222* ***www.holidayinnkeys.com*** (rooms US$120–US$170/£60–85).

The Everglades

On the west side of the Everglades, accommodation options are limited to Everglades City and it's important to book in advance in high season (January to April). A basic option, with a lovely pool overlooking the glades, is the Captain's Table 102 East Broadway ☎ *239 695 4211* ***www.captainstablehotel.com*** (rooms US$60–US$170/£30–85) while the Ivey House 107 Camellia Street ☎ *239 695 3299* ***www.iveyhouse.com*** runs a friendly B&B (rooms US$85–US$140/£42.50–70) and rents a basic small two-bedroomed cottage (US$120–US$170/£60–85 per night, minimum two nights' stay) and offers guests discounts on its canoe and kayak rentals and eco adventure tours (see p. 221).

On the east side of the Everglades, the only accommodation option for families is the collection of motels on Hwy-1 at Florida City. Recommended are the Best Western Gateway to the Keys ☎ *305 246 5100* ***www.bestwesternflorida.com*** (rooms from US$115/£57.50), Holiday Inn Express ☎ *305 247 3414* ***www.holidayinn.co.uk*** (rooms from US$100/£50) and the budget Fairway Inn ☎ *305 248 4202* (rooms from US$60/£30).

At the time of writing, Flamingo Lodge, the only accommodation inside the Everglades National Park, is closed due to the hurricane damage it received during the 2005 season. For up-to-date information check ***www.flamingolodge.com***.

MODERATE

Everglades Spa and Lodge ★★

SR-29, Everglades City ☎ *239 695 3151* ***www.evergladeslodge.com***

Housed in what was once Everglades City's old bank, Everglades Spa and Lodge is an unexpected gem of a B&B far from any well-beaten tourist track. The curiosity factor alone

Everglades Spa and Lodge

is engaging for children, as the hotel is full of relics from its past life, not to mention a beguiling old world charm. All the suites are named with money in mind – such as the Mutual Funds Department – and have their own kitchen facilities. The friendly staff can provide advice on the region's activities and book tours, or if you simply want to relax, the hotel's library and board games are free to use along with a guest computer with Internet access.

Rooms *7.* ***Rates*** *US$110–US$135 (£55–67.50).* ***Credit*** *AmEx, MC, V.* ***Amenities*** *Complimentary breakfast. Spa. Free use of bicycles.* ***In room*** *A/C. Cable TV. Wi-Fi Internet. Kitchen or kitchenette.*

FAMILY-FRIENDLY DINING

Key West

MODERATE/EXPENSIVE

Conch Republic Seafood Company

631 Greene Street, Key West ☎ 305 294 4403 ***www.conchrepublicseafood.com***

Housed in a large open-sided building on the edge of the marina, this popular seafood restaurant is infused with Key West's chilled-out ambience and blessed with one of the best views of any restaurant in the city. All kinds of people dine here, including boaters, tourists and locals, and the friendly atmosphere is accommodating for all ages. On the menu, speciality starters include almond brie and cracked conch and mains are a mix of sandwiches, salads, pasta and seafood. If children get tired of watching life on the marina outside, there's a number of inside TV screens to keep them entertained.

Open *For lunch and dinner daily.* ***Main Courses*** *US$8–US$33 (£4–16.50).* ***Credit*** *MC, V.* ***Amenities*** *Highchairs.*

MODERATE

Mangia Mangia ★

900 Southard Street, Key West ☎ 305 294 2469 ***www.mangia-mangia.com***

Decorated with wooden panelling and colourful artwork, there's a warmth and vibrancy to this seafood and pasta restaurant housed in an old wooden Key West building. Mangia Mangia is perfect for evening family dining because it's located away from the main drag of Duval Street and, although full of life itself, the restaurant is surrounded by a peaceful neighbourhood. The food is delicious and displays a more imaginative take on seafood than many Keys restaurants and there's something in its range of pastas to appeal to all tastes.

Open *5.30am–10pm daily.* ***Main Courses*** *US$10–US$25 (£5–12.50).* ***Credit*** *AmEx, MC, V.* ***Amenities*** *Disabled access.*

INSIDER TIP

Easily identified by its large mural of underwater sealife, the Waterfront Market, located at the marina on William Street, is a superb deli supermarket and takeaway. A recommended place for self caterers to shop, the market also sells a good range of take out sandwiches, salads and sushi and includes an upstairs juice bar and Internet café. **Open** 8am–6pm daily and Fridays until 8pm.

INEXPENSIVE/MODERATE

Caroline's Café

310 Duval Street, Key West ☎ 305 294 7511

Tucked away in a small courtyard off a bustling section of Duval Street, Caroline's is an inexpensive and cheerful haven away from the often more adult-orientated options in this part of the city. The Caribbean-influenced cuisine features a range of salads, sandwiches and seafood and the portions are more generous than most. Caroline's is great for children because its courtyard is also full of hair braiding, jewellery and craft stalls.

Open *10am–11pm daily.* ***Main Courses*** *US$7–US$15 (£3.50–7.50).* ***Credit*** *MC, V.*

The Rest of the Keys

MODERATE/ EXPENSIVE

Morada Bay ★★★

Hwy-1 at MM81.6 (Bayside), Islamorada ☎ 305 664 0604 ***www.moradabay-restaurant.com***

If you only ever eat out at one restaurant in the Keys with your children, make it this one. Too often in restaurants that focus on families, the food goes down a notch, however, the cuisine at this beachside bistro is full of Caribbean and Mediterranean influences and utterly fabulous. The genius of this restaurant, however, is its location. Spreading out over a small, child-friendly beach, children are free to play in the sand while adults relax and enjoy the food, company and breathtaking sunsets. However, if you've arranged a babysitter, don't miss a night out at the adjacent sister restaurant Pierre's *☎ 305 664 3225* ***www.pierres-restaurant.com***, a more formal option reminiscent of the Ivory Coast, whose fine dining starts with cocktails on the veranda and ends with speciality coffee overlooking the torch-lit beach.

Open *11.30 am–10pm Sun–Thurs and until 11pm Fri and Sat. Bar open until midnight.* ***Main Courses*** *lunch US$10–US$15 (£5–7.50), dinner US$10–US$32 (£5–16).* ***Credit*** *MC, V.* ***Amenities*** *Highchair. Children's menu. Disabled access.*

INEXPENSIVE/MODERATE

Key Fisheries ★

End of 35th Street, Marathon at MM49 (Bayside) ☎ 305 743 4353 ***www.keyfisheries.com/restaurant.htm***

This unpretentious, inexpensive family-friendly waterfront restaurant situated halfway along the Keys is a laid-back place to stop for lunch or dinner, when the sunsets are superb. Diners order at a window and sit at picnic-style tables facing the water, and the last time I was here, staff were asking punters to identify their order by the name of their favourite

Key West seafood platter

song. The mainly seafood menu is hearty value for money and an added extra is the chance to feed the nearby fish and birds.

Open *11.30am–9pm.* ***Main Courses*** *US$4–US$19 (£2–9.50).* ***Credit*** *MC, V.* ***Amenities*** *Disabled access.*

Key Largo Coffee House ★★ FIND

Hwy-1 at MM100.2 (Oceanside), Key Largo ☎ 305 453 4844 ***www.keylargocoffeehouse.com***

Key Largo Coffee House is the place to head if you're missing a proper cup of tea. It serves a good range of English teas along with delicious smoothies (including bubblegum flavour) and speciality coffees. The food is also fabulous; breakfast dishes range from raisin pecan French toast to spicy Cajun omelette and lunch includes an array of seafood, paninis, wraps and tacos. Tuesday nights are legendary all-you-can-eat Mexican buffets (US$10/£5 per person, children half price) and Fridays and Saturday evenings are seafood feasts. Diners eat on a shady wooden porch overlooking a courtyard where the resident Labrador – known as The Chief – keeps an eye on events, or inside the rustic old Colonial-style house.

Open *7am–10pm Mon–Sat, 7am–3pm Sun.* ***Main Courses*** *lunch US$8–US$11 (£4–5.50), dinner US$10–US$24 (£5–12).* ***Credit*** *MC, V.* ***Amenities*** *Children's menu. Highchair.*

INEXPENSIVE

Mrs Mac's Kitchen ★

Hwy-1 at MM99.4 (Bayside), ☎ 305 451 3722

This very popular with the locals 1950s-style diner serves inexpensive seafood, steaks, burgers and sandwiches and is the kind of place that once you've discovered you'll bring your children back to again and again. Diners eat in small booths or on stools at the counter and the décor, crammed with old-fashioned licence plates and folk art, is a magnet for

The Everglades

Dining options are limited in the Everglades. At Florida City, a number of chain and very average seafood restaurants, including the Mutineer ☎ *305 245 3377* ***www.mutineer.biz***. line Hwy-1. Tucked away on N Krome Avenue, one block west of Hwy-1, is the Farmer's Market Restaurant ☎ *305 242 0008* (open 5.30am–9pm). Don't be put off by appearances, this basic restaurant located inside the Farmer's Co-operative is clean and family run and set up to cater for the region's agricultural workers. The food is good, inexpensive and fresh, and their hearty breakfasts are an excellent way to start a day in the Everglades.

In Everglades City, restaurants tend to serve early to accommodate early-rising fishermen. The food at Susie's Kitchen on S. Copeland Avenue ☎ *239 695 0704* is excellent, but the hours are erratic; the Seafood Depot on Collier Avenue ☎ *239 695 0075* (open 7am–9pm) looks intimidating because the building is damaged, but the insides and staff are pleasant and it has a large wooden platform overlooking the glades; there's also a pizzeria takeaway ☎ *239 695 3665* (open 4pm–9pm) located behind the supermarket.

Along Hwy-41 the only restaurant is at the Miccosukkee Indian Village ☎ *305 223 8380* west of Shark Valley.

children's attention. The menu is large and food delicious, just make sure you leave room for dessert, when you'll be hard pushed to decide between peanut butter pie and Hawaiian wedding cake.

Open *7am–9.30pm Mon–Sat.* ***Main Courses*** *US$4–US$10 (£2–5).* ***Credit*** *AmEx, MC, V.* ***Amenities*** *Children's menu.*

INSIDER TIP

There are limited supermarket options in Everglades City. If you're self catering or picnicking, stock up before leaving Naples.

MODERATE/EXPENSIVE

Oyster House Restaurant

901 S Copeland Avenue, Everglades City ☎ *239 695 2073* ***www.oysterhouserestaurant.com***

Nestled on the edge of the National Park and adjacent to a marina, the Oyster House is a friendly restaurant, popular with fishermen and forms part of a wider complex containing holiday cabins, a campsite and canoe hire. The rustic interior is decorated with hunting trophies and a screened porch and wooden seating booths provide beautiful views of the surrounding glades. The menu contains mostly seafood, fresh from local suppliers, and also the chance to sample local alligator meat.

Open *11am–9pm daily and until 10pm Fri and Sat.* ***Main Courses*** *US$10–US$23 (£5–11.50).* ***Credit*** *MC, V.* ***Amenities*** *Children's menu. Highchair.*

9 The Panhandle & Big Bend

THE PANHANDLE & BIG BEND

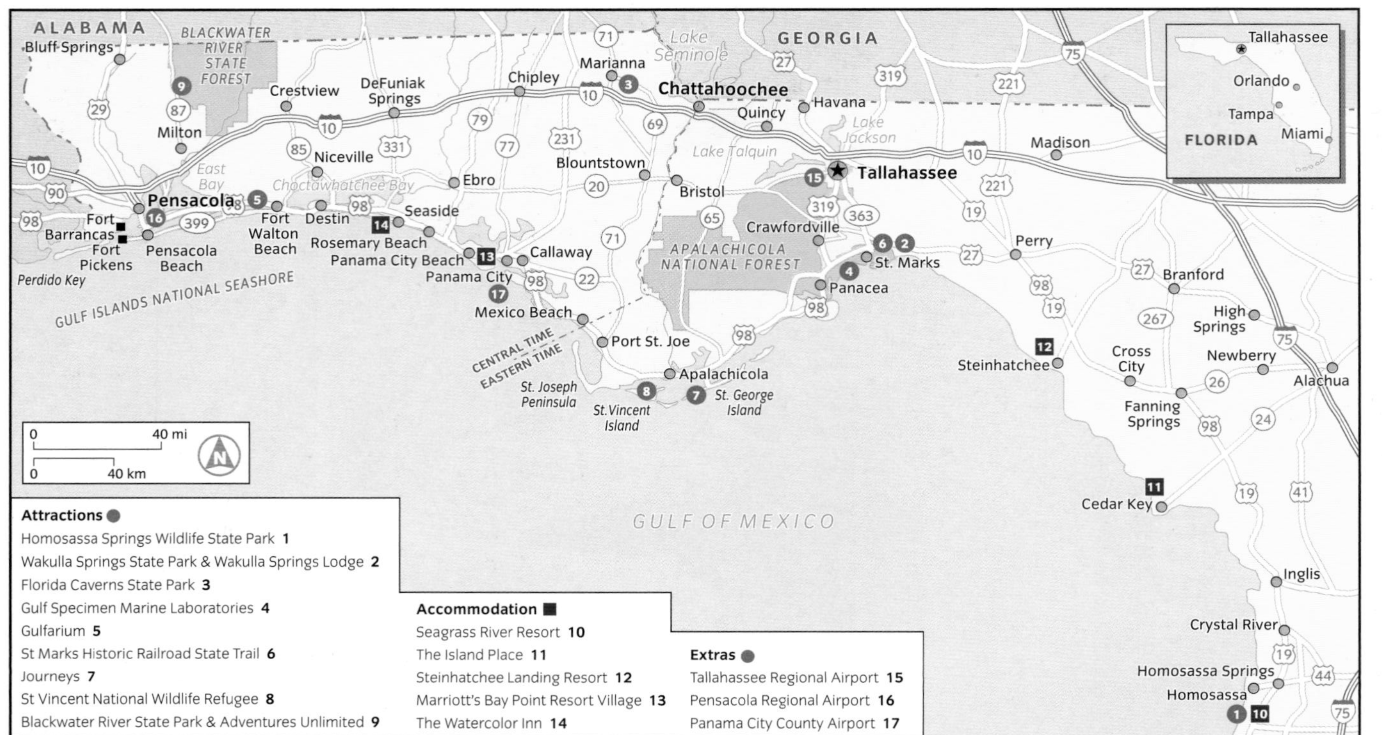

A firm holiday favourite with American families, the north west region of Florida is as far from the foreign tourist track as European families can get. However, the ever-increasing number of British travelling this far are discovering just how much this region has to offer. Curving gently north from Tampa, the Big Bend, made up of 150 miles of coastal wetlands, is a place to mess around on the water and watch lazy sunsets drop into wide horizons. While nestling beneath Georgia and Alabama, the Florida Panhandle has more in common with its Deep South neighbours than the rest of Florida. For active families, both regions offer some of the best kayaking in America and fantastic swimming in the aquamarine seas that lap the Panhandle's pristine yet wild beaches. With more than its share of old towns, there are plenty of opportunities to explore Florida's history – from the relics of Native American Indians to the site of recent controversial presidential elections. As well as museums, there are water parks and gulfariums to entertain all age groups, while those who simply want to relax, can enjoy a way of life as slow as the old rivers that this region is famous for.

ESSENTIALS

Getting There

By Plane Tallahassee Regional Airport ☎ *850 891 7801* ***www.talgov.com/airport/index.cfm*** is 12 miles south of the city and receives internal flights from Miami, Orlando, Fort Lauderdale and Tampa. Continental, Delta, British Airways and Virgin Atlantic provide services from London airports, Manchester and Edinburgh with stops in either Atlanta or Orlando.

Pensacola Regional Airport ☎ *850 436 5000* ***www.flypensacola.com*** is a 15-mile drive from downtown Pensacola and receives internal flights from Orlando, Tampa and Fort Lauderdale.

Panama City County Airport ☎ *850 763 6751* ***www.pcairport.com*** is a small facility 4 miles north of the city, serving a few cities in the south, including Orlando.

By Car From the south, you can drive Hwy-19 along the Big Bend's coast from St Petersburg, or the faster I-75 further inland and reached from Orlando via the Florida Turnpike. From the east, I-10 leads across the state from Jacksonville to Tallahassee and on to Pensacola, while Hwy-98 travels along the Panhandle's Gulf Coast.

VISITOR INFORMATION

The region's main tourist office is the FlaUSA Visitor Information Center ***www.visitflorida.com*** located on the ground floor of the New Capitol Building in Tallahassee (see p. 234). Open 8am–5pm Mon–Fri.

Orientation

Use Hwy-19 to explore the Big Bend's coastal communities and Hwy-98 along the Panhandle, although some smaller roads such as SR-30A break off from Hwy-98 to hug the coast. Arching across the top of the Panhandle, I-10 is the fastest way to travel between Tallahassee and Pensacola and the only way to reach Florida's most northerly state parks.

Getting Around

With limited public transport options, the only feasible way to travel around the Big Bend and Panhandle with children is by car. For details of car hire, see p. 29.

Child-friendly Events & Entertainment

Fiesta of Five Flags

Pensacola ☏ *850 433 6512* ***www.fiestaoffiveflags.org***

This annual festival is one of the longest running and largest in Florida and celebrates the founding of Pensacola by the Spanish in 1559. The festival takes place over a number of days around May or June and includes parades, a Spanish fiesta and all kinds of activities for children, including treasure hunts and a sand-sculpture contest.

Florida Seafood Festival

Apalachicola ☏ *888 653 8011* ***www.floridaseafoodfestivalfestival.com***

Located in Apalachicola's Battery Park, this 2-day festival in November is the oldest seafood festival in Florida. Starting with the Blessing of the Fleet, the festival includes a parade, a race through town, arts and crafts stalls and live music. It's the oyster-eating contest held on the Saturday afternoon of the festival that locals flock to see. Contestants have 15 minutes to eat as many oysters as they can without being sick. Get there early for a front row seat!

Halloween Howl

Tallahassee Museum of History and Natural Science, 3945 Museum Drive ☏ *850 575 8684* ***www.tallahasseemuseum.org***

Advertised as a 'howling good time', ghosts, goblins and things that go bump in the night are out in force in the museum grounds during this annual two-evening event around Halloween. There are haunted trails for children to explore, including a not so scary one for younger children, and a programme of trick or treating, storytelling, live music and magic shows, – all of which are great for pre-teens – and even adults!

October. ***Admission*** *US$10 (£5) adults, US$8 (£4) children.* ***Credit*** *MC, V.*

WHAT TO SEE & DO

Children's Top Five Attractions

❶ Kayaking in Blackwater River State Park; p. 248.

TALLAHASSEE

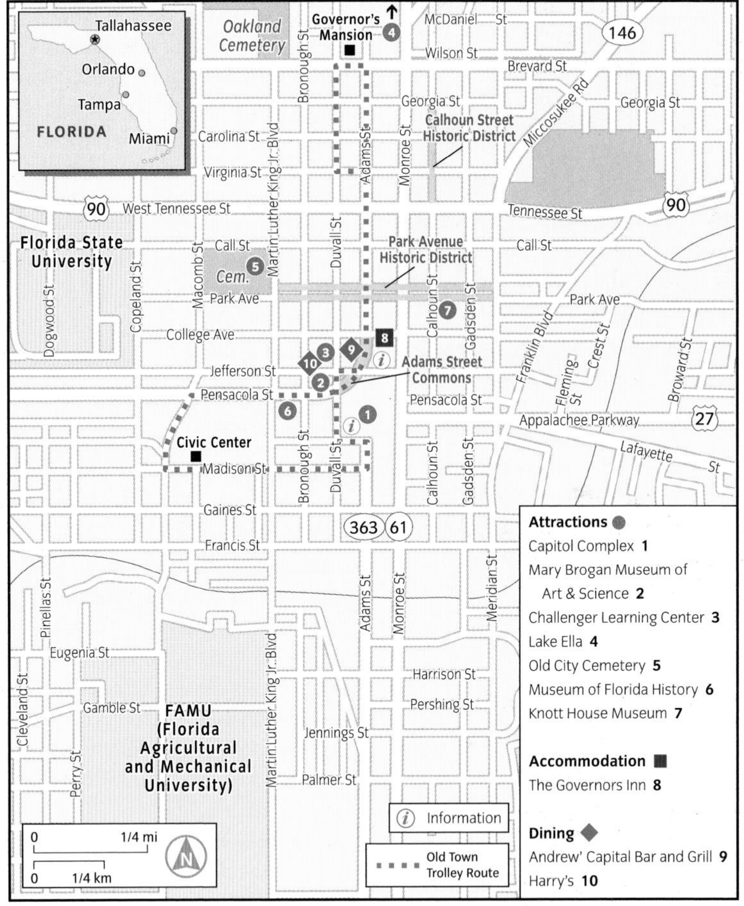

❷ Getting up close to the resident manatees at Homasassa Springs State Wildlife Park; p. 247.

❸ Swimming the emerald-green waters at Wakulla Springs; p. 246.

❹ Taking to the high seas aboard a Pirate Cruise in Panama City Beach; p. 244.

❺ Undertaking a night-time critter hunt with Journeys on St George Island; p. 248.

Historic Towns & Cities

Tallahassee

Chosen as state capital in 1824 due to its position halfway between St Augustine and Pensacola, Tallahassee today seems more than geographically distant from the more dominant cities in the south.

The name 'Tallahassee' is derived from the Muskogeon Indian for 'old town' and true to

Tallahassee

its name, the city is as focused on its history as it is on managing the modern state it governs. It's this distinctive mix of old and new that makes Tallahassee a fascinating place to explore; an excellent free walking guide can be picked up from the visitor information centre (see p. 231).

At the heart of the city, and on one of its highest spots – Tallahassee is surprisingly hilly for Florida – stands the Capitol Complex, which embodies the city's characteristic marrying of old and new. Built in Greek Revival style, the Old Capitol Building (☎ *850 487 1902* 9am–4.30pm Mon–Fri, 10am–4.30pm Sat, noon–4.30pm Sun. Free) contains exhibits featuring artefacts and reproductions detailing Florida's political history and that of the building itself.

Construction on the New Capitol Building (☎ *850 488 6167* 8am–5pm Mon–Fri. Free) began in the 1960s after the failure to move the capitol to Orlando to be closer to the boom cities of Tampa and Miami. Completed in 1977, the building houses Florida's executive and legislative offices and towers above the whole city. The observation floor on the 22nd storey provides visitors with panoramic views of the city and beyond.

Fanning out from the Capitol Complex is Tallahassee's historical and cultural district. Here the streets, known as 'canopied roads' are shaded by rambling oak trees laden with Spanish Moss, which arch across the roads and buzz with politicos and lawyers on weekdays.

Directly behind the New Capitol Building is the Supreme Court, scene of the infamous battles that decided the 2000 presidential elections when Bush was finally elected in Florida by a margin of 537 votes and the phrase 'hanging chad' made its introduction into political vocabulary.

Kleman Plaza is north of the Supreme Court on Duval Street and is filled with benches and fountains. It is a central place to

FUN FACT **Log Cabins**

Three log cabins served as Florida's first Capitol Buildings in Tallahassee until 1826 when a two-storey masonry building was constructed. This was replaced by the 'Old' Capitol Building in 1845.

Tallahassee's Museums & Attractions

Of Tallahassee's numerous museums and attractions, these are the most interesting for children.

Mary Brogan Museum of Art and Science ★ on Duval Street ✆ *850 513 0700* ***www.thebrogan.org*** makes learning fun. Its two floors feature interactive science displays, a programme of changing art exhibitions and touring shows, complemented by education-based activities. (10am–5pm Mon–Sat, 1–5pm Sun. US$6/£3 adults, US$3.50/£1.75 children 3–17, under 3s free)

The Challenger Learning Center ★ ✆ *850 645 7796* ***www.challengertlh.com*** opposite the Mary Brogan Museum, is an aerospace-based attraction containing an IMAX cinema and planetarium (call the above number for show times. IMAX US$7/£3.50 adults, US$5.50/£2.75 children, planetarium US$5/£2.50 adults, US$4/£2 children).

The Tallahassee Museum of History and Natural Science ★★ ✆ *850 576 1636* ***www.tallahasseemuseum.org*** is located south east of downtown, near the airport on Museum Drive and consists of 52 acres of historic buildings and nature trails. Exhibits include historical recreations, art galleries and a science-based Discovery Center. Use booklets and interpretive boards to discover the history and environment of the Big Bend, or join an educational tour. (9am–5pm Mon–Sat, 12.30pm–5pm Sun. US$8/£4 adults, US$5.50/£2.75 children aged 4–15, under 4s free).

park, enjoy a packed lunch or grab lunch at Harry's ✆ *850 222 3976* ***www.hookedonharrys.com***, a New Orleans-style restaurant serving wraps, burgers, salads and seafood from US$9 (£4.50).

A number of museums and attractions are clustered in this area (see above box) including the old-fashioned Museum of Florida History **OVERRATED** (✆ *850 245 6400* ***www.museumoffloridahistory.com*** 9am–4.30pm Mon–Fri, 10am–4.30pm Sat, noon–4.30pm, Sun. Free) on Bronough Street, which displays the history of Florida from dinosaurs to the present day.

On Park Avenue, leading east from the Old City Cemetery, you'll find a chain of attractive parks that host a vibrant Saturday market from 8am–2pm March–November. Stalls sell

FUN FACT Olympic Courtyard

Just south of the City Hall is Olympic Courtyard, dedicated to the British Olympic team who competed at the 1996 Atlanta games and chose Tallahassee as their official training site.

Tallahassee's Black History

Around 70 plantations once occupied approximately 300,000 acres of land between Tallahassee and Thomasville, 28 miles to the north in Georgia. Mostly growing cotton, these plantations and the slave trade that supported them are an integral part of the region's history. To explore further, head for the **Black Archives Research Center and Museum** (*☎ 850 599 8564* ***www.famu.edu/acad/archives*** 9am–5pm Mon–Fri. Free) at Florida State University, and **Knott House Museum** (*☎ 850 922 2459* ***www.taltrust.org/knott*** 1–3pm Wed–Fri, 10am–3pm Sat. Free) on Park Avenue, a lovingly restored Victorian house thought to have been built by George Proctor, a free black who became Florida's first coloured physician. However, the most poignant memorial of segregation is the Old City Cemetery on Park Avenue, where blacks are buried in the western half, and whites the east.

local arts and crafts and regional produce alongside a range of activities for children, including storytelling and live music. For a break from downtown, Lake Ella is north of the centre on Monroe Street (Hwy-27), and a pleasant recreational area around a scenic lake with a string of wooden cottages housing quirky shops. Four miles north east of downtown on Thomasville Road is the Maclay State Gardens ★ (*☎ 850 487 4114* ***www.floridastateparks.org/maclaygardens*** daily 8am–sunset US$4/£2 per car), a large ornamental garden where families can swim, picnic and explore nature trails. At the time of writing, Maclay House, furnished as it was when the Maclay family lived there in the first half of the 20th century, is closed for renovations.

Visitor Information Center: 106 Jefferson St, Tallahassee; ☎ 850 606 2305 ***www.seetallahassee.com***

Pensacola

Five miles inland of its beautiful beach, Pensacola is the second-oldest city in Florida and one lucky to exist at all after an ill-fated settlement established here by the Spanish in 1599 was destroyed by a hurricane two years later. Pensacola's nickname – the City of the Five Flags – symbolises the historic power struggles that have caused ownership to change hands many times over the centuries.

History is Pensacola's main draw, but delving into it is more of an adult-orientated pursuit, as the city's historical museums contain little to engage young children.

That said, Pensacola's charming streets are lined with colonial French-style balconies and filled with offbeat shops, laid-back cafés and piped Dixieland jazz – they are a pleasure to explore and reminiscent of New Orleans, a 3-hour drive away.

PENSACOLA

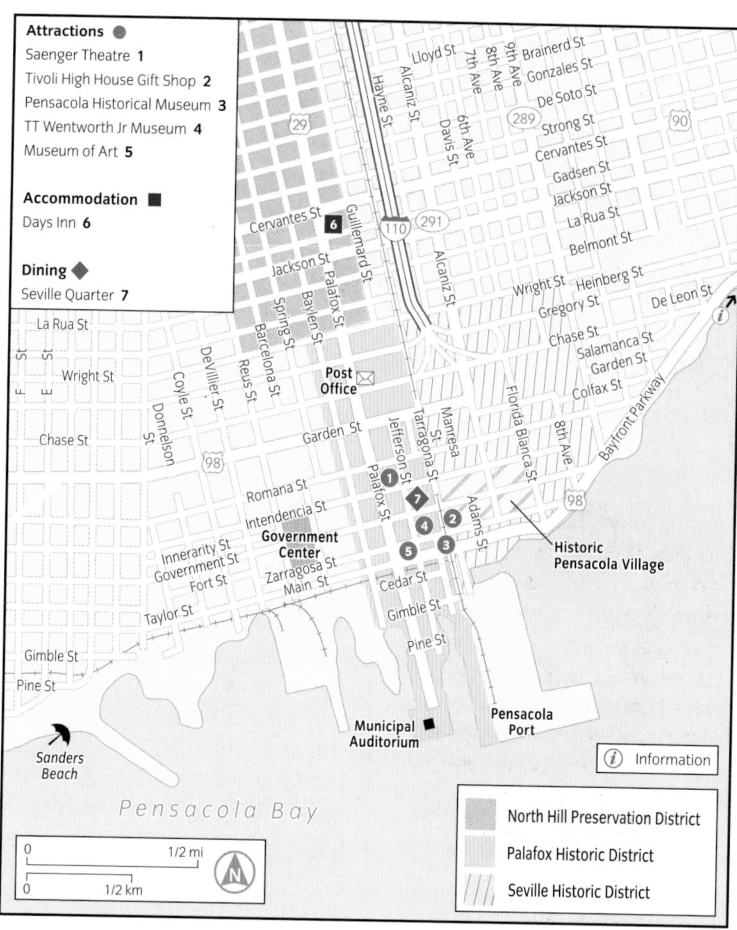

INSIDER TIP

Downtown Penascola is quiet at weekends and all the museums are closed on Sundays.

There are three distinct historic areas to explore: North Hill west of Hwy-29 as it leads south into downtown with its elaborate late 19th-century houses. The Palafox District, a commercial centre with a number of striking early 20th century buildings including the Saenger Theatre 📞 *850 434 7444* ***www.pensacolasaenger.com*** a Spanish Baroque theatre. More interesting is the Seville District and Pensacola's Historic Village 📞 *850 595 5985* ***www.historicpensacola.org***, an appealing cluster of old properties around Zaragoza and Tarragona Streets, a number of which are open to the public. Tickets can be bought from the Tivoli High House Gift Shop

Pensacola

(☎ *850 595 5993* 10am–4pm Mon–Fri. US$6/£3 adults US$2.50/£1.25 children) on Zaragoza Street.

INSIDER TIP

The car park at the junction of Zaragoza and Tarragona Streets is the best place to park when exploring the Seville District and Historic Village. It contains a small archaeological dig of a commanding officer's compound from the 1800s, where it is believed that Civil War general and President Andrew Jackson came to sign agreements that ceded Florida to the United States.

The city's two main museums are the Pensacola Historical Museum (☎ *850 433 1559* **www.pensacolahistory.org** 10am–4.30pm Mon–Sat. US$4/£2) on East Zaragoza Street and the T.T. Wentworth Jr Museum (☎ *850 595 5990* 10am–4pm Mon–Sat. Free) on Jefferson Street. T.T. Wentworth is the more interesting and child friendly. An unusual lunch stop is the Museum of Art (☎ *850 432 62 47* **www.pensacolamuseumofart.org**), housed in an old jailhouse and containing Portabello Market, a small restaurant serving fresh sandwiches and salads, all accompanied by light jazz. A number of cafés and restaurants cluster around the junction of Government and Alcaniz Streets and children can look out for the colourful ornamental pelicans dotted around the area.

South west of downtown Pensacola, just off the Gulf Breeze Parkway, is the National Museum of Naval Aviation ★★ (9am–5pm daily. Free ☎ *850 453 2389* **www.navalaviationmuseum.org**). Worth a visit with older children, this collection of historic naval, marine and coastguard aircraft spans the history of flight from 1911 to the exploration of space. The museum contains more than 150 aircraft, 100 scale models and aviation memorabilia and the simulated test flight is a big hit with children.

Visitor Information Center: 401 E. Gregory St, Pensacola ☎ 850 434 1234 ***www.visitpensacola.com***

Cedar Key ★

www.cedarkey.org

Situated on an island 3 miles from the mainland and halfway between Tampa and Tallahassee, Cedar Key is one of the oldest communities in Florida.

Today this town of ramshackle streets and weathered old wooden houses promotes itself as a place where time stands still, and its slow of pace of life will not appeal to every family. However, for those wanting to get off the beaten track and discover a small pocket of Florida history, it's worth breaking your journey here or spending some time discovering the region's natural beauty.

Cedar Key's atmospheric downtown is home to a number of one-off gift shops and art galleries and is easily explored on foot. A booklet detailing a historic walking tour can be bought for US$4.50 (£2.25) from the Historical Society Museum (☎ *352 543 5549* ***www.cedarkeymuseum.org*** 1–4pm Sun–Fri, 11am–5pm Sat, US$1/50p adults, 50¢/25p) children, on the corner of SR-24 and 2nd Street). You can also explore by bike, as the speed limit drops to 15 mph in places, making cycling safe and stress free. Bikes can be rented from the grocery store on the corner of SR-24 and 3rd Street for US$4 (£2) an hour or US$15 (£7.50) for a whole day.

Cedar Key's waterfront, with its small beach and play area, is one of the most photogenic in Florida and the best place in town to find somewhere to eat. Try Frogs Landing ☎ *352 543 9243* ***www.frogslanding.net*** for a selection of seafood dishes from US$10 (£5) and an outdoor, sea-facing balcony from which to look out for dolphins. Most accommodation is located along the short waterfront. You won't find any chain motels, just a series of small, locally run establishments with rates starting at US$55 (£27.50) a night.

INSIDER TIP

Cedar Key gets very busy at weekends so if you plan to stay here on Friday or Saturday night, book by Wednesday.

The 12 small islands that make up Cedar Key National Wildlife Refuge ***www.fws.gov/cedarkeys*** lie within a 5-mile radius of Cedar Key's shore. Now an official wilderness area, these islands were once home to Native American Indians and are rewarding places for families who enjoy exploring the outdoors. A number of tour operators are on Dock Street; try Island Hopper ☎ *352 543 5904* ***www.cedarkeyislandhopper.com*** whose 1½-hour tours include time to explore an island (US$20/£10 adults, US$15/£7.50 children under 12). If you'd rather explore alone, kayaks can be rented from Kayak Cedar Keys ☎ *352 543 9447* ***www.kayakcedarkeys.com*** for between

US$25 and US$40 (£12.50–20) for three hours, while Wild Florida Adventures ☎ *352 528 3984* ***www.wild-florida.com*** lead half-day kayaking tours along the coastline for US$50 (£25) per person.

Apalachicola ★

www.apalachicolabay.org

Made rich by the cotton that poured through its port from the plantations (not exclusively Florida plantations), Apalachicola's economy and tourist trade relies on the surrounding estuary, one of the most productive sources of seafood in the northern hemisphere. Sampling Apalachicola's excellent oysters is reason enough to stop here but there's more to this sleepy town than shellfish. Apalachicola is also famous for its abundance of antebellum houses. Unlike the town's fortunes, these old southern beauties with their wrap-around wooden balconies, rocking chairs and swings have changed little over 150 years. Take time off the SR-98 as it steams through town to explore the tree-lined avenues leading to Lafayette Park, a beautiful landscaped refuge with a children's play area and picnic tables – the perfect place to break a journey.

It doesn't take long to explore Apalachicola's working waterfront with its fishing fleet and peaceful river views or the downtown area full of craft shops and art galleries. If you want to discover more about the region's wildlife, spend an hour or so at the Apalachicola National Estuarine Research Reserve at the north end of Market Street (☎ *850 653 8063* open 8am–5pm Mon–Fri. Free), where you can follow a nature trail and access bird-viewing areas.

Apalachicola

FUN FACT **Oysters**

90% of all the oysters eaten in Florida are harvested in Apalachicola's estuary.

Apalachicola is one of the best places in the Panhandle to eat; for an authentic 1950s American experience, visit the Old Time Soda Fountain on Market Street ☎ *850 653 8000*, with its milk bar where you sit on old-fashioned stools and enjoy milkshakes, ice creams and floats from US$3 (£1.50). Café Con Leche ★ FIND on 32 Avenue D ☎ *850 653 2233*, is a rustic Internet café with wooden floors, world music and daily newspapers, serving healthy breakfast dishes and sandwiches and cakes from US$7 (£3.50). With only one chain motel – the Best Western Apalach Inn (☎ *850 653 9131*, rooms US$90/£45) – there are limited places for families to stay, so consider finding accommodation on nearby St George Island instead.

Best Beaches & Beach Communities

Beaches along SR-30A ★★★

www.discover30a.com

SR-30A, otherwise known as the scenic highway, is an 18-mile stretch of memorable coast road that winds its picturesque way through undeveloped beaches and quaint communities.

The largest and most unique of them all is Seaside *www.seasidefl.com*, whose one and a half mile stretch of beach and distinctive wooden pavilions is stunning – don't expect to paraglide or jet ski, but do expect to enjoy a child-friendly beach where the sand is like sugar. Take time to explore Seaside's shops and cafés; Sundog Books ☎ *850 231 5481* on Central Square stocks a large range of fiction and children's books, and sells walking tours of Seaside for US$5 (£2.50), Modica Market ☎ *850 231 1214* *www.modicamarket.com* is a superb deli supermarket selling fresh sandwiches, breads, cakes and upmarket groceries (including PG Tips) along with an impressive selection of beer and wine. Clothes shoppers should head for the speciality shops off Cinderella Circle near the waterfront, where you'll also find Café Spiazzia ★ ☎ *850 231 1297*, serving fresh pizza, pasta and sandwiches for around US$15 (£7.50) and a children's menu from US$5 (£2.50).

One mile west of Seaside is Grayton Beach State Recreation Area (8am–sunset. US$4/£2 cars, US$1/50p pedestrians and cyclists), whose quartz white sands are wilder than Seaside's and walking trails lead through dunes and pinewoods.

Further west still is secluded Grayton Beach, a favourite with local artists and one of the oldest

An All American Seaside

With a website that encourages you to enjoy the 'life of your time', Seaside is no ordinary town, but definitely a family-friendly one. Developed in the 1980s by award-winning builder/developer Robert Davis, the theory behind this immaculate white picket-fenced community is that a town built of pseudo-Victorian wooden cottages constructed with traditional building methods will nurture a positive community spirit. There is a sense that this town, and the folk who call it home, are almost too good to be true and it comes as no surprise that Seaside was chosen as the location of Jim Carrey's film *The Truman Show*, in which an insurance clerk discovers that his whole life is entirely fake. However, it's easy to be cynical about a community that's simply trying to make the world a better place and there's a lot more than a great beach and good shopping to enjoy in the uniquely American seaside town. But be warned, if your children are into graffiti, make them leave their spray cans at home.

communities in the area. Keep travelling along SR-30A to reach Gulf Place, a collection of unusual shops and funky cafés, including the recommended Smiling Fish Café (junction of SR-30A and SR-393 ☎ *850 622 3071*) and The Red Bar at 70 Hortz Avenue ☎ *850 231 1008*. Both are open for lunch and dinner and serve main courses starting at US$8 (£4).

Beaches along the SR-399 from Navarre to Pensacola

The powdery sand and mile upon mile of stark white dunes that line SR-399 create an almost surreal arctic landscape that's unlike any other strip of beach in Florida. Unfortunately, SR-399 is currently inaccessible beyond Navarre due to extensive hurricane damage during the 2005 season. At the Pensacola end of SR-399 a large number of motels, restaurants and shops are accessible by car, but Fort Pickens is not. Repairs to SR-399 and the Fort Pickens Road began at the end of 2007. For updates on their progress ☎ *850 934 2600* or check ***www.nps.gov/guis***.

Panama City Beach

A firm favourite with American college students on spring break (don't bring children here at this time), Panama City Beach is one of the most popular and tackiest party towns in Florida and a rampant display of commercialism by the seaside. As Alt-98 (Front Beach Road) stretches along the vast beach, it becomes one long cruising strip for hot rods and souped-up cars and any view of the sand quickly disappears behind a string of down-market high-rise resorts. On the other side of the road, cheap gift shops and fast-food joints jostle for attention. That said, this is one of the few places in the Panhandle where families can have good old fun and enjoy numerous distractions from crazy golf to go-carts.

Popular with teenagers are the six acres of wild flume rides, wave pools and water rapids that make up Ship Wreck Island Water Park on Middle Beach Road (📞 *805 234 3333* ***www.shipwreckisland.com*** admission over 50 inches US$29/£14.50, 35–50 inches US$24/£12 – with some ride restrictions for children under 48" – under 35" free. Children under 12 only admitted with an adult). Ripley's Believe It or Not (see p. 94) (9907 Front Beach Road, 📞 *850 230 6113* ***www.ripleyspanamacitybeach.com*** open daily from 10am, US$15/£7.50 adults, US$10/£5 children aged 6–12, under 6s free) is good for a rainy day and housed in a replica beached ocean liner. All children who love the weird and wonderful enjoy this museum of the eccentric and unbelievable.

Like all the Panhandle beaches, Panama City's is wide, white and beautiful. Public access points are marked with blue and white semicircular signs. However, a more chilled-out option for families who want to spend time on the sand is St Andrews State Recreation Area ★ (8am–sunset, car US$5/£2.50, pedestrians and cyclists US$1/50p) to the east of the main beach.

This is one of Florida's most popular state parks and locals and visitors alike flock here to enjoy miles of sand, nature trails and picnic areas. A small artificial reef protects part of the beach, making the water safe for small children, while over the headland, an unprotected beach is perfect for teenagers. Catch a shuttle to Shell Island – an isolated island with a splendid beach where visitors can kayak or hike – which leaves hourly between 1pm and 5pm. Tickets (US$12.50/£6.25 adults, US$6.50/£3.25 children) are bought from the visitor centre, where you can book snorkelling packages (US$20/£10 adults, US$15/£7.50 children) or rent kayaks (US$35/£17.50 per day for a single, US$45/£22.50 for a double).

Bike SR-30A

A cycle path runs the length of SR-30A and offers some of the most scenic cycling in Florida plus 8 miles of off-road biking along a forest trail. Bikes can be rented from various places along the route, including Big Daddy's at Blue Mountain Beach 📞 *850 622 1165* ***www.bigdaddysrentals.com*** and Seaside Bike Rentals on Central Square in Seaside (📞 *850 231 2314* open 8.30am–4.30pm daily) for US$15/£7.50 per half day, US$20/£10 per day and US$60/£30 per week.

Pirate Cruise aboard the Sea Dragon

Visitor Information Center: 17001 Panama City Beach Parkway ☎ *850 233 5070* ***www.thebeachloversbeach.com***

St George Island ★★

www.apalachicolabay.org

Approximately 15 miles east of Apalachicola, SR-300 branches south from SR-98 and leads to St George Island, whose glorious beaches are some of the most outstanding in Florida. Families, including many Brits, come here to kick back, mess about on the sand, snorkel, cycle and kayak.

The island's best beaches are in the state park at the far eastern tip (open 8am–sunset, cars US$5/£2.50, pedestrians and cyclists US$1/50p), where the endless white dunes are home to

Cruising with the Children

If you're looking for entertaining ways to take your children out onto the waters around Panama City Beach, its vast array of watersport activites and themed tours, won't let you down. Head for the marinas at the east end of North Lagoon Drive to book boat tours, snorkelling trips, parasailing and dolphin encounter cruises. Located in Lighthouse Marina, and one of the most popular trips with families, is the Pirate Cruise aboard the Sea Dragon ★ (☎ *850 234 7400* ***www.piratecruise.net*** US$19/£9.50 adults, US$15/£7.50 children aged 3–14, US$9/£4.50 children aged 1–2, babies free). Their ticket booth sells toy swords, hooks and bandanas so children can look the part, while adults enjoy the complimentary rum punch.

many nesting birds and are accessible via a 2½-mile nature trail. You can explore the park, and the whole island, by bike – hire them from Island Adventures ☎ *850 927 3655* ***www.sgislandadventures.com*** on East Gulf Beach Drive for US$10 (£5) a day. The range of activities and trips, many just for children, organised by Journeys (see p. 248) is reason enough to come to St George Island. If you've packed your children off with them for the day, Eddy Teacher's Raw Bar ☎ *850 927 5050* next door to Journeys is the perfect place to enjoy a beer and dish of fresh oysters while your youngsters wear themselves out.

State Parks and Historic Sites

Florida Caverns State Park ★★

3345 Caverns Road, Marianna ☎ *850 482 9598* ***www.floridastateparks.org/floridacaverns***

The main reason to visit this 1,300 acre state park is to explore the amazing series of interconnected caverns crammed with formations ranging from the beautiful to the bizarre. Rediscovered in the 1930s, the caverns have been used by Native American Indians for burials and as a hiding place for Union soldiers during the American Civil War, while the presence of shark teeth, sand dollars and shells embedded in the ceiling serves as a reminder of the geological history. A popular day out for local school children, any child happy to go underground – the caves drop to 55–60 ft below ground – will enjoy the 45-minute guided tour (US$8/£4 adults, US$4/£2 children, last tour at 4.30pm) of this unique environment.

Claustrophobics and tall people with bad backs (adults have to bend double in places) should stick with the swimming and nature trails also offered in the park.

Open *8am–sunset daily.* ***Admission*** *US$4 (£2) cars, US$1 (50p) pedestrians and cyclists.* ***Amenities*** *Shop. Picnic area.*

Homosassa Springs Wildlife State Park ★

Hwy-19 ☎ *352 628 5343* ***www.floridaparks.org/homosassasprings*** *75 miles north of Tampa.*

This delightful state park has a mission to preserve Florida's native wildlife and its winding wooden boardwalk provides a viewing platform into different natural habitats showcasing a variety of animals including black bears, cougars, alligators, river otters, Key deer and many different species of birds.

The highlight is a small underwater observatory providing intimate viewing of the endangered West Indian manatee, making it one of the best places in Florida to get up close to these lovable creatures.

The park's daily Wildlife Encounter Programmes (check times when buying your ticket) focus on education rather than entertainment, although feeding time for Lu the hippo makes up for this – watch out for the splash zone!

***Open** 9am–5.30pm daily (ticket counter closes at 4pm). **Admission** US$9 (£4.50) adult, US$5 (£2.50) children aged 3–12, under 3s free. RAC and AA members receive a 20% discount. **Credit** AmEx, MC, V. **Amenities** Café. Picnic area. Shop. Disabled access.*

INSIDER TIP

Situated on the side of SR-490, 2½ miles from its junction with Hwy-19, the ruins of Yule Sugar Mill are an excellent place to break a journey. Interpretive boards detail how sugar was made at this steam-driven mill from 1851 until 1864, and picnic tables are available for public use. Pop into the adjacent Old Mill House Gallery and Printing Museum (*352 628 1081.* Open 10am–3pm Tues–Sat), whose small café houses old printing presses, a Wurlitzer juke box and old wooden Ford pick-up van, and serves delicious Cuban sandwiches.

Wakulla Springs State Park ★

*SR-267 850 224 5950 **www.floridastateparks.org/wakullasprings** 14 miles south of Tallahassee*

Wakulla Springs State Park is home to one of the world's biggest and deepest freshwater springs and is a glorious place for families to mess around by the water. Fringed by a small beach, the swimming is calm, making it safe fun for younger children. The park's abundant wildlife can be discovered via nature trials (bring mosquito repellent between April and October) and, if the water's clear enough, glass-bottom boat tours (US$6/£3 adults, US$4/£2 children) provide fascinating views of the 180-ft underwater cavern, through which half a million gallons of water bubble out each day.

***Open** 8am–sunset daily. **Admission** US$4 (£2) cars, US$1 (50p) pedestrians and cyclists. **Amenities** Café. Gift shop. Picnic area. Toilets.*

Gulfariums

Gulfarium

*Hwy-98 Fort Walton Beach 850 244 5169 **www.gulfarium.com***

Open since 1955, the world's oldest marine show aquarium remains one of the best in the state. Highlights include the Living Sea exhibit, a panorama of sealife found in local waters. Children get to feed a variety of birds, and resident species include tropical penguins (not all penguins live in cold places) and injured birds receiving care. Daily dolphin and sea lion shows, and penguin and otter feeding times are a chance to learn more about the animals, while for US$150

FUN FACT Follow That Dream 

Just north of Inglis, SR-40, otherwise known as Follow That Dream Parkway, branches west from Hwy-19 towards Yankeetown. Elvis came here in 1961 to make *Follow That Dream*, one of his best-loved films.

Seeing Manatees in the Wild

The Crystal and Homasassa rivers are home to a large number of manatees, particularly during the winter months, making this area of the Big Bend excellent for encountering them in the wild. **Sunshine River Tours** *352 628 3450* ***www.sunshinerivertours.com*** operate from Homasassa Riverside Resort in Homasassa Springs and organise glass-bottom boat tours and swimming trips, and the **American Pro Diving Center** *352 563 0041* ***www.americanprodiving.com*** on Hwy-19 at Crystal River runs snorkelling and diving trips.

(£75) anyone over 5 can book a 30-minute encounter with a spotted dolphin.

Open *9am–6pm daily, last admission at 4pm.* ***Admission*** *US$11 (£5.50) adults, children under 3 free.* ***Credit*** *MC, V.* ***Amenities*** *Disabled access. Café. Shop.*

Gulf Specimen Marine Laboratories ★

222 Clark Drive, Panacea 850 984 5297 ***www.gulfspecimen.org***

How can a sea squirt be related to a fish? What is a sea cucumber? These are the questions that a visit to this environmental exhibit can answer. There's a focus on the small animals and plants that contribute to the ecological diversity of the north Florida coast and the seawater-filled tanks allow visitors the opportunity to get up close to about 1,200 different marine species, including sea

Wakulla Springs

horses, hermit crabs and sea anemones. Families that enjoy rock pooling will love this place.

Open *9am–5pm Mon–Fri, 10am–4pm Sat, noon–4pm Sun.* ***Admission*** *US$6 (£3) adults, US$4 (£2) children.* ***Credit*** *MC, V.* ***Amenities*** *Shop. Disabled access.*

INSIDER TIP

A good lunch stop near Gulf Specimen Marine Laboratories is Hook Wreck Henry's Dockside Café FIND *850 984 5544*. Named after the owner's son's favourite pirate, this rustic waterfront restaurant serves everything fresh and nothing fried. Sandwiches start at US$9 (£4.50) and there's a children's menu from US$5 (£2.50) plus live music at weekends.

For Active Families

Blackwater River State Park

850 983 5363 ***www.floridastateparks.org/blackwaterriver***

Blackwater River State Park, with its pure sandy bottom, slow-moving rivers surrounded by ancient oak, pine and juniper forests is one of the best places in Florida to get out and canoe or kayak. The park's main entrance (8am–sunset US$3/£1.50 per car) is situated 3 miles along Deaton Road Bridge after it turns off Hwy-90 at Harold, where you will find nature trails, picnicking and swimming.

However, the best way to go kayaking as a family is through Adventures Unlimited ★★ at Coldwater Creek, 12 miles north of Milton off Hwy-87 *850 623 6197* ***www.adventuresunlimited.com***. Adventures Unlimited is set in 88 acres of woodland and offers a range of canoeing, kayaking and tubing trips from US$20 (£10) per person. They also rent cabin accommodation from US$79–US$149 (£39.50–74.50) per night – some with full kitchen, but none with TVs, telephones, clocks or radios. With biking, hiking, challenge rope courses and swimming also on offer, this is an opportunity for wilderness-loving families to enjoy the outdoors in a uniquely American way.

Journeys ★★★

240 East 3rd Street, St George Island *850 927 3259* ***www.sgislandjourneys.com***

With over 13 years' experience of leading tours on to the water and deep into the wilderness surrounding St George Island, Journeys is one of the most experienced companies around to help your family explore this region. Journeys organises a large range of trips including narrated nature cruises, kayaking with manatees and night-time critter hunting for children, with prices starting at around US$30 (£15) per person. Call in advance to see what's on offer. You can also rent canoes and kayaks.

St Marks Historic Railroad State Trail

850 245 2052

Once a rail link between Tallahassee and St Marks until its closure in 1984, this flat, straight 16-mile bike path starts at a car park on SR-363 just south of Tallahassee and leads past the Apalachicola National Forest to the coastal community of St Marks and the nearby San Marco de Apalache Historic State Park, where the St Marks and Wakulla rivers meet. Bikes can be rented from St Marks Trail Bikes and Blades 📞 *850 656 0001* at the start of the trail for around US$16 (£8) per half day – family rates available.

St Vincent National Wildlife Refuge

You can't get much further off the beaten track than exploring this 10-mile barrier island to the south west of Apalachicola, only reached via the St Vincents Island Shuttle Service (📞 *850 229 1065* ***www.stvincentisland.com*** US$10/£5 adults, US$7/£3.50 children) at Indian Pass on SR-30. Once on the island you can laze on deserted beaches or discover inland freshwater lakes, both of which are abundant in native wildlife including deer and bald eagles.

Explore the island by bike, rented for US$25 (£12.50) from the Shuttle Service – rates include travel to the island. There's a small store at Indian Pass selling drinks, snacks and fishing equipment and, if you fancy a night or two on the edge of a deserted beach, you can rent waterfront cabins from US$95 (£47.50) a night 📞 *850 227 7203* ***www.indianpasscamp.com***.

FAMILY-FRIENDLY ACCOMMODATION

The Big Bend

Accommodation options in this region are limited to small communities along the coastline. Homosassa Springs, Crystal River and Cedar Key all have a number of options, of which the locally owned businesses are the best family bet. A cluster of chain motels can be found at Perry, 52 miles south east of Tallahassee, but the only reason to stay here is to put your head down for a night.

EXPENSIVE

Steinhatchee Landing Resort ★

SR-51, Steinhatchee approximately 90 miles south of Tallahassee 📞 *352 498 3513* ***www.steinhatcheelanding.com***

Nestled in 35 acres of moss-draped oak, pine and silver palm trees, the charming Steinhatchee Landing is the kind of place that families return to again and again – and it's easy to see why. The resort consists of a collection of one- to four-bedroomed old-fashioned individual cottages that sleep between two and ten and have all the modern conveniences you expect of upmarket, self-catering accommodation. The amount of activities for children available at this resort (canoeing, kayaking, cycling, tennis, archery, basketball, swimming and even shuffleboard) puts it on the family-friendly map – even younger children are catered for, with a petting zoo and playground area. Each cottage has its own screened porch with a charcoal grill – perfect for evening barbeques.

***Cottages** 56. **Rates** US$142–US$180 (£71–90) per night in winter, US$278–US$438 (£139–219) in summer. **Credit** AmEx, MC, V. **Amenities** Sports facilities. Pool. Spa. **In room** A/C. Cable TV. DVD/VCR. Washer/dryer. Full kitchen.*

MODERATE

Seagrass River Resort ★

10386 W. Halls River Road, Homosassa Springs ☎ *352 628 2551* ***www.seagrasspub.com***

Homosassa Springs is a place where American families come to fish, kayak, snorkel and simply enjoy the outdoors, and a number of laid-back resorts dotted around the river cater to them.

My favourite is Seagrass River Resort, perched right on the riverbank and two miles west of Hwy-19. It's livelier than other options in the area and its waterfront restaurant and bar is a friendly focal point for guests to relax, meet new people and often enjoy live music. Families can rent, on a nightly or weekly basis, spacious villas or smaller cottages. Affiliated to the American Pro Diving Center (see p. 247), manatee tours and diving trips can be easily arranged through the resort, as can fishing trips, boat rentals and river cruises – some of which include lunch or dinner at the resort's restaurant.

***Rooms** Villas 14, cottages 4, efficiencies 7. **Rates** Cottages US$89 (£44.50) Sun–Thurs, US$99 (£49.50) Fri–Sat for two people plus US$10 (£5) extra for each additional person; villas US$99–US$129 (£49.50–64.50) Sun–Thurs, US$109–US$139 (£54.50–69.50) Fri–Sat. **Credit** MC, V. **Amenities** Bar. Restaurant. **In room** Cable TV. A/C.*

The Island Place

550 1st Street, Cedar Key ☎ *352 543 5306* ***www.islandplace-ck.com***

Just minutes from Cedar Key's marina with its restaurants and shops and right on the waterfront, The Island Place is central enough to be within easy walking distance of the centre of town, yet far enough away to maintain a sense of privacy. All the one- and two-bedroom suites at this friendly resort are comfortable and airy, have fully equipped kitchens and private sea-facing balconies and the ground floor waterfront patio area has a decent sized pool, jacuzzi and communal charcoal grill.

***Rooms** 30. **Rates** One-bedroom suites US$105–US$135 (£52.50–67.50) for up to two people, two-bedroom suites US$150–US$190 (£75–95) for up to four people; all units sleep up to five people and each additional person costs US$5 (£2.50), children under 6 free. **Credit** AmEx, MC, V. **Amenities** Outdoor pool. Jacuzzi. **In room** Wi-Fi Internet. Cable TV. DVD/VCR. Washer/dryer.*

The Panhandle

Most families visiting the Panhandle want to stay on its beaches. Prices are highest from mid-May to mid-August, during public holidays and spring break (see p. 242). The best times to visit are late spring and early autumn, when the prices are low, beaches quiet and temperatures still high – October/November half term is a particularly good time for British families to visit this region. Winter rates are still lower, but many tourist-focused restaurants and attractions close and the temperatures cool off.

VERY EXPENSIVE

WaterColor Inn ★★ GREEN

34 Goldenrod Circle, Santa Rosa Beach nr Seaside 32459 ☎ 850 534 5000 ***www.watercolorinn.com***

For those families willing to splash out for somewhere special to stay, this stylish, intimate and surprisingly casual luxury resort has it all. The understated rooms – just a few for a resort this size – all face the ocean, have private balconies, bags of space and a walk-in shower with a window overlooking the beach. The biggest attraction for families, however, is Camp Watercolor and its daily range of activities for children aged between 4 and 12, including nature lessons, arts and craft sessions, a water play area and much more. Leaving parents free to enjoy the resort's many other facilities such as its sunny library, golf and tennis courts, swimming pool (where towels are mango-scented), or simply spend time on the beaches that this region is so famous for.

The WaterColor Inn is a member of Florida's Green Lodging programme in recognition of its environmentally friendly practices.

Rooms *60.* ***Rates*** *US$325–US$505 (£162.50–252.50) for two adults and two children sharing, depending on type of room and time of year.* ***Credit*** *AmEx, MC, V.* ***Amenities*** *Pool. Complimentary sports equipment. Fitness facilities.* ***In room*** *CD/DVD player. Cable TV. Internet.*

MODERATE

Marriott's Bay Point Resort Village VALUE

4200 Marriott Drive, Panama City Beach ☎ 850 236 6000 ***www.marriottbaypoint.com***

The range of accommodation options in Panama City Beach is mind boggling, especially for the

Villa Rentals

Many families rent holiday villas along the coastal Panhandle. For holiday homes on St George Island try Collins Vacation Rentals ☎ *850 927 2900* ***www.collinsvacationrentals.com*** who have around 300 properties to choose from. Further west, Seaside Cottage Rental Agency ☎ *850 231 1320* ***www.seasidefl.com*** and Rosemary Beach Cottage Rental Company ☎ *850 278 2100* ***www.rosemarybeach.com*** both rent hundreds of holiday cottages.

Staying in Tallahassee

At certain times of the year it can be almost impossible to find a place to stay in Tallahassee. The 60-day sitting of the state legislative begins on the first Tuesday in March, at which time accommodation options are full on weekdays, while weekends in May are busy at graduation time and in autumn, when the Florida State University football team plays at home. During these periods expect to pay very high rates and book well in advance. In terms of chain motels, there are a number clustered on North Monroe Street (Hwy-27) near the junction with I-10 – Cabot Lodge North is recommended *850 386 8880* ***www.cabotlodgenorthmonroe.com*** – and Apalachee Parkway (Hwy-27).

first-time family not wanting to get caught in the madness of this party-loving town. Prices tend to be higher than anywhere else along the coastal Panhandle and this resort's reasonable rates make it one of the better options in town. Sitting on the edge of a lagoon at St Andrew's Bay, the resort is tucked away from the high energy of the main drag. And what it lacks in proximity to the ocean, it makes up for with the large range of activities on offer. For children wanting to have fun outside of the resort, seaplane rides, wave-runner tours to the nearby Shell Island and dolphin-spotting tours can all be booked for guests.

Rooms *356.* ***Rates*** *From US$143 (£71.50) in summer, US$134 (£67) in winter.* ***Credit*** *AmEx, MC, V.* ***Amenities*** *Four restaurants. Two bars. Two pools. Jacuzzi. Two golf courses. Health club. Spa. Water sports equipment and bike rental. Babysitting service. Valet parking.* ***In room*** *A/C. Cable TV. Fridge. Movies and Playstation for a fee.*

Around Tallahassee

EXPENSIVE

The Governors Inn ★★

209 South Adams Street, Tallahassee *850 681 6855* ***www.thegovinn.com***

Despite its business feel, this friendly, luxurious hotel, situated in the historic heart of Tallahassee is welcoming for families wanting the buzz of downtown and well worth the extra cost if you don't fancy staying in a chain motel. Each room or suite is named after a former Florida governor and decorated in the style of the period when they held office – some with four-poster beds, oak writing desks and even wood-burning stoves. After a hard day entertaining the children in the city's museums, parents can enjoy free evening cocktails in the pine-panelled Florida Room. This hotel is very popular so book in advance.

Rooms *41.* ***Rates*** *Doubles US$159–US$239 (£79.50–119.50), suites US$189–US$309 (£94.50–154.50) based on two people sharing, extra*

Wakulla Springs Lodge

person US$10 (£5) per night. ***Credit*** *AmEx, MC, V.* ***Amenities*** *Valet parking.* ***In room****: Wi-Fi Internet. Cable TV.*

Wakulla Springs Lodge

550 Wakulla Park Drive, Wakulla Springs ☎ *850 224 5950* ***www.floridastateparks.org/wakullasprings/Lodge.cfm***

Built in 1937 and one of the few places to stay between Tallahassee and Apalachicola, this elegant hotel won't appeal to families whose children need a lot of stimulation (there are no TVs in the rooms). However, for those fed up with bland motel accommodation, this simple, old-fashioned, elegant hotel with its antique furniture and marble bathrooms is a charming alternative. The real draw, though, for families is the hotel's location. Situated deep inside a popular and pretty state park, guests can roam the grounds and swim in the springs long after day trippers have gone home.

You can lounge in deep sofas and play checkers in the hotel's lobby, and the old Ball Room is now a reasonably priced restaurant. The best bit for kids is the old-fashioned soda fountain which serves ice creams and snacks throughout the day.

Rooms *27.* ***Rates*** *US$85–US$105 (£42.50–52.50).* ***Credit*** *AmEx, MC, V.* ***Amenities*** *Restaurant.* ***In room*** *A/C.*

Staying in Pensacola

Pensacola has a string of decent motels on Pensacola Boulevard (SR-29) south of the junction with I-10 – try the Quality Inn 6550 ☎ *850 477 0711* ***www.qualityinn.com/hotel/fl732***. The best downtown option is the Days Inn on Palafox Street ☎ *850 438 4922* and for Pensacola Beach try the Hilton Garden Inn ☎ *850 916 2999* ***www.pensacolabeach.gardeninn.com***

FAMILY-FRIENDLY DINING

MODERATE/ EXPENSIVE

Bud and Alley's ★★

SR-30A, Seaside ☎ *850 231 5900* ***www.budandalleys.com***

Named after a cat and dog, this waterfront restaurant and bar is a firm favourite with locals and visitors alike. The food, with its distinct Mediterranean influence, is all fresh and consistently fabulous. The menu features healthy options for children, including noodles with creamy cheese sauce and grilled chicken with veggies – a welcome alternative to the usual hot dog and fries deal dished up for children at most restaurants. You can eat in contemporary surroundings inside, or on the rooftop bar, where the sunset views are as good as the food and live jazz plays at the weekends. It's advisable to make reservations, even for lunch, as this place is always busy.

Open *Lunch 11.30am–3pm, dinner from 5.30pm daily.* ***Main Courses*** *lunch US$8–US$15 (£4–7.50), dinner US$27–US$35 (£13.50–17.50).* ***Credit*** *AmEx, MC, V.* ***Amenities*** *Children's menu.*

The Treasure Ship

3605 Thomas Drive, Panama City Beach ☎ *850 234 8881* ***www.thetreasureship.com***

It's impossible to miss this 200-ft-long wooden pirate ship – a full-scale replica of the *Golden Hind*, and one of the funkiest places for children to eat. There are three levels to this restaurant complex offering different styles of dining, all with a pirate theme. Hook's Grille and Grog on level one is open for lunch and dinner, while the more expensive main dining room on level two is open only for dinner from 4pm. At the top of the ship, on level three and with panoramic views, is Captain Crabby's, which contains indoor and outdoor bar-style dining and is famous for its all-you-can-eat crab legs. There are early bird specials between 4 and 5pm and acoustic music on Fridays and Saturdays.

Open *Daily from 11am.* ***Main Courses*** *US$7–US$30 (£3.50–15).* ***Credit*** *MC, V.* ***Amenities*** *Children's menu. Highchair.*

MODERATE

Andrew's Capital Bar and Grill ★ FIND

228 S Adams Street ☎ *850 222 3444* ***www.andrewsdowntown.com***

This New York-style deli in the shadow of the Capitol Complex has been a firm favourite with the city's white-collar workers for over 30 years and makes for a pleasant change from the Panhandle's beachside bars and seafood restaurants. I eat lunch here as businessmen and women are out in force and this infuses a sophisticated buzz to the conversation and company. However, children are still very welcome, as this is the kind of place people come to take a break from the office and relax, while out of town visitors come to soak up the ambience, eavesdrop on the politics and enjoy the delicious food. Many of the items of the menu are named after politics and politicians – my favourite is Bill Law (and order) Veggie Quesadilla – and the all-you-can-eat Sunday buffet (US$12.95/ £6.48 a head) is recommended if you're in town at the weekend. The shady outside terrace is the best place to eat (weather permitting) but expect to wait for a table between noon and 1pm on weekdays.

Open *11.30am–10pm Mon–Thurs, 11.30am–11pm Fri–Sat, 11am–2pm Sun.* ***Main Courses*** *US$8–US$30 (£4–15).* ***Credit*** *AmEx, MC, V.* ***Amenities*** *Inside TV featuring sporting events.*

Boat Yard Restaurant ★

5323 North Lagoon Drive, Panama City Beach ☎ 850 249 9273 ***www.boatyardclub.com***

Perched on the marina waterfront of Grand Lagoon, well away from the main drag, The Boat Yard is one of the most pleasant family dining options available in Panama City Beach. The front of this spacious and airy restaurant opens out onto the water – perfect for watching boats come and go – and there's a Key West feel to both the ambience and varied menu – the Key Lime Garlic Shrimp is particularly good – and the children's – or Yard Puppies' – meals (all US$6/£3) are served on a Frisbee, which they can keep.

Open *11am–11pm daily, later at weekends.* ***Main Courses*** *US$8–US$27 (£4–13.50).* ***Credit*** *AmEx, MC, V.* ***Amenities*** *Children's menu. Highchair.*

Boss Oyster ★★

125 Water Street, Apalachicola ☎ 850 653 9364 ***www.apalachicolariverinn.com***

All the seafood served in this waterfront restaurant is fresh from the fishing fleet that docks right outside. The seafood chowder is legendary and they claim that folk come from miles around for the ultimate seafood experience – the Journey's End sandwich, a steal at US$12 (£6) and packed with buckets of shrimp, crab and scallops. But it's oysters that make this – and most other restaurants in town – famous, and there are so many different ways to eat them (with bacon, cheese, jalapenos, artichoke and even sherry) that even children might give them a go. Add to this the laid-back ambience and never-ending river views and you can see why this is a local favourite.

Open *11.30am–10pm Sun–Thurs, 11.30am–11pm Fri–Sat.* ***Main Courses*** *US$8–US$15 (£4–7.50).* ***Credit*** *AmEx, MC, V.* ***Amenities*** *Highchair. Children's menu.*

Oysters

Chemical tests indicate that oysters are made up of water, protein and carbohydrates along with small amounts of fat, sugar and minerals, none of which, despite the claims of folklore, are known to have aphrodisiac qualities.

Harry A's

28 West Bayshore Drive, St George Island 850 927 3400 **www.HarryAsRestaurant.com**

Yes this is yet another seafood restaurant, but it's hard to escape them and there's more to the menu of this super-friendly restaurant than the ubiquitous oyster. This place appears a bit rough and ready, but that's in keeping with the island and what it lacks in neatness it makes up for with a lively atmosphere and child-friendly attitude. It's open for lunch and dinner with a daily happy hour from 4pm until 7pm and there's often live music in the evenings.

Open *11am–11pm daily.* **Main Courses** *US$7–US$27 (£3.50–13.50).* **Credit** *MC, V.* **Amenities** *Children's menu. Highchair.*

Peg Leg Pete's

1010 Fort Pickens Road, Pensacola Beach 850 932 4139 **www.peglegpetes.com**

Known for being laid back and friendly, this beachside restaurant has a decent-sized menu which features sandwiches, seafood, burgers, pasta and, of course, oysters, all reasonably priced and with a Cajun slant. The children's menu (US$5–US$6/£2.50–3) is standard cheeseburger and fried shrimp fare, but they make it fun by serving the food in a beach bucket and providing an unusual range of children's frozen drinks. However, what makes this restaurant stand out for families is that it encourages children to play by providing a large playground in the sand right outside.

Open *Daily for lunch and dinner.* **Main Courses** *US$8–US$28 (£4–14).* **Credit** *AmEx, MC, V.* **Amenities** *Children's menu. Highchair.*

Seville Quarter ★

130 E Government Street, Pensacola 850 434 6211 **www.rosies.com**

Tucked away in the heart of Pensacola's historical district, this place might play up to the tourists but it's so much fun and so friendly that it just doesn't matter. A rambling antique brick restaurant and bar complex, the Seville Quarter consists of a number of different themed areas – some more family orientated than others – and two beautiful courtyards, one with a striking fountain. This family-run establishment with its big wooden bars, large ceiling fans and Dixieland jazz has a New Orleans feel and is best enjoyed for lunch or an early evening meal with children (families catered for until 8pm) – take a wander round and see which area appeals to you the most. Visitors love Lili Marlene's, a themed WW1 aviators' pub and a favourite with locals – Brits will appreciate the genuine old English pub tables.

Open *Daily for lunch from 11am and for dinner from 5–8pm for families, until 10pm for parties without children.* **Main Courses** *US$3–US$17 (£1.50–8.50).* **Credit** *MC, V.* **Amenities** *Children's menu. Highchair.*

Index

See also Accommodations and Restaurant indexes, below.

General

A

B

C

D

E

K

L

M

N

O

P

Q

R

S

Accommodations

Restaurants